Prologue to Violence

Child Abuse, Dissociation, and Crime

Psychoanalysis in a New Key Book Series
Volume 5

Psychoanalysis in a New Key Book Series

DONNEL STERN, PH.D., SERIES EDITOR

Prologue to Violence

Child Abuse, Dissociation, and Crime

Abby Stein

THE ANALYTIC PRESS
2007   MAHWAH, NEW JERSEY   LONDON

Names, dates, locations, and other unique characteristics of
crime scenes and criminals have been changed to shield the
identity of subjects.

Parts of this book previously appeared in *Contemporary
Psychoanalysis*: Vol. 37, #3, July 2001, pp. 443–451; Vol. 39, #2,
April 2003, pp. 179–197; and Vol. 40, #4, October 2004,
pp. 495–517.

Dedication quote on page v is from Gerrard, N. (2003). Holly and
Jessica—We'll never know. *Observer*, Sunday, December 21.

Parts of this research were funded by the Harry Frank
Guggenheim Foundation.

Published by
The Analytic Press
10 Industrial Avenue
Mahwah, NJ 07430
www.analyticpress.com

Cover design by Kathryn Houghtaling Lacey

Library of Congress Cataloging-in-Publication Data

Stein, Abby
Prologue to violence : child abuse, dissociation, and crime/
Abby Stein.
  p. cm.
Includes bibliographical references and index.

ISBN 978-0-88163-416-7 — 0-88163-416-6 (cloth)

Printed in the United States of America
10 9 8 7 6 5 4 3 2 1

Pedophiles are other people; rapists are other people; murderers are other people. It's hard for the mind to know itself as wicked. It tells itself a different story, keeping the darkness at bay.

—*Nikki Gerrard*

Contents

Foreword

I edit the journal *Contemporary Psychoanalysis*, and that is how I learned about the work of Abby Stein. Perhaps you can imagine how unusual it is for remarkably insightful, creative, and beautifully written submissions from unknown writers to come in over the transom. Such events are among the best things that can happen to an editor. You begin to read, without any particular expectations, and suddenly, to your surprise, you find yourself in the firm and confident authorial grip of someone you have never heard of. Who *is* this person? On the very best of these already rare occasions, you are taken to a place you did not know existed. Abby Stein's writing came to me that way, and I was taken by it that way, too. After the second or third of these papers from Stein, I proposed to her that she write a book on the subject that she was digging into more and more deeply with every installment of her work.

And what a subject it is! In the book that resulted, *Prologue to Violence*, which you hold in your hands, Stein addresses one of the most daunting problems of contemporary life: the role of childhood trauma (and she means *serious* trauma: violent, physical, sexual) in the creation of violent adolescents and adults (and, again, she means violence in the most serious way—beatings, rape, and murder). The existence of this developmental picture is hardly news, of course. We all know that violence in one generation begets violence in the next. But Stein, having studied violent adults, both in person and in the files of law enforcement agencies, draws a radically unfamiliar set of conclusions from this distressingly familiar developmental history. The key observation Stein makes, over and over again, is that violent crime is very often carried out in a state of dissociation. The offender either does not know he has done the crime or feels as if someone else inside him did it; or he presents in a kind of daze about the act. Stein quotes such a profusion of utterances of this kind from her subjects that the reader is left with no doubt at all about the dissociative processes involved.

All by itself (that is, even without the heart of Stein's argument, which I will get to), this observation amounts to a challenge to the most common interpretations of criminal violence. Most often, Stein tells us, violent criminals are not conscienceless; they are not, in other words, what we are used to thinking of as psychopaths or sociopaths. They are not simply evil; or rather, if they are evil, theirs is a complex kind of evil, an evil that seems desperate not to know itself. It is an ashamed and guilty evil, not proud or entitled. Stein suggests not only that we consider the possibility that these people do have consciences, but also that, because of the insanely brutal disciplinary measures they suffered at the hands of their "caretakers," their consciences may actually be especially, crazily severe, so severe that the people who commit these acts may be even less willing than the rest of us to know what they have done.

But, of course, they *have* done awful things. And the case could be made that the reason they cultivate a lack of awareness or lack of appreciation of their deeds is that they could not otherwise allow themselves to carry out these horrific acts. If that were the case, we would have to conclude that their dissociations exist only to make it possible for them to do what they "really want" to do. This state of affairs, if it exists, is simply and directly evil. To evade awareness so as not to offend one's conscience is a corruption, nothing more than a way to grease the tracks for the enactment of the worst kinds of violent, exploitative impulses. That would not really be psychopathology, but the grossest failure of morality.

Stein offers us a more complex picture than that, though, one that we simply cannot divorce from psychopathology, however appealing it can be to dehumanize violent criminals. Stein's revelation of the dissociative process is just the beginning of her argument. More important than the dissociation itself, she recognizes, is *why* violent offenders dissociate. It is in answering this question that Stein makes her greatest creative leap, one that has critical implications not only for psychotherapy, psychoanalysis, and psychiatric nosology, but also for forensic psychology, traumatology, criminology, and the entire criminal justice system.

The leap Stein takes is to apply to the dissociation of criminals the work of Harry Stack Sullivan (e.g., 1940, 1953) and the contemporary theory of dissociation formulated by writers from within relational and interpersonal psychoanalysis (Mitchell, 1993; Davies & Frawley, 1994; Stern, 1997; Bromberg, 1998). Contemporary relational writers hold that it is not only people suffering from dissociative identity disorder (DID, or what used to be called multiple personality) whose identities are fragmented. The "normal" self, too, is fragmented and multiple, not the stable, unitary self we are used to thinking we are. But, unlike the situation in the relatively rare diagnosis of DID, most "selves" or "states of self" in what we call a "normal" personality are accessible to one another. Dissociations in such personalities are relative, not absolute. For example, I may not be able to feel angry under certain interpersonal circumstances, but I am certainly able to feel that way when the context changes. As the context changes, self-states that were dissociated can once again access one another.

For generations in psychoanalysis, drive and its psychic representation, intrapsychic fantasy, were the engines of the mind. The entire psyche was understood to be constructed on the foundation of the conflict between drive and defense, between instinct and the demands of civilization. This was Freud's overarching perspective, and it remains dominant today in many quarters. In this way of seeing things, the meanings of the external world are structured according to the compromises that shape the internal one.

But increasingly, especially among interpersonal and relational psychoanalysts, the actual events of life, experienced according to our personal interests, conscious and unconscious, are the sources of the personality we become. Trauma, therefore, has become paramount in the theorizing of this group. What happens in the so-called external world matters, and the bad things have particular import. The external and the internal shape one another incessantly, very much like the M. C. Escher image of two hands, each in the act of drawing the other. It was this image, as a matter of fact, that Stephen Mitchell (1988) used on the dust jacket of the book in which he announced his vision for psychoanalysis.

We all dissociate. All of us have suffered enough trauma to feel parts of our subjectivity as not-self, or in Sullivan's (e.g., 1953) wording, "not-me." It was the genius of Stephen Mitchell (1993) and Philip Bromberg (1998) to bring this insight, drawn from the most severely traumatized, to those of us who have also suffered, but much less. It was their insight that mind is always multiple, divided by the impact of trauma. And it is now Abby Stein's genius to take this formulation about the "expectable," "normal" multiple self and apply it in reverse, to those much more damaged people who have committed the most terrible violent crimes. Dissociation has come full circle in relational psychoanalysis.

The idea is this: when experience is dissociated, it is because one cannot tolerate being the self who went through that awful experience. That self is isolated, separated, kept apart. That self is "not-me." But not-me does not merely take up invisible residence in a hidden corner of the mind. Not-me is enacted. Dissociated experience is enacted, always. That is the only way that such experience puts in an appearance in life, because it has never been symbolized and cannot be, not by a mind that rejects it. As Stein tells us, such experience has never been made into a narrative form. It cannot be thought. In psychotherapy and psychoanalysis, this absence, this dissociation, is the source of the enactments between therapist and patient that must somehow be negotiated if treatment is to go forward. In fact, we can say that, for the many relational theorists who think in these terms, enactments and their breach lie at the heart of psychotherapeutic work.

And so, bringing these ideas back to their origins in severe trauma, Stein tells us that, when children are badly traumatized, parts of them are dissociated. These parts are never explicitly known. They become not-me. But they are enacted; they find their way into life through action. If the dissociated self was the victim of violence, the enactment is also violent. The victim of this new violence is attacked for many reasons, often to avoid what would otherwise feel to the perpetrator like one more humiliation at the hands of those who hurt him.

Stein has done too good a job of laying out her point of view for me to do more than offer its broadest outlines. I must emphasize that Stein has brought back within the human realm acts that are often thought to be inhuman. She shows us how these most terrible of human acts are magnifications of reactions we can recognize in ourselves. There but for the grace of God go I. The most awful things people can do to one another are committed in some terribly distorted attempt to create meaning. There may be meaningless events in life, but violent enactments are not among them.

Prologue to Violence brings up the most difficult moral questions. What do we do with violent criminals? At the book's end, Stein tells us about the psychotherapies that have had some kind of success with them. But what about culpability? Don Greif (2004), who is both a psychoanalyst and a forensic psychologist and who therefore has a valuable and unique perspective on these issues, wrote a heartfelt and revealing commentary on a paper of Stein's (2004) concerning sexual homicide. In the context of the knotty problems of culpability, understanding, and evil, Greif's thoughts are worth quoting at length:

> Early in my experience evaluating sexual offenders, after hearing an especially grisly account, told in a matter-of-fact way, of the chronic, sadistic abuse and torture of an inmate by his parents when he was a child, I left the prison with tears in my eyes and realized I had no reason to think I wouldn't be where he was if I had had his parents. There but for the grace of God go I, I thought. He had been imprisoned for twenty years for repeat offenses against children, and his meager internal resources made it unlikely he would change sufficiently to ever be released from prison. With most men I was primarily infuriated and saddened by the pain and damage they inflicted on innocent human beings, but this time I was struck most by the ghastly details of this man's childhood victimization, and the inevitability of the path by which his own abuse, and the profound developmental failures resulting from his awful childhood, led to his offenses. I was shaken for the rest of that evening.
>
> It would have been consoling to think this man was simply bad or evil. It might have comforted me to believe that the two of us were intrinsically different, and that it would therefore be inconceivable for me to have become a pedophile, even if I were subjected to his miserable childhood. I would have preferred to think this, to tell you the truth; but I couldn't quite believe it. I realized how large a role luck plays in determining the kind of life one can have, and I just felt sad. We have no control over who our parents are or, up to a certain age, what they do to us. This is a terrible truth for the unlucky.
>
> In the case of murderers like those Stein writes about, or the children who murder children, we tend to think they have free will and choose their paths. I believe it is true, at least according to the legal definition of criminal responsibility, that most violent individuals know the wrongfulness of their actions. It is also true, however, as Stein emphasizes, that severe, early maltreatment begets violence. The "reproduction of evil" (Grand, 2000) does not usually seem so mysterious.
>
> If evildoers are simply bad people, then the proper response is punishment and protection of society. Both punishment and protection are vitally important if we are to do a better job of preventing violence. It is understandable that people respond to violence with moral outrage and blame those we think should have prevented it. But punishment of offenders and protection of the innocent is insufficient. If we want to prevent violence, we must understand and address its roots in trauma [pp. 524–525].

That is the grim and straightforward message of Stein's book. We must understand what trauma does to children and to the adults they become, and we must decide what to do about it. Will we simply let it go on? Do we really have a choice? But must we not *try* to do something different? What is our moral responsibility here? Rehabilitation? Treatment? Punishment? Retribution? Protection of the innocent? How do we even *know* when the innocent are protected? How do we know when a dissociated trauma is defused? Can that happen?

Stein has written a brave, brilliant, and thoroughly innovative book about the most terrible things in life, and she has done this without once succumbing to either sensationalism or despair. Neither does she backpedal the horror and the pain. *Prologue to Violence* is an extraordinary piece of work. It will be recognized as a landmark contribution.

Donnel B. Stern
October, 2005

REFERENCES

Bromberg, P. M. (1998). *Standing in the Spaces: Essays on Clinical Process, Trauma, and Dissociation.* Hillsdale, NJ: The Analytic Press.

Davies, J. M. & Frawley, M. G. (1994). *Treating the Adult Survivor of Childhood Sexual Abuse.* New York: Basic Books.

Grand, S. (2000). *The Reproduction of Evil.* Hillsdale, NJ: The Analytic Press.

Greif, D. (2004). Discussion of Stein's "Fantasy, fusion, and sexual homicide." *Contemp. Psychoanal.,* 4:519-526.

Mitchell, S. A. (1988). *Relational Concepts in Psychoanalysis.* Cambridge, MA: Harvard University Press.

————(1993). *Hope and Dread in Psychoanalysis.* New York: Basic Books.

Stein, A. (2004). Fantasy, fusion, and sexual homicide. *Contemp. Psychoanal.* 40: 495-517.

Stern, D. B. (1997). *Unformulated Experience: From Dissociation to Imagination in Psychoanalysis.* Hillsdale, NJ: The Analytic Press.

Sullivan, H. S. (1940). *Conceptions of Modern Psychiatry.* New York: Norton.

———— (1953). *The Interpersonal Theory of Psychiatry.* New York: Norton.

Preface

This is not the book I set out to write.

Schooled in the 1990s, interning at Bellevue Hospital in New York, I was enamored of the medical model of diagnosis and intervention. I was fixated on discovering pathology in the men I visited on the prison unit, and, indeed, psychiatric illness was remarkably easy to find. The unit was a tinderbox of untreated signs and symptoms: of mania, suicidality, paranoia, neurological impairment, and, most disquieting, ignored or dismissed evidence of pathological dissociation. Tutored by the pioneering forensic psychiatrist Dorothy Otnow Lewis, I came to recognize the characteristic trajectory of dissociated violence—introduced during childhood beatings, facilitated by mental illness, and ultimately enshrined in adult perpetration.

It was fashionable at that particular social moment to diagnose multiple personality disorder in adult survivors of childhood trauma, and our prisoner/clients certainly fit the bill. A nightmarish childhood both shadowed and illuminated each man's polyglot narrative of destruction and redemption. I wanted to write a book about these inmates and whether or not their multiplicity rendered them incapacitated before the law. The book would be about cognition and volition, the prongs of sanity recognized by the criminal justice system. The question was: to what degree is a multiple whose "alter personality" commits a crime to be held accountable for his or her extralegal activities?

It was the wrong question.

Not that it is not an important question to raise. Many noted attorneys and psychiatrists, among them Ellen Saks, Ralph Slovenko, Marlene Steinberg, and D. O. Lewis herself have addressed the issues of competence and culpability that surround a defendant's diagnosis of what is now called dissociatve identity disorder. But, by the end of the 90s, I had come across a body of thought that I believed superseded a medicolegal inquiry into the topic and forced a new kind of question. Informed by mounting clinical evidence of the ubiquity of dissociative rejoinders to threat, many psychoanalysts were reinvigorating a theory of mind that named dissociation, rather than repression, as the critical defensive operation. Contemporaneous with this stream of thought, laboratory research increasingly point[ed] toward a novel model of the mind that envisions waking, sleeping and dreaming as distinct neurodynamic states that lie along a continuum and are separated by imperfect, sometimes porous, boundaries. States can get "dissociated," or mixed together in the way script from one program can hang up in another when you're shifting between the windows of a buggy computer [Brown, 2003].

How does such a theory of mind affect the estimation of psychological disorder? Arguably, in this formulation, everyone is "multiple." Only the rigidity of the system, the impermeability of those cubicles of affect, desire, behavior or cognition, determine the gravity, and perhaps the intractability, of dissociation. The inability to negotiate facilely between and among self-states, or to access them simultaneously, became the criterion for emotional illness (Stern, 1997b; Bromberg, 1998;). Reading the contemporary psychoanalytic literature, I finally opened a window onto the uneasiness I had experienced with criminological theories about perpetrator motivation and methodology; I came to understand why the medical model had never fully relieved me of that discomfort. This more nuanced version of dissociation theory seemed to explain many of the conundrums in my data set, particularly as they pertained to the simultaneous knowing and not knowing of one's history. I became quite driven to look more closely at the stories of assault, rape, and murder I had collected, either through direct interview or by access to law enforcement files, through the lens provided by analysts articulating the theory.

Some of the crime theories I dispute are questionable on their face, like the one about serial killers being attractive, articulate, and charming (have you seen or heard John Wayne Gacy or Otis Toole?) or the one that says most felons engage in particular criminal specializations, much like scions of business (believe me, to read a rap sheet is to scan the heights of diversification). Other theories that have helped to create a mythology of violent perpetration are far more difficult to dispute because they contain elements of truth. Some involve the centrality of consciously indulged fantasy as a trigger for criminal activity; others offer a reductionistic genetic interpretation of data regarding the origins of expressive deficit in criminals; still others are built on questionable assumptions about the supposedly random way that many perpetrators choose their victims.

One of the most difficult concepts to untangle is the notion of criminal "psychopathy" as it regards attributions of conscience, or, more specifically, the lack of it. The "mine is bigger than yours" theory of conscience has undermined attempts to profile, investigate, interrogate, understand, and rehabilitate criminals ever since Krafft-Ebing (1886) applied his particular ethical slant to the diagnoses of lust murderers, child molesters, rapists, and necrophiliacs and recommended that simply abstaining from the behavioral manifestations of their desires might somehow reweave their moral fiber. A psychological model that appreciates the verticality and rotation of defenses need not resort to an all-or-nothing interpretation of moral or empathic faculty and failure. Conscience and remorse are present—maybe even abundant—in the criminal, but are unseen, by turns, just as they are for most of us encountering the trivial and extraordinary traumata of existence. Moral disengagement characterizes much of human action, both by choice and by unconscious necessity; in people who were horribly maltreated in childhood, selective disengagement is tantamount to survival.

As you see, most important to me is to make the case for the criminogenic impact of physical and sexual abuse when it is imposed on a self-system already marked by neglect, external disorder, and internal chaos. Such a self is largely habituated to attending to threats selectively; it cannot fully develop the capacity for object constancy and narrative continuity that might inform an unvaryingly empathic arc toward others. Instead, the arc is as fractured as the elaboration of self and other objects from which it is derived.

In the stories I tell here, dissociation is both the harbinger of violence and its consequence. The material presented showcases the extremes of human behavior because that is the train that brought me here. In a broader sense, though, the paradigm is as applicable to the boy who pulls the wings from flies as it is to the one who pulls the panties off his protesting date as it is to the woman who slaps her child in a fit of pique. None of these "perpetrators" may ever see the inside of a jail cell or a psychiatrist's office. All stories of violence are stories of dissociations, large and small. I hope that these most horrid tales will illuminate something about tales not so horrid and will spark a different way of imagining abused children and abusive adults in the protracted winter of their discontent.

1

Who, me? Locating Agency in Violent Narratives

Matias Reyes, now designated as the "real" attacker in the Central Park jogger case, capped a career of muggings and serial sexual assaults by raping and stabbing a pregnant woman to death as her children listened from the next room. A short time later, he left the jogger, Trisha Meili, for dead in the park, the victim of a rampage so brutal that NYPD detectives still have trouble accepting that a single offender perpetrated the crime. Yet Reyes steadfastly rejects portrayals of himself as aggressive. "I always say no to violence," he is quoted as saying. As if to punctuate the assertion, Reyes shared with his defense team's psychologist that he once surreptitiously called 911 to get help for a victim of his own sexual sadism. Such seemingly contradictory behavior is not incompatible with reports that Reyes was known to take showers with his rape victims, apparently so that he could imagine their intimacies as consensual (Flynn, K. 2002).

Revitch and Schlesinger (1989) report the case of a 15-year-old boy charged with the unprovoked stabbing of a 63-year-old woman. The boy seems divorced from the consciousness of his own vicious intentions, as he apathetically describes his actions: "I just started stabbing her. I really did not think about it. I really did not want to stab anybody. It was just bad luck" (p. 14).

A once-aspiring law student and dedicated suicide hotline volunteer told a psychiatrist to whom he had earlier confessed the grisly details of myriad murders, "The man sitting before you never killed anyone." The convict's name was Theodore Robert Bundy, a prolific serial murderer executed in Florida's electric chair in 1989 (Lewis, 1998 p. 3).

A man in Brainerd, Minnesota was questioned about the disappearance of a woman with whom he had left a bar at closing time. "I don't know if something happened. I hope it didn't," he told police, before leading them to the pit where her body was buried (Haga, C. 2003). Although not charged at the time of her disappearance, William G. Myears eventually pleaded guilty to the killing of Erika Dalquist, and was sentenced to 21 years behind bars (McKinney, M. 2005).

That crime note was emailed to me by a Midwestern writer friend who knew that I was embarking on an analysis of criminal narratives, some elicited during depth interviews and others culled from law enforcement files.

The Brainerd perpetrator's dissociated account, nervy and darkly laughable to uninitiated eyes, seemed routine to me.

INITIAL RESEARCH

In the 1990s, as part of a project on memory, I interviewed 64 men awaiting medical evaluation on a hospital prison ward. The inmates' crimes ranged from petty larceny to double murder. Eighty percent reported having been physically assaulted during childhood. Almost half of that 80 percent had endured truly grisly episodes of maltreatment at the hands of caregivers: many had suffered severe burns, broken bones, loss of consciousness, ongoing sexual molestation, and threatened, as well as actual, attempts on their lives by parents or parental surrogates.

I documented intense episodes of depersonalization, derealization, and amnesia in almost a quarter of the men with whom I spoke. Dissociative signs and symptoms were most frequently recorded for those inmates prone to extreme violence. Of note, the 11 most pathologically dissociative offenders had committed the most vicious crimes: kidnapping, attempted matricide, murder, arson, serial rape, aggravated assault, and armed robbery. Five of these men professed amnesia for their offenses, although none claimed to be innocent of the crimes with which they were charged. Thus, in stark contrast to their nondissociating counterparts, who often denied their offenses, dissociative men were abundantly willing to assume guilt even when they were unaware of what they had done. And, although these perpetrators claimed not to remember committing their crimes, they had no difficulty confessing to them or presenting investigators with incontrovertible evidence of their guilt (Stein, 2000). My observations dovetailed with the findings of numerous forensic clinicians and researchers who have recognized pathological levels of dissociation among offenders, particularly those incarcerated for violent crimes (Allison, 1981; Bliss, 1986; Lewis & Band, 1991; Lewis et al., 1997, 1998; Snow, Beckman, & Brack, 1996).

As my research agenda expanded to cover archival data in police case files, I made it a point to note information that might be relevant to the study of links among childhood trauma, dissociation, and adult violence. I was surprised to find that, even in a database collected without this purpose in mind (no specific questions regarding child abuse or dissociative signs and symptoms had been uniformly asked), there was much to read about both maltreatment and dissociation.

Since the completion of that initial research project in 2000, at least five quantitative studies, highlighting the link between dissociation and crime, found extremely high levels of dissociation among a variety of offender populations. Moskowitz (2004a, b) in his reviews of these and earlier studies, found that 25% of jail and prison inmates assessed had scored over 30 on Carlson & Putnam's (1986) Dissociative Experiences Scale (DES), with between 7.0 and 9.5% scoring above 50, a total that often indicates the presence of severe dissociative pathology. While preferring more open-ended and dialogic methods to self-administered survey instruments like the DES[1], I have to admit that Moskowitz's tallies are

---

[1] I did give my interview subjects DES questionnaires to fill out, but found that problems—ranging from illiteracy to noncompliance to incomprehension—made the findings ambiguous at best.

quite provocative and closely align with my own observations regarding the dissociative capacities of incarcerated persons.

CHILD MALTREATMENT AND DISSOCIATION

Clinicians and researchers have fairly well-grounded suspicions that the more serious dissociative illnesses are closely related to chronic physical, sexual, or psychological abuse (or a combination of types of abuse) during childhood, although such abuse may not be the only determinants of dissociative illness (Zelikovsky & Lynn, 1994). Tillman, Nash, and Lerner (1994), for example, caution that the failure of researchers to control for other pathogenic influences in the abusive environment leaves us ignorant of the true nature of the maltreatment-dissociation connection. Clearly, these researchers are correct in assuming that the association is not simply linear. Violent, sexually inappropriate, or negligent families are usually dysfunctional in a variety of ways; it is difficult, if not impossible, to tell which particular combination of conditions contributes most to members' specific psychopathologies (p. 407).

Research concerns aside, having spoken with many victims of domestic violence, I am convinced that in the thick of a beating, a rape, or a vicious psychological attack by an intimate the most archaic of defenses are called forward. In such straits, a brain in overdrive will boomerang incoming information: deny it, disavow it, depersonalize it, derealize it—turn away from what is happening even before it is translated by the nervous system into something readable as experience. That is the core of dissociative process, and it is the most primitive, essential way of dealing with the world, particularly those events or interpersonal engagements that seem potentially disintegrating.

Of course, we all dissociate defensively at times as a way of attenuating anxiety. But people growing up in extremely neglectful or abusive homes habitually resort to dissociation—not only defensively, but preemptively too. It becomes a way of hosting aggression without acknowledging its toll.

CHILD MALTREATMENT, DISSOCIATION AND ADULT VIOLENCE

According to the most recent National Institute of Justice studies, experiencing early abuse and neglect increases the likelihood of juvenile arrest close to five-fold, doubles the rate of arrest for adults, and makes it 3.1 times more likely that the victim will go on to commit a violent crime, as compared with matched controls (English, Widom, & Brandford, 2001). Indeed, almost anyone I have known who works in the courts, the prisons, or the treatment facilities that oversee violent offenders admits informally to being acutely aware of the degree to which violence is a transgenerational phenomenon. The fact that familial violence so often antecedes stranger violence, although borne out by research (Widom, 1989), is largely ignored in the highly politicized arena of criminal justice policy, despite its centrality to both prevention and rehabilitation.

Studies of clinical populations have shown that proactive aggression tends to be elevated among highly dissociative people, with pathological dissociation in some studies being an even better predictor of assaultiveness than a history of childhood abuse alone (e.g., Moskowitz, 2004b). Prison and jail populations, as already noted, are home to a large number of highly dissociative men and women, some of them very violent. With all the conceptual and epidemiological overlaps that occur in child abuse, violence, and dissociation, the field is ripe for an integrative analysis of the three.

The premise of this book is that offenders, because they have with high frequency been the victims of maltreatment in childhood, are likely to have dissociated—and subsequently reenacted—those childhood traumas. Dissociation is not the *only* way that violent induction is translated into violent enactment: children may model the actions of their caretakers, sustain central nervous system injuries that make it difficult to moderate behavior, or, being unable to retaliate against their abusers, simply seek out weaker prey to victimize. However, it is the pathological disengagement precipitated by early, intense, and repetitive trauma that most strongly facilitates the streaming of an unprocessed violent past into the present. Because dissociative processes circumvent symbolization (Bucci, 1997), attacks cannot be reflected on or learned from (Davies & Frawley, 1994; Stern, 1997b; Bromberg, 1998). Consequently, urges toward aggressing are difficult to mediate and are frequently impossible to diffuse. Dissociated violence seems destined to be replayed in an endless loop, like the very cheapest pornography.

I hope to move away from the current medical model of dissociative disorders, which, in many ways, mimics Robert Louis Stevenson's (1896) Manichean take on consciousness. Instead, I turn to the more nuanced understandings of dissociation and enactment available in contemporary neuroscience as well as in the relational and interpersonal schools of psychoanalysis.

THE TRAUMATIZED BRAIN

Post-Cartesian models of consciousness move beyond the idea that the mind is simply a correspondent of specific brain functions that record the objective world. Arnold Modell (2003) has said that the mind is "embodied," in the sense that symbolic thought requires sensory-affective charging from the more primitive areas of the brain. Severely traumatized persons may undergo a kind of defensive cauterization, so that highly charged somatosensory data remain diffuse and inaccessible for higher levels of neural processing.

Bioarchitects of trauma theory, like Bessel van der Kolk and his colleagues, have lent empirical credence to clinical hunches about the way that the brain formats abusive experiences. These researchers posit that the perceptual-affective flood engendered by a traumatic encounter is configured mainly as an autonomic response to danger; people may experience lasting hormonal and neurochemical changes, as well as deformations of neuroanatomical structure, following intense or prolonged exposure to threatening stimuli (van der Kolk, 1996, p. 220). Of particular interest are regions of the brain that are implicated in the ability to reflect upon mental contents, first by attaching emotional significance to them and then by representing intentions symbolically, as a rehearsal for action. These areas have been shown to be compromised during trauma, and leading to a disabling of normal integrative function:

The experience is laid down, and later retrieved, as isolated images, bodily sensations, smells and sounds that feel alien and separate from other life experiences. Because the hippocampus has not played its usual role in helping to locate the incoming information in time and space, these fragments continue to lead an isolated existence. Traumatic memories are timeless and ego-alien (p. 295).

Alterations in mindfulness manifest as posttraumatic defenses with a distinctively dissociative flavor, including amnesias, derealizations, depersonalizations, alexithymias, and somatizations. In a healthy personality, dissociation will still assert itself defensively, but an underlying sense of psychic unity and temporal stability will prevail as the parts of the self speak to one another and assess reality; philosopher Jennifer Radden (1996) calls this kind of dissociativity "the unremarkable heterogeneity of the singular self" (p. 23). At the other end of the continuum, in dissociative disorders proper, symbolic thought—most often expressed through language—is unavailable as a referent for experience. Dissociators feel imperiled and act to diffuse the threat, which, in many of the cases detailed here, had deadly consequences. Without language, action itself announces intention.

There is an interesting convergence of clinical and experimental findings on the relationship between language and crime. Herve Cleckley (1941) the psychiatrist whose early, groundbreaking writings on both criminality and dissociation (Thigpen & Cleckley, 1957) have become classics, recognized the degree to which "the mask of sanity" worn by criminal psychopaths disguises not only atypical psychosis, but a kind of "semantic dementia" affecting receptive and expressive language. Cleckley (1941) hypothesized that language deficits impacted negatively on the processing of emotional stimuli, divorcing action from description, potentially subverting value judgments, and precluding consensual meaning-making (see Richards, 1998).

It never ceases to amaze me that Cleckley's (1941) classic, *The Mask of Sanity*, revered in forensic circles for its supposed revelations about the conniving nature of criminals, is usually cited without its even more revealing subtitle: *An Attempt to Clarify Some Issues About the So-Called Psychopath*. Indeed, on the publication of the first edition of his book, Cleckley "was so much impressed with the degree of maladjustment in these patients that he felt at the time, and said, they should be called psychotic." In later editions of the book, fearing that his words would be used to absolve offenders of legal responsibility, Cleckley reworked his diagnosis. In the 1988 edition, Cleckley offered that the psychopath differed from an "integrated personality" in that the former did not enter reality in quite the same way, owing to an unconscious, "far-reaching and persistent blocking, absence, deficit, or dissociation" (p. 370–371)[2]. Cleckley felt that one of the more robust clinical indications of criminals' dissociation fell in the language sphere, where "so-called psychopaths" demonstrate a kind of

---

[2]Although I think that Cleckley was remarkably prescient in his later analysis, I regret the subtle shift of position. In the original work it was clear that the criminal's "mask" was a thin veil tentatively covering true psychosis; in the later work, "the mask" is understood only as the offender's intention to deceive, an interpretation I do not think Cleckley would endorse.

evaluative aphasia, an inability to differentiate different kinds of feelings within themselves or decipher the emotional expressions of others.

Operationalizing and testing Cleckley's clinical observations, researchers have abundantly documented abnormalities in semantic processing among criminals tested on a variety of psychophysiological measures, particularly as such mental activity pertains to the recognition and valuation of affectively charged words, pictures and stories (Hare & Jutai, 1988; Raine et al., 1990; Damasio, Tranel, & Damasio, 1990; Patrick, Bradley & Lang, 1993; Patrick, Cuthbert, & Lang, 1994; Rieber & Vetter, 1994; Blair et al., 1995). Criminals' semantic ineptitude is often mired in a general kind of physiologic under-arousal, as demonstrated by their failure to learn avoidance responses to electric shocks used to reinforce learning during experimental trials (Lykken, 1955, 1957). At least one forensic psychiatrist, Dorothy Otnow Lewis (1992), has wondered if the imperviousness to pain is a result of early abuse.

Attending to chronic or extreme physical pain is an assault on sanity; the hurt is compounded when the purveyor of pain is a loved one on whom the child is dependent. Thus, children who have suffered repeated beatings may retain them simply as somatosensory intrusions, never conceptualized or articulated in an internal dialogue as "pain." Unfortunately, when forswearing pain becomes habitual, it does not enhance survival; if a two-year-old did not experience the pain of touching a hot stove, she would simply leave her hand there to burn. (Indeed the perception of pain is so integral to existence that people born with dysautonomia, a congenital insensitivity to pain, rarely live to adulthood.) Because circumstance dictates that an abused child must leave his hand on the burning stove (sometimes quite literally), he becomes adept at not acknowledging the heat. When analgesia for pain is coupled with a loss of descriptive ability, the pain will often initiate a displaced reaction bereft of moral intention.

PUNISHMENT AND GUILT

Since it is the work of the traumatized self to dissociate victimacy (in self and other) and agency (in self and other), the part of subjectivity that might house some kind of evaluative moral scale—classically as well as colloquially known as conscience—is functionally segregated. Many offenders do not acknowledge empathic pangs or suffer conventional expiatory guilt because the emotions aroused are too potentially disintegrative to heed. As a consequence, these offenders cannot verbally express remorse in the way that the criminal justice system demands in exchange for judicial munificence.

The presence of guilt is eschewed in the many writings about violent criminals, and its absence is considered a necessary criterion for the diagnosis of sociopathy or antisocial personality disorder. Yet it is unlikely that any child, no matter how dysfunctional the parents' child-rearing practices, has not been introduced to at least a basic notion of right and wrong (Whitman & Akutagawa, 2004). If anything, in an abusive home, ideas of right and wrong are exponentially amplified and twisted; they are seldom if ever absent. In fact, just as capricious and painful punishments in childhood inculcate anxiety and guilt (Sullivan, 1953, p. 344), many perpetrators tend to preserve guilt in the form of a sense of pervasive culpability—one that extends even past their actual crimes. For example, one man I interviewed insisted he had shot someone during an armed holdup, although he had only robbed the victim. It was relatively common for subjects either to reveal crimes for which they had not been arrested, or to question the magnitude of the destruction they had wrought, assuming it to be greater than the charges reflected. Of course, U.S. jails host many people who have falsely confessed to crimes, often voluntarily (Kassin, 1997).

The pervasive guilt that envelops the victim-perpetrator becomes a vehicle for disavowing the persecution—or at least the malicious intent—of the loved caretaker. In what follows, I have italicized an inmate's undoing of his abuse and his invalidation of the agency of his abuser.

In the islands, grandma did the disciplining with her husband. We were beaten with belts, most likely with the buckle. We were beaten until it welted, *but never on the head.*

It was my mother who had the temper. Everything set her off. She threw things at me, threatened to kill me. In the summer of 1977, she beat me and my brother all day long. She made us take our clothes off and kneel and then beat us. That's why my brother left home, because she would beat him instead of talking. *But she never knocked him out.*

She would get mad if we played after school. My grandmother said mom was abusive and couldn't raise kids. My uncle claims that she used to torture the cat. *But I was never hospitalized for a beating.*

When I asked this man about the origins of an old burn mark on his arm, he explained perfunctorily, "It's a brand—all babies got to get it to keep from being stolen." In his Orwellian narrative, being burned is a kind of security; the scar becomes a talisman against separation or abandonment. Usually, though, criminal narrators are not so lyrical. They directly assume responsibility for their victimization:

I had more welts from a garrison belt . . . my mother had to raise four kids by herself—she ran my father out with a knife. She once shoved a lit cigarette down my throat when she caught me smoking. My mother was a beautiful person, so lovely. If I said no, she beat me from one end of the house to another. I was only beaten if I did something wrong—like not eating.

Rethinking abuse as a self-initiated act confers the illusion of control; it is as if potential predators can be monitored and restrained through active choice. Moreover, as most of us are more concerned with consonance than with accuracy in the overall arc of our stories, it is reasonable to fable the past according to our current self-assessment. For an offender, it makes sense that an abusive caretaker's earlier valuation would echo the criminal justice system's later verdict, providing the retrospective corroboration of the offender's contemporary badness. Freud (1916) was not wrong in opining that criminals may be born from a sense of guilt, instead of the other way around.

SEXUAL HOMICIDE: AN ATTACHMENT THEORY

What distinguishes a rigid, pathological kind of dissociation from an adaptive plurality of selves may be that in the former there can be no imaginative or fruitful discourse among the parts of subjectivity, only static and sequential monologues, drained of art and resource (Hermans, 1996; Stern, 1997b). As Pye (1995) suggests, traumatized persons are so persecuted by their own thoughts that "imagination [itself] becomes a place of assault" (p. 162). Productive reverie is absent and cathartic fantasy cannot be woven.

Although offenders, particularly those who commit violent sexual crimes, are said to be indulging their perverse aggressive fantasies (Burgess et al., 1986), my work suggests that they have almost no talent for actual fantasy, although they are often sidetracked by obsessive rumination, dissociative reverie, or border-line delusions. Although deviant, even sadistic, sexual fantasies are a staple among the noncriminal public (Crepault & Couture, 1980), I see no evidence that most sex offenders engage them exclusively, or even at a level of symbolization that deserves the label fantasy.

Even when something more closely resembling symbolization processes occurs (and it does only briefly and intermittently, as the offender cannot main-tain this higher order organization of ideas for long), it appears that what is lusted after is much more a relational attachment than a sexual release. As Donald Meltzer (1992) has so movingly articulated in his exploration of claus-trophobic phenomena, for those terrified of abandonment, the precondition for any object relation is object merger, the powerful need to "sleep inside the mother" thus displacing potential rivals. But the defensive remedy itself activates additional splitting and projective identification as the pleasure of fusion gives way to the dread of entombment.

It is no accident that murder is referred to as the taking of a life; murderers often describe their acts as somehow reifying their own unfelt existence. Bollas (1991) alluded to it as a companionship of corpses. Killing makes the killer both omnipotent and immortal—murderer and victim are eternally bound. Indeed, the leitmotif of "ownership" of the victim's body as well as the accumulation of "trophies" (personal belongings of victims) that runs through scenes of serial murder may be the eerie manifestation of life-affirming themes.

In Patrick Suskind's (1991) novel *Perfume*, a serial killer born with no body odor methodically murders to appropriate the scent of a lovable human being. The killer, Grenouille, distills human perfume from the skin and hair of his cherished victims in the hope of becoming one of them. Less metaphorically, Ted Bundy offered the following treatise on the satisfactions of violent behavior:

> [Murder] becomes possession. They are a part of you, and you [two] are for-ever one. Even after twenty or thirty it's the same thing, because you are the last one *there*. You *feel* the last bit of breath leaving their body. You're look-ing into their eyes and, basi-cally, a person in that situation is God! You then possess them and they shall forever be a part of you (Geberth, 1996, p. 752).

It seems that many sexual murderers, far from having primarily sexual goals, seek the kind of merger that Ted Bundy so creepily and elegantly details in his treatise on victim possession. Indeed, sex murders are often logged as such because evidence at the crime scene suggests that a variety of primitive actions have *substituted* for sexuality, such as biting, ritual body arrangement, or pene-tration with inanimate objects. For many of these offenders, early abuse and abandonment may have become sexualized as a defense against recognizing the malevolence of the assaulting caretaker. Anxiety and arousal, thus conflated, became the cornerstone of perversion, boomeranging offenders back to a diffuse pregenital sexuality, a regressive stance from which adult conventions regarding gender, age, and bodily integrity can be violated with impunity.

Less frankly sexual than primitively incorporative, most sex murders demonstrate both the need for, and the terror of, engulfment by a figure onto whom one's primary attachment needs have been projected. The seamless cycling of projection and introjection in sexual homicide eerily mirrors early caregiver-child interactions that predate true individuation. A startling example of this can be drawn from the trial transcripts of serial killer Dennis Rader, self nicknamed BTK for his method of operations: "bind, torture, kill" (Wilgoren, J. 2005).

Rader, given a chance to speak after being sentenced to 10 consecutive life terms in prison, took advantage of it by strolling down memory lane with some of his victims. He spoke about all the things that he had in common with those he had killed: the concern for dogs he shared with Dolores Davis, the Air Force service he had in common with Joe Otero, the abiding love for poetry and drawing he shared with Joe's 11-year-old daughter, Josie, whom he had hung naked from a sewer pipe prior to masturbating. Rader even spoke of being reunited with his victims in the afterlife some day, where they might continue to answer his needs. It was as perverse a twinning as I had ever heard—this grandiose identification with victims, pronounced not in sorrow or regret, but as a dispassionate observation about entwined destinies. Clearly, this is a man for whom the prehomicide method of binding had significance far beyond mere victim control or sexual sadism. Rader has said that "bonding" (sic) was the "big thing" for him, the most exhilarating part of his rituals (*Dateline NBC*, 2005).

Rader delivered his courtroom speech nonchalantly, almost as if his victims would have appreciated the irony and agreed with his conclusions. His dreamwish of similitude exemplifies the extent to which victim-objects may furnish a canvas for idealized, as well as persecutory, identifications for the perpetrator. The end product of such elaborate fusion is the enshrinement of a dyadic self-state in the offender that preserves an otherwise fleeting attachment to his chosen victim.

PERSONAE NON GRATAE

Throughout this book, I discuss the myriad ways dissociation presents itself to the forensic clinician. In my original set of 64 interviews, roughly one third of the inmates functioned at a borderline level of dissociative process; they chronically used dissociation to deflect anxiety but were likely to be at least partially conscious of their behaviors. They were capable of using, in addition to dissociation, some higher order defense mechanisms such as projection (as opposed to simply projective identification or its cousin, projective pseudoidentification)[3]

---

[3]Projection consists of projecting onto another person that which is intolerable in the self and thereby externalizing the source of threat. Projective identification is a more primitive defense wherein a person—losing all sense of boundary between himself and the object—makes the other experience the terror, dread, rage, and so on that is too disintegrating to experience oneself (Kernberg, 1992). Projective pseudoidentification is a term that identifies an even more regressed level of dissociative maneuvering where "not-me" aspects of subjectivity are evacuated into potential victims, often at the cost of their lives (Meloy, 1997a).

and could, at times, straddle the split in their psyches enough to feel momentary concern for their victims or even a fleeting sense of guilt. They were capable of some fantasy activity, albeit underdeveloped and redundant, more like fixation than imagination and often not volitional.

A second group of interviewees, comprising just under a quarter of my sample, were more manifestly dissociative; 11 even met the criteria for dissociative identity disorder. The overwhelming majority (92.8%) of these offenders carried a previous psychiatric diagnosis, although none had been recognized as primarily dissociative. These inmates displayed such a confusing concurrence of symptoms that each intervening diagnostician interpreted their presentation differently: half the severely dissociative subjects had at least four previous, but divergent, diagnoses. In chapter four, I discuss these offenders, who seemed least able to differentiate real from imaginary, self from victim, and metaphors for things from the things themselves. I explore the ways that the men negotiated precarious identities within an overarching narrative of self-and-other loss, loathing, and occasional love.

Early psychoanalysts writing about dissociation conceived of a process in which dissociated parts of the self went to sleep at the wheel and left the driving to highly aroused (but unlicensed) agent-provocateurs (Janet, 1889; Freud, 1896; Laing, 1959; Sullivan, 1953). Sometimes these unprocessed experiences are enacted with a frequency and force that raises them to near-characterological standing.

Sullivan's (1953) vision of dissociation seems most sensitive to the subtle interplay of conscious, unconscious, and interpersonal forces in the consolidation of defenses:

> The first security operation for the maintenance of selective inattention is found in the dramatization of roles which a person knows to be false ... Second, a person may use parataxic you-me patterns which are incongruous with the actual interpersonal situation; and in this instance he has no clear realization of the multiple "personalities" involved and of the instability of his behavior ... Third, a person may use substitutive processes [from very subtle shifts in the communicative set] to the utmost absorption in intense preoccupation with covert processes [which] may be with or without behavior which is, or borders on being, totally inexplicable ... [F]inally, there are transient or enduring "transformations of personality" [pp. 346–347].

Sullivan's theory is compatible with much of what we see clinically in abused children and violent adults abused in childhood. These psychologically compromised persons sometimes compensate for affective or cognitive lacunae with an exquisitely confabulated autobiography; they write a past that defensively serves the present with which it is conflated. "Emplotting" one's life in such a way lends coherence to fragmented affect or cognition, serializes life events in a manner that grants the illusion of causality (Sarbin, 1989), and makes meaning from the mayhem of brutal interactions with caretakers. Emplotment can also make sense of the acts of an accused perpetrator, whom a criminal may regard as "not-me" even while acknowledging complicity in violent enactments.

I hesitate to call these alien aspects of personality "false," as other observers (Winnicott, 1960; Laing, 1959) have, because those aspects delineate the real, though bankrupt or banished, voices of subjective experience. Dissociated aspects of the self are false only in the sense that they represent the defensive façades of children during early interactions with others who refused to recognize and validate the fledging communications of an emergent, authentic self.

Unconflicted selves often borrow their visages from an available cast of social characters—the innocent, the avenger, the savior, and the like—which is why they seem so artificial, so "faked" to the clinicians or attorneys who encounter them. With so much secondary gain to be realized, it is not a far stretch to imagine that people are exaggerating their pathologies. Of course, they may be: the ease with which many perpetrators suspend conscious attention—and shift agency—is an example of both extreme sensitivity to threat and extreme habituation to a particular defensive mode.

A case in point is that of Kenneth Bianchi, convicted of the brutal "Hillside Strangler" murders. Bianchi's multiple personality disorder diagnosis— roundly eschewed by the prosecution's psychiatric experts at his trial as the antics of a malingerer trying to avoid the gas chamber—is even today, 25 years into his 118-year prison term, debated among certain forensic clinicians. One of the turning points in the prosecution's unraveling of the defense's insanity case rested on the presentation of evidence indicating that Bianchi's alternate "personalities" had sometimes been appropriated from real people in his life. This appropriation is not at all unusual: clinicians who work with criminal psychopaths suspect that their apparent talent for mimicry is trussed by the static verticality of their defensive structure. Even clinicians who staunchly believe that Bianchi's multiple personalities were malingered (e.g., Meloy, 1997a, pp. 172–181), recognize the complex interweaving of conscious deception and unconscious self-deception that occur in cases like Bianchi's, where the criminal patient is likely prone to splitting and dissociation:

> The verticality of defenses is most helpful when alternative, and perhaps very contradictory, affects and ideations are imitated or simulated; for there is no sense of conscious ambiguity or contradiction in the psychopath's phenomenal experience of self. This may account for the chameleon like effect of certain psychopathic individuals [p. 144].

> What we are dealing with here is not a complete man at all but something that suggests a subtly constructed reflex machine which can mimic the human personality perfectly (Cleckley, 1988, p. 369).

In survivors of maltreatment, disembodied voices become almost hyperconscious, positing reparative images to countervail abuse and death symbols. The images have been termed incipient personalities in the trauma literature (Fagan and McMahon, 1994), but they usually do not exhibit the complexity, variation, and depth of true personality constructs. A clearer way to envisage them is as subnarrators created to interface with the world (and articulate an acceptable narrative history) without risking the loss of the few shards of authentic identity that remain.

There is an almost generic quality to the self-portraiture of abused, dissociating persons: an immobilized child; a "protector" character, often violent; and a shaman, or healer (Stein, 2000). Similarly, Dell and Eisenhower (1990) describe three core personality types in dissociative identity patients: fearful, protective, and avenging. Deidre Barrett (1994) also notes the caricatured nature of personality subtypes in dissociative persons and likens them to the archetypes of the collective unconscious described by Carl Jung. She finds that Jung's main archetypes: Persona (the compliant host self), Shadow (the evil self), Puer (the child self), and Anima/us (the cross-gender self) appear with startling frequency in the personality constellations of dissociative patients. Both Fritz Perls and Jung saw nighttime dream characters as dissociated parts of the self, trying to be heard; Barrett asserts that "trauma seems to give dream characters more autonomy . . . with extreme cases [of abuse], they move into the waking world." (p. 130).

Barrett deftly bridges the Jungian analytic model with a narrativist tradition that emphasizes autobiographic construction mainly through the plagiarism of available cultural scripts (Albright, 1994). Confabulatory narratives and their authors may be modeled on confederates, enemies, and even victims, real people that typically demonstrate the archival traits to which Jung referred. In this way, culturally available "dramatistic" forms are absorbed, later to be resuscitated as narrative guideposts for schematizing amoral engagements and assigning agency (Sarbin, 1989, p. 194).

WHERE DO WE GO FROM HERE?

The final chapter of the book is not about every patient who wishes his mother's back to break or dreams of murdering his psychoanalyst and feels troubled in some way by his own aggression. Most of these patients will be all right, at least as concerns the public's safety. Conceivably, much of what they have dissociated has been made sufficiently conscious as to engender conflict; psychic restitching becomes immeasurably easier after this.

The chapter deals with people who have already committed criminal violence, whether or not they have been confined for it, and with those who seem perilously close to crossing over into overt demonstrations of irreversible harm. The first group I have already discussed at length; the latter are the "other" aggressive people. They are the ones who never get to jail, but arrive in treatment rooms—family mandated or self-motivated—because they autocratically rule their wives and children, kick the cat, drink to make their obsessive longing for a coworker abate, or are in the habit of hiring 15-year-old prostitutes. Maybe they are a hair's breadth from a monumental enactment, or maybe they are lucky enough to get help when they are still young, before the stories have calcified and the endings have become predictable.

Statistics are always sobering, so I will offer a few, just to familiarize you with the magnitude of the problem. There are over 5.6 million adults in the U.S. who have served time in a state or Federal prison. In jails and state prisons, roughly half those incarcerated were sentenced for committing violent crimes. Eighty percent of those who commit violence against an intimate seriously injure or kill their victims. According to victim surveys, there are more than two million violent female offenders. There are over a quarter million sex offenders under the supervision of the correctional system. The number of children maltreated in the course of a year is close to one million yet, given the fact that so much neglect and abuse goes unreported, this may be a gross underestimation of the problem.

Undeniably, there are at least 1400 fatalities each year from child abuse or neglect; it is difficult to argue about the statistical validity of small dead bodies.[4]

Is it naïve to suggest that aggressive or violent people can be helped? Is this even a legitimate goal, especially as concerns those who are already imprisoned? Well, it has to be because most offenders, including the most violent ones, will be back on the streets. They will return: sooner than you think and angrier than before their entanglement with the law. With little to appease their blood lust (as the gothic novelists and quite a few modern criminal profilers say) except more violent crime.

Given the sweep of the modern panopticon,[5] it is amazing how little we see about aggressive engagements. Leman-Langlois (2003), writing in *Police and Society*, avers that our observations of criminals are "myopic" because they shrink crime to its most obvious behavioral manifestations (p. 43). Interventions with offenders in surveillance-based systems usually consist of confrontation and containment. As disciplinary incidents occur, they are responded to with force. If the prisoner rebellion ratchets upward too steeply, total lockdown is imposed. While these intercessions may quash a particular incident or even a more general uprising, they are unlikely to deter future violence. Most worrisome is the increased use of controversial "corrective" interventions with electroshock, injectibles like Depo-Provera, and guided hypnosis for offenders, geared toward installing phobic reactions to criminal cues in the environment. (By the way, the response to more common forms of social aggression—ranging from road rage to domestic assault to schoolyard bullying—is similarly reactive and reductive, if somewhat less like Anthony Burgess's (1988) *Clockwork Orange*.)

Cognitive approaches to criminal behavior became popular in the 1970s, following Yochelson and Samenow's (1976) identification of "fifty thinking errors" of criminals. Cognitive behavioral technique allows a therapist to keep a greater distance from the potentially corruptive wellspring of aggressive offenders' perversion and hatred, but it "risks depicting violent men as faulty thinkers, normal in theory but abnormal in action" (Gadd, 2004, p. 187). These programs ignore the complex underpinnings of human behavior and the inevitability that the urge toward violation will assert itself again and again if its genesis is not addressed. Moreover, they proceed from the assumption that the part of the self committing the crime is readily accessible for conversion.

The therapeutic programs that do exist for violent adult offenders are based primarily on some combination of cognitive-behavioral techniques, like "firewalling." This popular strategy for treating sex offenders suggests that, on encountering a potential victim or similarly arousing circumstance, a rapist or pedophile should construct a mental block between his offensive thoughts and his more benign ones—sort of a purposeful dissociation. I argue that dissociation

---

[4]Statistics from the Bureau of Justice Statistics, Health and Human Services, and the National Crime Survey.

[5]Panopticon is a term coined by criminologist Jeremy Bentham (1791) to describe the architecture of his ideal prison, which would have a central viewing station perched over a spoke-like cell structure, allowing relatively few custodians to watch over many prisoners. Foucault (1979) wrote of the internalizing function of such surveillance in a more general program of social control.

is where all the trouble starts and that until aggression is appropriately integrated, offenders will have no reprieve from its blind enactment.

U.S. programs contrast unfavorably with many prison programs in the U.K., which are largely administered by personnel who have been heavily influenced by Kleinian psychoanalytic models that rely on expanding reflection, imagination, and expression through art, writing, drama, group, community or milieu therapy, and individual psychotherapy. It is the watchword of many of these initiatives that the work of mourning and consequential remorse (for one's self and one's victims) is achieved only in dynamic relationship with others, who can both witness and contain that which feels shamefully out of control. To quote British therapist Michael Parker (2003), who has worked with offenders in group analytic situations, "catharsis is arguably not an autistic activity, but one needing to be received by another person" (p. 179).

Unfortunately, practitioners who chose to treat psychodynamically in a prison environment face a triple whammy: an unwelcoming system, a potentially dangerous and inarticulate clientele, and their own dissociated aggression. These issues and others are discussed in greater depth in the final chapter.

METHODS AND SOURCES

I am always astounded by the absence of narrative that enfeebles many criminals' recitation of violent events. At one time, this kind of cognitive or emotional vacancy was ascribed to the inherent human tendency to repress knowledge of threatening experiences once they had occurred. In recent years, however, neurological and psychological paradigms have begun to shift, suggesting that much of our interaction with the world, rather than being known and then somehow "unknown," is simply not attended to in the first place; it is archived as raw biological data rather than as symbolized, articulatable experience. Dissociation, the nonpathological weeding out of stimuli through inattention, may become habitual and defensive in people who face chronic overstimulation, in the form of assaultive engagements with others.[6] In potentially annihilative moments (whether one is the recipient or the dispenser of injury) dissociation becomes the default position; hence, the memories that would inform a detailed narrative are not fully fashioned.

In a situation that presses for certainty—because the stakes can be so high—a forensic interviewer cannot always be sure exactly whose experiential world is reflected in the words of the interviewee. Offenders' stories often seem artificial and constructed, as if they had borrowed a generic life script on which were overlaid a few distinguishing details. Because narratives can be so impoverished (or, conversely, overembellished) much that is related about both child abuse and the sensation of deferred agency for criminal activity is difficult to believe. Understandably, those of us who evaluate offenders are concerned about being conned and manipulated by our charges. When the credibility bar is set too high, however, it may impede the scope of inquiry and color the interpretation of

---

[6]It is less clear, but probable, that chronic neglect, or understimulation, triggers the same kind of dissociative mechanism, particularly when it alternates with aggressive engagements (Shengold, 1989).

whatever information is received. As is the case with other populations, a neutral curiosity is more strategic than is incredulity and constant contest.

Sullivan (1970) admonished interviewers to remain aware that their own defensive "self-systems" would always be standing in the way of gathering anxiety-provoking information, just as the subject's cautionary apparatus might forbid the conscious formulation of those data, much less their articulation. Without some attention to one's own censor, it becomes almost impossible to muster the experiential worlds of criminals in a way that illuminates the path to their horrific crimes.

It is a common human tendency, especially on hearing shocking or sordid information about experiences of child abuse, suicidality, sexual sadism, or criminal violence, to assume that one has "heard everything" and to abandon prematurely a particular line of questioning. To avoid this problem, in both the research and the clinical work done on the hospital prison ward, follow-up questions were written into the interview rather than left to the discretion of individual interviewers.

Unlike clinicians dealing with traumatized or aggressive patients in a typical therapy situation, forensic practitioners do not have the luxury of time to develop trust or encourage the slow trickle of information that is tolerable for many persons. Teasing the "truth" from defense and deception is a long-term endeavor; but, since access to prisoners may be severely restricted, those doing evaluation or research in correctional facilities must find a way to develop trust, disarm defenses, elicit sensitive material, and utilize countertransference reactions in a collapsed time frame.

Much can be learned when the flow of information remains unrestricted, but such a method has definite limitations (MacKinnon & Michaels, 1971; McCracken, 1988; Della Femina, Yeager & Lewis, 1990; Kruttschnit & Dornfeld, 1992; Stein & Lewis, 1992). First, left to their own devices, subjects will omit information they perceive as irrelevant but that may, in fact, be integral to analysis. Second, subjects may consciously suppress information that is painful to remember, difficult to articulate, or, if revealed, might have deleterious consequences on the adjudication of their cases or on the circumstances of their incarceration. Finally, the most salient clues are often the most tenaciously repressed or, as is often the case with highly threatening material, completely dissociated. In the absence of repeated probes, such experiential markers may never surface, depriving us of true insight into individual perceptions and motivations. Sensitive material is always difficult to uncover. This is all the more true of investigations into the genesis of criminal activities, which by their very nature are veiled, even independent of more covert psychological processes. Sullivan (1990) an innovator of methods of tapping repressed or dissociated material, likened the early stages of a good interview to a reconnaissance mission where data are gathered and weighed, and earmarked for finer investigation:

When people find themselves recurrently in obscure situations which they feel they should understand and actually don't, and in which they feel their prestige requires them to take adequate action (a somewhat hypothetical entity, since they do not know what the situation is), they are clearly in need of psychiatric assistance. This assistance is by way of the participant observation of the psychiatrist and the patient. A great many questions may be asked and answered in the psychiatric interview before the patient sees much of what the psychiatrist is exploring; but, in the process, the patient will have experienced many beginning clarifications of matters which will subsequently take on considerable personal significance [p. 23].

The instrument that yielded much of the data for this book was a semi-structured interview protocol (Stein, 2000, appendix A). The interview has a carefully scripted format but easily accommodates the insertion of additional nuggets of information, and allows each interviewer to take subjects down separate predesigned paths. Much like interactive novellas for the computer, the interview allows the writing of a story with twists, turns, and false endings, but a story that moves inexorably onward.

For a variety of reasons, witting and not, offenders' stories can seem as distorted as the head of Medusa in Perseus's shield. Elusive narratives can only begin to be pinned down as the interviewer presses toward an increasingly sharper recitation of events. In long-term treatment situations certainly, but even in briefer interventions, the reconstruction of events in meticulous subjective detail may help to bring the "not-me" aspects of the personality into the consultation room, where they can be vetted (Bromberg, 2005, pp. 413–414). I always hoped, when interviewing violent people, that "the devil" would emerge in the details and become accessible for intimate conversation.

Secondary Sources

Quite a different situation exists when examining the archival data found in law enforcement files. At that point, one's research agenda must be superimposed on extant information. Since the broad goals of a police interrogation or competency/sanity evaluation are often antithetical to the objectives of a social science researcher, scanning official documents for clues about perpetrators' interiority can seem like using a dimestore magnifying glass to examine protozoa. Law enforcement grillings, expert witness interviews, confessions, victim statements, eye-witness reports, autopsy photographs, and the like offer a very different body of evidence about the accused and the alleged crimes than would be gleaned through person-to-person contact. Archived narratives are static and so can be interrogated only textually, decoded inferentially as one might a piece of literature.

Throughout the book, I distinguish narratives recorded in police files, from personally elicited ones, by labeling them as such. Although I fully believe that my interpretations hold for both kinds of data, I am the first to point out that assertions about the dissociativity of offenders I have not personally interviewed, of necessity, rest more on conjecture than do those based on the findings of a detailed, personally conducted, inquiry.

trauma and Trauma

Definitions of trauma range from the all-inclusive (i.e., anything subjectively experienced as overwhelming) to the narrowly restrictive (i.e., objectively discernible events, like surviving a war or a plane crash). The literature on trauma is vast and is not revisited here; specialists have produced significant work in this realm, and have examined trauma from myriad perspectives, including biological, social, psychological, cultural, and historical. Psychological theories regarding trauma both predate and have outlived Freud and are currently enjoying a renaissance of sorts as empirical evidence mounts that, on physical and emotional plains alike, trauma annuls selfhood with a special, disintegrative force.

Since charges first surfaced indicating that Freud may have been politically motivated to suppress his seduction theory of traumatic neurosis (Masson, 1984), the psychoanalytic field has vigorously embraced the controversy surrounding its replacement with oedipal theory, which foregrounds the significance of unconscious fantasies of sexual union in the production of incestuous memories. The reexamination of Freud's cases has led to many contemporary clinical analyses that foreground actual abuse and its dissociation rather than imagined impropriety and its repression.[7] Clinicians have widely commented on the way dissociated traumatic material remains aloof from autobiographical integration and thus is prone to be robotically reenacted under stressful conditions (Davies & Frawley, 1994; Stern, 1997b; Bromberg, 1998). Attachment and developmental theorists, connecting additional pieces about aggressive behavior, have bridged current empirical findings about the cognitive effects of child maltreatment with older relational notions of internalization and projection (Fonagy et al., 2002).

Defining abuse is somewhat easier than defining trauma. In research, I was taught to stick to a conservative definition of abuse, so as to avoid weakening findings through overinclusiveness. Thus, in my early quantitative work, only the most villainous mistreatment was coded as child abuse: knuckle punches, burns, starvation, broken limbs, violence precipitating unconsciousness, threatened or attempted murder, forcible rape or sodomy, sex under the age of 12 with someone at least five years senior. Qualitative work has given me slightly more leeway to include even borderline cases of maltreatment, inasmuch as I give the reader enough information with which to judge for themselves the relative severity of the childhood circumstances presented.

Largely, though, I still write about people who have endured the extremes of maltreatment. So, while I acknowledge that subtler forms of interpersonal aggression are indeed potentially traumatic, even the most offensive cases of purely psychological abuse are, of necessity, underreported here. This conservative research schema serendipitously aligns well with ego theorists, who separate catastrophic levels of trauma from lesser levels of threat and assume a hierarchy of possible adaptive reactions from the neurotic to the psychotic (Solnit & Kris, 1967; Krystal, 1988). A theme I return to again and again in these chapters is that *all traumas are not created equal.* Neither is their symptomological expression.

---

[7]Although more consistent attention has been paid to sexual molestation than to physical maltreatment in the psychoanalytic literature, I regard them both as progenitors of violent enactment, including those violent sexual crimes that so demonstrably link childhood pain, excitement, and disavowal with defensive sexualization.

2

Conversing with Mutes

I sometimes felt that it was a cruel and unusual punishment to make them speak at all. Not, as is often the case with traumatized persons, because the reactivation of a painful memory schema swarmed the senses, swamping psychological reserves. Actually, despite the fact that my discussions with perpetrators unstitched acts of voluminous cruelty, I almost never saw offenders cry or rage. It was just that there seemed to be so few words to retrieve. Analytically considered, most criminal narratives I collected were illusory or, at best, derivative. One murderess, explaining why she had disposed of her boyfriend's body parts in sundry locations, said—*without irony*—"I didn't want to put all my eggs in one basket." Such banality chills the soul, no matter how you parse it. I guess that the unemotional, clichéd reiteration of villainy is what, perhaps, imbues many observers with the nearly universal urge to dehumanize offenders.

For the most part, the silver-tongued manipulators of criminal lore have been distinctly underrepresented, both in the groups I have interviewed personally and among those whose confessional accounts I have read in police files. For many aggressive offenders, the very act of speaking is incredibly labored. Mouths move out of sync with words, like a badly dubbed Godzilla movie. Or they wrap around irrelevancies, or swear no memory of what has happened, just before relating every disowned, dreadful detail in b-flat.

THE TEXT OF MUTENESS[1]

When language fails to capture or convey experience, memoranda are expressed through other registers, from pantomime to ululation, and psychiatric sign to criminal signature. Often only the residue of violent gestures, recorded at the crime scene, provides interpretable data.

One child murderer, himself molested and beaten in childhood, did not even possess the linguistic capacity to verbally spirit away his tiny prey. Instead he trilled, uncannily mimicking the soulful whistle of steam engine trains. The children followed him from state fairs to wordless deaths by railroad tracks.

---

[1]From Brooks (2001).

He covered them with cardboard, a shield against the battering sun and the prying eyes of other transients. Eight days later, in police custody, he told investigators that he had "seen the murderer put the rope around the boy's neck, but I couldn't save him in time." This is the dissociated self as a paralingual apparatus. External pressures generate a metered disavowal, accompanied by an acknowledgment (Freud, 1940). Perpetration is psychically exiled (an embodiment of Sullivan's, "not-me") toward the end that conflict is externalized, dissipating anxiety. As long as the locus of the conflict remains external to the self, only part of it is available for internal representation and articulation; the other part is enacted (Bucci, 1997; Bromberg, 2004; Stern, 2004). When evocation of older traumata—in this case, fear and rage attendant to the victimization of a young boy—goes unrecognized, it is acted out instead (Bucci, 2002; 781).

The observation that "not-me" selves are embodied in perpetration, and that they are so often counterposed by heroic selves seeking to right dissociated enactments, suggests that there may be less of an amnesiac barricade between self-states than has been supposed. This possibility is important to considerations of criminal responsibility. Someone in the self-system formulates the dissociated acts in whole or impart, the implication being that even the most pathological persons exert a mix of what Stern (1997b) calls "weak and strong dissociation." Though linkages are tenuous and scant, they do exist, underlying the curious ability of dissociative patients to witness and judge unformulated states even when those states are not, strictly speaking, accessible in conscious domains.

For this perpetrator, the strangulation of the young boy choked off his own words, recreating the imposed silence of his own horrific childhood. The struggle to control that rage—the perpetrator's perception that he was a bystander trying to avert tragedy—gives voice to conscience, however distant and diminished. There emerges (and I have seen this again and again); a reparative narrator who attempts attunement or reconstitution on behalf of the part who can neither hold nor repair objects and thus obliterates them. Sometimes the subnarrators vie for dominance (as in the foregoing story); other times they effect the same enactment with divergent goals, as did the confessant who told police that his friend had stabbed the victim first, but she was still alive, and "I couldn't stand to see her like that," and so he had to stab her again to "finish her off." My college research assistant wrote a note to me in the margin of this narrative: "Seemed as though he felt he was saving her, or helping her!" Indeed, it's another version of true selflessness (irony intended). In a suicide note, this despairing perpetrator wrote of his ongoing "troubles" with women. He concluded, "This is why I am a ghost." Clearly, *somebody's* misery needed to end; the perpetrator, caught in an eddy of projective identification, just could not decipher whose.

FORKED TONGUES

If any single traumatic moment radiates an obfuscating latticework of alarm and undoing, then serial traumas generate multiple, diversionary webs. Although one school of psychoanalytic thought understands identification with the aggressor in the abuse matrix almost as total, undiscriminated introjection, a kind of "swallowing whole," it may be that primary objects ensnared during the course of abusive interactions are assimilated in smaller bites. Forensic psychologist J. Reid Meloy (1997) has written that the anticipation of malevolence from care-takers, rather than engendering full introjection, leads to a partial *failure* of incor-poration and an ultimate forswearing of the need for pacifying objects in the internal world. A "malevolent transformation" is effected, wherein the child develops elaborate ways to jettison vengeance, often through dissociative means (Sullivan, 1953). Subsequent identifications revolve around the parent's awesome power (Fairbairn, 1952), internalized as a sense of entitlement that finds expres-sion in perpetration (Meloy, 1997b).

According to the Kleinian (1946) paradigm, in normal development inter-nalized objects are fractionated because the child cannot tolerate the notion of so good and so malignant coexisting in the same body. Splitting is the best defense against persecutory anxiety: the good object is introjected while the bad is projected and vice versa. In more pathological characters, however, the object has never been securely enough anchored to precipitate splitting, and so there can no firm demarcation of good and bad. According to Fairbairn (1952), these powerful relational paradigms, represented internally, substitute for actual relationships as the maltreated child increasingly dissociates from exter-nal reality. In such a situation, one inherits only a fluctuating ability to assess the morality of people and positions; as a young patient once told Melissa Ritter (personal communication, 2000) she never knew when someone would "unzip," revealing their true malignant self.

One of the earliest encounters I had with the eerie enactment of partial objec-tification in trauma took place when I was a student intern at Bellevue Hospital. A lovely, delicate-looking preschooler in braids was brought in for an evaluation; her mother was suspected of selling the child's sexual services in exchange for drugs. Doll-play proceeded conventionally until a male doll was introduced, at which point the child became very agitated, eventually picking the male doll up by the ankles and banging his head furiously against the table's edge, while screaming "You bastard" at the top of her little lungs. The enactment was so violent that we feared the girl would injure herself. The quick-witted psychiatrist doing the evaluation, Dorothy Lewis, quickly grabbed another male doll and announced, "Hello. I am a police officer. I am going to arrest this bad man." The girl looked up, relaxed (almost trancelike, we all agreed later), and—rubbing her stockinged foot against the crotch of the policeman doll—implored, "Please don't take him away, I *need* him."

Fairbairn (1952) might have seen that episode as presaging or reflecting a second-order split of the ego, with one part being pulled inexorably toward danger and the other languishing in an irremediable longing for succor. Fonagy et al. (2002) suggest that this type of dissociation stems from the piecemeal internalization of inconsistent objects, mentalized alternately as benevolent or malevolent so that the child can attempt to forecast the object's behavior. To affix discrete intentions to one's object, even if erroneously, empowers the child caught in a frightening, unpredictable reality. Though such mentalizations assuage anxiety, attributions of others' intentions based on these partial inter-naliztions are largely inaccurate (pp. 361–362). The projections tend to be but dismal facsimiles of early parental threats or reparations, the responses to them a violent compensation for past impotence or a desperate attempt at reunion.

SILENT FILMS

If this split organization occludes any vision of an integrated moral landscape, the loss of descriptive capacity virtually condemns people to stereotypic moral or amoral behaviors. Language creates the textured truth that underlies subtler forms of decision making and action. Morality and language are so mutually constitutive that linguistic deficits directly handicap one's ability to make moral meaning and engage the world empathically. Indeed, the quality of post-maltreatment symptoms in violent criminals suggests a moral bipolarity that often seems melodramatic rather than appropriately tragic.

Melodramatic characters have no psychological complexity or depth, no internal conflict. They instead "exteriorize conflict and psychic structure, producing [a world] built on an irreducible manichaeism, the conflict of good and evil as opposites not subject to compromise" (Brooks, 2001, pp. 35–36). In a traumatized patient, the default to primitive, protective defenses likewise inhibits affectivity in favor of affectation. Amnesia is the point of departure where manifold, sometimes nefarious, subjectivities become trauma's handmaidens.

I am continually struck by the *absence* of narrative in the tales told by violent offenders. Like Muller's (2000) alexithymic patients "with no story to tell", many inmates I have interviewed purported not to remember their offenses. Professed amnesia for criminal activity is well documented: researchers variously report that between 10% and 50% of violent male offenders claim to have no memory of committing the crimes with which they are charged (Bradford & Smith, 1979; Taylor & Koppelman, 1984; Parwatiker et al., 1985; Stein, 2000). Murderers fall in the upper range of those figures (O'Connell, 1960; Holcomb & Daniel, 1988).

In a similar vein, offenders' histories of nightmarish maltreatment are often blandly recited and absurdly interpreted, if indeed the abusive events of childhood are remembered at all (sometimes only the old scars and burn marks on a man's back, or a yellowing abuse and neglect petition in his file, survive to tell the story). Criminal pasts are rendered inaccessible by a strange combination of memory gaps, historical revisionism, and what appears to be a kind of existential absenteeism on the part of the narrator. In its most extreme manifestation, the psychic departure is absolute and resolute: the doer *knows nothing*; he is a dumb terminal for others' data:

> The more severe the dissociation, the more difficult the problem of learning to symbolize. In some cases the threat embodied in the dreaded schemas is experienced as so extreme that the individual turns against the symbolizing process itself in a more pervasive way [Bucci, 1997, p. 208].

The recitation of potent events appears in a surrealistically offhanded manner, sometimes in language that is regressed or in word inventories that are urged from the staccato narrator. As Bucci points out, alexithymia, a poverty of descriptive capacity, is best understood as a "crisis" of symbolization. For example, I here is a part of my psychiatric intake with a depressed prisoner who could not articulate the connection between feeling suicidal and trying to kill himself. After adamantly denying that he had attempted suicide, the prisoner allowed:

Inmate: I tried to cut myself with a razor here in jail. [Over] some garbage . . . I tried to tell my lawyer.

Interviewer: When else did you try to hurt yourself?

Inmate: That was it, just here.

Interviewer: When was the first time you tried something like that?

Inmate: I took these pills, brown pills from the bathroom cabinet when I was "on punishment." No one knew.

Interviewer: You were how old?

Inmate: I was eight, I think.

Interviewer: Did you try to kill yourself other times?

Inmate: No.

Interviewer: When else did you try to hurt yourself?

Inmate: I jumped in front of a car or bus in 1990 because my daughter's mother wanted to leave me. They took me to Bronx Lebanon Hospital. I left that same night in a wheelchair. My legs and arms were cut and stitched.

Interviewer: And what other times? Were there other times that something like this happened?

Inmate: I drank some bleach in 1991.

Interviewer: You tried to kill yourself?

Inmate: I don't know. I "hung up" in 1991 or 1992. I was sent to the clinic.

Interviewer: You have tried to hurt yourself a lot.

Inmate: Sometimes I cut my arms or chest.

The inmate went on to describe over 30 suicide gestures or attempts. For these he posited external agency, by way of what is usually conceived as command hallucinations evidentiary of psychosis. I have come instead to regard such externalizations as dissociative reverie when it appears in those who are otherwise not psychotic.

Interviewer: What do you think makes you do these things?

Inmate: It didn't sound like any other voice—maybe my voice, like "do it or don't do it." One time I was looking over a bridge and I heard a deep voice, a man's voice: "Go ahead, you could do it—jump." I thought it was my voice, maybe.

     I could do it without feeling pain. On my own. I just don't think about it. It's unexplainable. I just think about other stuff.

PSYCHIC LAW: LETTER AND SPIRIT

As Emmanuel Tanay (1976) observed of the murderers he had interviewed during a lengthy psychiatric career, they are most often in a dissociated state akin to dreaming, except that "we may dream all the murders we wish and no one will punish us" (p. 19). Barrett (1994) notes that many early theorists recognized the similarities between dreaming and a variety of psychopathologies: conversion hysteria (Freud), hypnoid states (Janet), altered consciousness (Prince), and schizophrenia[2] (Fischer & Dement, 1963). Barrett herself has argued an explicit connection between the chronic disruption of REM sleep in ongoing trauma and the tendency of dream characters to "wake up" and become agentic (pp. 132–133). Sullivan (1953b) called dissociative reverie a kind of "dreaming while awake" that permits the disavowal of agency without suspending the security operations that are usually attenuated during real sleep.

I have adopted the term psychosomnia to capture the quality of the crazy dream states that perpetrators have described to me as the perceptual position from which they view their crimes. Psychosomnia allows the perpetrator to hew to the letter of the superego's law by disavowing agency while grossly violating its spirit through enactment. In Freud's model (1900), the dream censor—a precursor to superego—distorts in part to dislocate hypothetical agency during sleep or repression[3]; in a dissociation model, autistic interlocutors may manifest in waking life through the "diminishment of self-consciousness" and a position of "somnambulistic" (Sullivan, 1972) lawlessness, both internally and externally.

That the lawlessness is gestural, autistic rather than voiced, anticipates and solidifies its dreamlike quality. Offenders work hard to exploit their natural talent for dissociative reverie; the default defense of a traumatic childhood becomes the preferred abode of the adult offender. The traumatic death of speech, foreclosing memory, entombs violent enactments along with their progenitors. Many criminals exist in what Yochelson and Samenow (1976) so aptly termed the "zero state," a place where nothing ever happened, nothing will ever happen, and you are nothing. While Samenow and Yochelson did not trace the path from childhood trauma to adult perpetration in their clinical sample of offenders, I cannot help but wonder whether, like the offenders with whom I spoke, "zero" implied, as much as anything, the nullification of self-reflective capacity, engendered by abuse.

Abusive, neglectful caregivers and their charges connect mostly through their aloneness or rage, if at all. More often they each retreat to an attitude of inattention and irremediable longing that will come to characterize their interactions in both external and internal space (Fonagy et al., 2002) What is "really" happening during toxic interactions with caregivers defies articulation. It is unsymbolizable; indeed, it cannot be functionally imagined in any transformative way (Davies & Frawley, 1994; Grotstein, 1995; Stern, 1997b, Bromberg, 2003). The inability to symbolize has grave implications for the way that traumatized persons draw inferences and construct meaning from situational cues and ultimately respond to perceived threats, injustices, or entreaties.

In the theatre, when characters lose their (literal) tongues through mishap or ordeal—or are struck dumb by scurrilous circumstance—we intuit the corruption of their purity. We automatically "get" why trauma effaces articulation. A similar understanding is extended in Grotstein's (1995) description of the traumatized person's lack of a "linguistic-conceptual filter" through which reality is encoded:

---

[2]Rosenham (1972) and Kluft (1987) have both noted the similarities between "positive" symptoms in schizophrenia and the symptoms of dissociative identity disorder.

[3]I refer here to Freud's (1900) discussion of the way that one's agency for forbidden acts "lies concealed, by identification, behind [another] person" (pp. 322–323) and his broader discussion of the diffusion of agency in dreams that disguise death wishes toward others (pp. 249–267).

Under this condition, the mind becomes deprived of the ordinary echoes, con-firmations, and reinforcements of the harvest of intersubjective discourse, and instead finds itself trapped in another dimension of time and space, trapped in an echo chamber without reflection, which could all the while be a virtual car-pet factory in which the cries of the dying remain mockingly unheard [p. 296].

If the core defense in trauma is dissociative amnesia, rather than repression, it makes sense that no symbols can arise. Tragically unmoored, traumatic perceptions cannot be liberated from libidinal impasse. Highly charged but psychically unassimilated, one's victimacy (a terrific designator of the self-state that opposes agency, coined I believe by Sarbin (n.d.) cannot be seamlessly woven into expressive discourse. Rageful impotence intersects myriad, seem-ingly minor, everyday degradations of the soul. Each experience is a split-off happening, not seen in moral relationship to other happenings, because no language exists to bridge them. Instead, the comforting pulse of gesture replaces voice. The criminal signature, so repetitive, is signed in silence.

THE LANGUAGE OF OFFENSE

Although the majority of the violent criminals I interviewed spoke with limited emotional erudition, an occasional few, initially at least, dazzled the clinical senses with penetrating looks and effusive speech. Such people are often clas-sified as criminal psychopaths[4], at least in part because of the way they turn lin-guistic vacuity to manipulative advantage. It is these supposedly intelligent, articulate criminals who are most likely to capture the public's imagination.

Although certainly not the first of his breed, serial murderers like the garru-lous Ted Bundy have contributed to an enduring mythology of the smooth-talking, cold-blooded predator. Violent psychopaths, so the legend goes, wield language in as dangerous a fashion as knives, ropes, or guns. Potential victims, evaluating psychiatrists, even law enforcement personnel are constantly being reminded of the considerable ability that psychopaths have to divert their prey's attention with verbal gymnastics. Robert Hare (1993) has even appended to his book on criminal psychopathy a handy "survival guide" for those who might encounter particularly engaging versions of the type in the course of their work or play. Hare recommends minimizing one's own vulnerability by not "paying attention" to the "fast talk" of the criminal psychopath, which may "distract you from his true intentions" (pp. 207–208).

While everyone who studies this glib subset of criminals admits that they are few and far between, theories about their intuitive and linguistic skills have

---

[4]One needs to be careful about the term psychopathy. Although convenient as a moralistic short-hand for abhorrent behaviors, the term has limited clinical value. The psychopathy construct, as operationalized by Robert Hare and his colleagues (Sutai et al., 1987; Hare, 1993), is used to describe an antisocial personality subtype whose predatory acts are accompanied by, among other things superficial affect, coldness, and a paucity of regret. As proponents of the construct are likely to declare, such people are "without conscience" (which has also served as a catchy title or subtitle for a number of books, including Hare's). As I argue throughout this book, the character traits asso-ciated with that rather terminal diagnosis are actually quite common in the general population of violent criminals, can be understood in a number a different ways, and may be subordinate to a variety of far more enlightening diagnoses.

disproportionately occupied the forensic imagination since Krafft-Ebing (1886) conjoined psychopathy and sadism in the late 19th century. Rather than seeing them as a breed apart, I would place these chattier criminals on an alexithymic continuum with their less conversational counterparts.

Forensic clinicians often aver that offenders purposely use language in dissimulative or obfuscatory ways, paying scant attention to the curious futility of most criminal oratory. We can note the meaninglessness of language in criminal narratives without *necessarily* ascribing a fully conscious deceptive intention to the speaker. For instance, I would underscore the second half of the following observation by Adrian Raines (1993): "Not only is [their] language unusual in the sense that [violent psychopaths] are loquacious and deceitful, but also because of the curious dissociation between what they say about themselves and how they actually behave" (p. 116).

The literature on alexithymia describes the way in which posttraumatic language may become a performative act rather than a communicative tool (McDougall, 1978; Krystal, 1988). Where catastrophic trauma has either prevented or undone symbolization processes, more astute alexithymics may lean toward affect imitation and expressive theft (Krystal, 1988), as do "chameleonlike" criminals (Meloy, 1997a). Both simply learn to describe emotions as they have heard others describe them. In their most pathological manifestation, deceptive "dramatizations" engender multiple subpersonifications of the self, preoccupied with the avoidance of anxiety (Sullivan, 1953).

Close listening and adroit interviewing exposes the decontextualized nature of a criminal's affective repartee. Krystal (1988) has noted that alexithymics' speech lacks nuance, metaphor, abstraction, and associative capacity. Similarly, as Cleckley (1941) realized early on, beyond the apparent connectedness of the facile criminal talker lies a sterile imaginative landscape, a kind of "semantic aphasia" that condemns speech to meaningless tautology.

Underlying—perhaps launching—the need for linguistic compensation is a matrix of undifferentiated affect, more easily somatized or projected than verbalized. Feelings, for alexithymic offenders, do not exist in a manner usable for reflection; they are experienced simply in the form of mounting tension, mitigated only through physical action. Assault, rape, and murder relieve the pressure.

The forensic community (clinicians, law enforcement personnel, legal analysts) tend to understand this unbearable tension as arising from an overindulgence in sadistic fantasy (Ressler, Burgess & Douglas, 1992; Schlesinger, 2000). I would argue just the opposite: that the tendency to experience affects as alarmingly diffuse and indecipherable suggests an *inability* to engage in imaginative reverie, and a collapse into physical expressions of anxiety and rage (Stein, 2004).

A FAILED CONNECTION

Despite psychopaths' supposed facility with language, studies of their linguistic processing reveal a number of abnormalities. Psychopaths make more hand gestures than do nonpsychopaths (Gillstrom & Hare, 1988), have more trouble discriminating between phonemes (the smallest phonetic unit) under conditions of stress (Jutai, Hare, & Connely, 1987), and, in a number of studies, show less brain lateralization of lingustic processes (Raine, 1993). The verbal I.Q.s of aggressive persons, delinquents, and psychopaths are strikingly lower than are their performance I.Q.s (Quay, 1987). Kenneth Dodge and his colleagues (Dodge, 1990; Dodge & Newman, 1981; Dodge & Somberg, 1987), applying information-processing theory to this glut of findings, asserts that underlying language deficits fuel the faulty encoding of environmental cues and the attribution of hostile intentions to others, and limit the response repertoire of violent delinquents, a conclusion that appears self-evident.

Verbalization is a crucial developmental milestone because a child defines reality through the consensual validation of events provided by caretakers (Sullivan, 1953; Siegel, 1996). The fledgling speaker of 18 months warbles a collection of sounds indistinguishable from animal grunts to the uninitiated ear, and mama chortles excitedly, "Oh, baby wants bottle" and proffers the bottle. The baby may actually have wanted a doll, or nothing at all, but she now will learn that this particular collection of sounds (refined over time) produces not only something tasty to drink but unconditional approval from her mother. This is the reality they agree upon, mother and child, that specific sound combinations mean something—the same thing—to both. Eventually this language will engender cause-and-effect reasoning, perspective taking, indeed the whole of rational thought.

Language further encourages the reconciliation of the opposing imagery on which the subpersonifications of the self are founded. In Sullivan's (1953) conceptualization, "good mother" and "bad mother" become "mother" through the linguistic filter of culture, foreshadowing the integration of self-states:

> [Because of] language it becomes quite impossible for the child to carry forward any striking surviving evidence of his earliest impression of two mothers—one who gives tenderness and cooperation in the satisfaction of needs and one who carries anxiety and interferes with the satisfaction of needs. [This dichotomy] can scarcely survive very long the high pressure acculturation which makes one person "mama" [p. 189].

Thus does language facilitate the fusion of "good me," "bad me," and "not-me," through the heightened recognition that the self, like individual others, is a single, symbolized entity.

CONFLATION AND DISTORTION:
THE UNDETERMINED SELF

What happens when there is no consensual validation of events between caretaker and child? What if, in an abusive situation, the reality of the traumatic event, already partially dissociated by the victim, is now also denied by the perpetrator (e.g., "You asked for it," "You imagined it") or by other adults (e.g.,"Liar! Daddy would never do that!")? We can easily see how the victim's already tenuous grasp of reality would be further loosened. It may, in fact, be that the denial of traumatic events by others is an even more crucial determinant of victims' lack or distortion of explicit memories for events (and the psychopathology they may trigger) than is the sensorial cacophony surrounding the abuse itself. Sue Crimmins (1995), in a landmark study of females incarcerated for homicide in

New York State, found that violent outcomes were highly correlated with the lack of an other-than-abuser confidante to validate the victim's belief that sexual abuse was occurring in real time. As it does at more primitive stages of development, consensual validation of trauma, at any juncture, may empower an integrated narrative that facilitates the "extended consciousness" (Bucci, 1997) critical for autobiographical self-determination (Davies & Frawley, 1994; Grand, 2000).

In his review of the attachment literature, Siegel (1996) found that the infants of emotionally rejecting parents[5] have a "unique paucity in the content of spontaneous autobiographic narratives" when reassessed at the age of ten. Notably, the parents of these insecurely attached children often exhibit a steadfast inability to recall their own childhoods (p. 517) and show little evidence of reflective capacity during interviews (Main, Kaplan, & Cassidy, 1985). Siegel concludes in his review that there in a robust-enough association between and among early relational conflict, mental schemas, linguistic disorganization or incoherence, and clinical indices of dissociation to warrant further investigation.

In addition to the defensive thrust toward amnesia, a kind of cognitive deconstruction of events takes place, rendering any *realistic* encoding of their own experiences unlikely. Instead, fanciful imaginings concerning the motives of neglectful or abusive caretakers come to be reified as alternative narratives. I again return to my initial learning experiences at Bellevue Hospital to offer an illustrative anecdote.

Maria was a 14-year-old hospitalized for depression and suicidality. She was, by turns, painfully shy and sexually exhibitionistic, provocative with staff and other patients but often almost catatonically withdrawn—a behavioral puzzle that, because our team was doing research on dissociation, we were called on both to verify and to explicate. The family history was unremarkable, and there was no indication of abuse or sexual abuse in Maria's background, although she did catalogue as high-normal on the dissociation scale of our screening instrument. After a number of meetings, we all felt as though we were treading water in the case.

One day we were asked to see Maria following a visit by her mother that had left her quite agitated. They had apparently argued over a boy that Maria fancied on the ward. Maria's mother was very strict and kept close tabs on all Maria's activities. Maria had no permission to date; she told us that she had never so much as kissed a boy—her mother simply would not allow it. Asked if she had never even stolen a kiss in secret, Maria insisted that she simply *couldn't*, her mother would *know*. I was ready to ascribe her belief in her mother's omniscience to adolescent magical thinking when the lead psychiatrist asked how Maria could be so certain that her mother would know. "Why,

---

[5]The attachment literature classifies parents as emotionally rejecting when, during experimental situations and home visits they exhibit a pattern of interaction characterized by blocking their infant's proximity seeking behaviors or permitting proximity only erratically. These parents, often rated as insecure with respect to their own early attachments, tend to devalue relationships, be preoccupied with dependency issues, or seem not to have completed the mourning process subsequent to losing their own parent(s) at an early age (Main, Kaplan, & Cassidy, 1985). An important implication of this type of parental rejection is that it produces children who feel "untouchable, repellent, or contaminated" (Hopkins, 1991, p. 197).

she checks, of course." "Checks what?" "To make sure I haven't done anything." "She asks, you mean?" "No, she checks." It took only another moment for us to learn about the mother's vaginal inspections to check if Maria's hymen was intact, examinations that had been going on since Maria was roughly four years old. "Well, you know, she was raped by her stepfather when she was my age so she needs to make sure that no one is hurting me" Maria said. In this linguistic-behavioral muddle, where invasion is defined as protection, no means yes, mine is yours, and assault is an expression of love. The only conceded meaning is that words are not recognizable symbols for action; they are ambiguous codes to be used in the service of those who can manipulate them most adroitly.

Prone to disbelieve the sadism of a caretaker, anxious to disavow one's own oddly complicitous victim status, the abused child learns, through the subversive use of language, that to her great relief what she thinks has happened may not have happened at all (or at least may be reconfigured in parallel universes where it happened and did not happen simultaneously). To survive the assault of nonsensical language, words—and by, extension, reality—are reconfigured, derealized. Both Shengold (1999) and Herman (1992) have likened the phenomenon to Orwell's (1949) "doublethink" where it becomes possible to hold completely contradictory ideas and believe them both, to forget and to remember coextensively in order to survive. Such transmogrification of language, encapsulated in memory, drives autobiographical narrative into particularly fossilized forms.

Narrative psychologists posit that a childhood memory is the shared linguistic construction of an event that becomes encoded through narration (Hermans, 1996). This concept seems all the more important for understanding traumatic memory to which no language—other than the abusers' or that of non believing others—has been attached. Memories are made credible, or become believed-in, through interactions with confirmatory others, such as friends, relatives, or even therapists (Sarbin, 1995). In this sense, split-off aspects of the self are reified (or disappeared) not simply because of internal defensive or cognitive processes, but in contract with significant others:

> The important point to note is that what the experience of trauma disrupts is not identity itself but the social process through which identity is constructed. Correspondingly, in this view, the phenomenon of multiplicity is a disorder of identity or identity construction … Multiple identity, like unitary identity, is performed-that is to say, it is dynamically constructed through social relationships (Lynn et al., 1998, p. 139).

The victims of predators must be added to the list of confirmatory others who unwittingly help reify or formulate the perpetrators' abuse narratives. A victim's perceived liability, visible terror, vain resistance, helpless submission, or imagined complicity authenticates an affective memory of the offender's own trauma. But, because the crime destroys the witness and with the witness the possibility of testimony, knowledge and memory are forfeited again. As in his own history of maltreatment, the offender's amnesia for violence is neither genuine nor confabulatory: it is inferential. How can he remember a happening potently externalized, synchronously undone?

INCOMPLETE SENTENCES: TRAUMA AND
LINGUISTIC FAILURE

The burgeoning field of developmental traumatology addresses the psychobiological sequelae of traumatic experiences across the life span. Neurological systems, in particular, are sensitive to the overwhelming impact of stress, especially when tension is chronic. The pervasive, elemental stressor in child abuse includes not only a disorganizing physical assault but also the relational paradigm of continued dependence on the abuser. Daily, nonabusive interactions with such a caretaker are heavily freighted; each "normal" engagement can contain multiple triggers for anxiety that, we now know, take a massive physiological toll (van der Kolk, 1996). These encounters may prompt a cascade of neuropathic interactions that negatively affect brain growth, lateralization and specialization (Debellis, 2001).

Multiple, overlapping spheres of neuronal dyfunction can blunt development in a variety of emotional, cognitive, and behavioral domains. Dissociation, for example, has been linked to the disruption of endogenous opiate systems, which may explain the analgesia for pain that often accompanies PTSD (van der Kolk, 1996). Dissociative symptoms in maltreated children have also been linked to shrinkage of the corpus callosum, signaling a possible disruption in connectivity between the hemispheres. In one study of maltreated children, the reduction in corpus callusom area, as assessed by MRI, was associated with the presence of intrusive imagery, hyperarousal, and dissociation at clinical intake (Debellis et al., 1999). Moreover, maltreatment has long-term effects on the human hormonal system. The brain adjusts to abuse through compensatory brain mechanisms by increasing the production of stress regulators like cortisol. This hormonal infusion may prime the brain to overreact to subsequent stressors, even those of minor import (Cicchetti & Rogosch, 2001; DeBellis, 2001).

How do the timing, chronicity, and type of trauma experienced affect children's aggression? While chronic maltreatment beginning in infancy or toddlerhood presages the most deleterious outcomes in terms of expressed violence (indeed, even when abuse abates after toddlerhood, aggression remains), abuse at any juncture leaves its telltale stain. Maltreatment beginning after the age of three years, at a time when children are mastering perspective taking and empathic skills, still has a profoundly destructive effect on expressive capability and the social interaction it might regulate. Most germane to an analysis of linguistic deficits in traumatized persons, PET scans of those with PTSD have demonstrated that trauma impedes oxygen utilization in the area of the brain responsible for associating words with affective experience and constructing semantic contexts for somatic states (van der Kolk, 1996). This impediment increases the likelihood that trauma will provoke alexithymia: []"trauma may lead to 'speechless terror,' which in some individuals interferes with the ability to put feelings into words, leaving emotions to be mutely expressed by dysfunction of the body" (p. 193).

The misrecognition of physiological states of arousal, and the misattributions of causality that are likely to follow, may make one more likely to act out in retaliatory ways. This is particularly true when reflective capacities have been short-circuited neurologically, as well as psychologically, by abuse (Cicchitti & White, 1990).

THE NEUROLOGICAL SUBTEXT

The representation of entities in their absence, in image or word, is the domain of the symbolic; immediate response based on intuitive, implicit processing is the function of the subsymbolic mode. Wilma Bucci In a fascinating treatise that explores the neurological underpinnings of dissociation, Bucci (1997) offers multiple code theory, an attempt to integrate current knowledge of neurocognitive processing with psychoanalytic models of memory, conflict, emotion, and defense. Bucci is particularly instructive in her discussion of the ways in which trauma may distort or abort reflective capacity through the transmogrification of language.

Bucci's thoughts are appealing and readily applicable to the study of criminogenesis, as they potentially both support theoretical links among child maltreatment, dissociation, and violence. While developmental theorists (DeBellis, 2001; Elin, 1995) have discussed how trauma that occurs at a very young age, prior to self-and object permanence, engenders gross linguistic poverty of the sort associated with the dissociative pathologies[6], multiple code theory allows a wider space to hypothesize about the ability of adolescent and adult trauma to sever linguistic forms from affect or evolved meanings (kinds of dissociation), even when some level of consciousness for those events adheres. The kinds of trauma relevant to adult aggression may include physical or sexual victimization in later childhood, adolescent traumatic recreations of earlier abuse (e.g., engaging in teenage prostitution), and even committing violence, itself a traumatizing event[7].

Multiple code theory begins with the idea that subsymbolic modalities—cognitive processes operating outside intention or formal volition but highly systematized nonetheless—engender habituated behaviors in the realms of sensation, intuition, and movement. Symbolized thought, on the other hand, is represented most compellingly by language, although it can also take nonverbal forms. A hieroglyph, a mathematical equation, an analyst's interpretation, a ballet, and a ballot—what makes each expression symbolic is that it is linked to an internal image that can be deconstructed to its basic components and reconstitiuted in new forms. The subsymbolic is merely impressionistic and cannot be recombined; these raw analogues of incoming information are fated for regurgitation, unless they become linked to higher order processes.

Both kinds of data—the subsymbolic and the symbolic—exist as firing potentials targeting specific neuroreceptors. Subsymbolic enterprise is essentially body centric, emanating from the more primitive brain structures and existing mainly in the sensory and motor realms. On the basis of Damasio's (1999) work on dispositional representations, Bucci (1997) concludes that there is a secondary structure superimposed on the basic neural circuitry that allows subsymbolic data

---

[6]Early abuse may also inhibit or distort the ability to recognize boundaries, in turn diminishing the capacity for object constancy and permanence. The repercussive enormity of this lack is enumerated in the bizarre attachment patterns noted in abused children and the partial projections common among violent predators.

[7]Dissociations during perpetration have been dubbed "red-outs" by researchers who posit that it is only the affective component of the violent act that is forgotten; left intact is a certain degree of consciousness for the crime but, conceivably, its meaning is destroyed (Swihart, Yuille, & Porter, 1999).

to attain psychological standing through a referential process that connects crude neurodata, first with images and then with increasingly higher levels of abstraction. Imagistic modes, conscious and unconscious, permit the recognition of feelings and the labeling of emotional states; without iconography, arousal simply triggers habituated responses in a thoughtless loop. The "unformulated" is articulated in rote ways, like an old phonograph needle stuck in particular verbal grooves (Stern, 1997b), or it is acted out without any mediating symbolization.

The failure to represent symbolically core affective experiences related to survival is one kind of dissociation: "[T]here is a self that is carrying out the activity, but it is not the integrated self of identity and personhood. The feeling is experienced as happening to oneself, but its meaning is not recognized" (Bucci, 1997, p. 780). The failure to tie a subjective self to a larger autobio-graphical consciousness that incorporates memory and emotional schemas is an even more profound severance. The avoidance or dismantling of symbols impedes proximal agency, and make one's own violence a voyeuristic encounter.

LANGUAGE SHORT-CIRCUITED: THE TIMING OF TRAUMA

It is probably true that very early neglect and abuse disrupts the laying down of neural connections critical to verbalization and perhaps even its forerunner, vocalization. These early experiences of threat may not become symbolized because the child has yet to develop the cognitive capacity to signify experience. Elin (1995), for example, has tied linguistic deficits in dissociative patients to particular neurocognitive substrates, so as to discern the age at which abuse may have occurred:

> In [dissociated] states, individuals often report memories in one word utterances. They use telegraphic speech style, early sentence structures, and agrammatical semantic and syntactical usage … In some cases, permanent injury to linguistic competency may occur during critical periods of language development in which it is bypassed, blocked, or severely repressed as a result of physical, sexual, and psychological abuse [p. 235].

According to Elin, early trauma may inaugurate synaptogenesis in the inchoate language centers of the brain. The trauma thus creates a parallel processing system for perceptions unelaborated by language, a system that remains intact, increasing the probability that subsequent traumas will also remain unsymbolized. In other words, all trauma resists ideography, but *early* trauma sets the neurological stage for particularly rigid memory capsules, where "words are suppressed and cut off from consciousness. Symbols are lost, embedded, or dampened, and the world of objects remains less available for affective linkages"(p. 237). In these cases, acts have no meaning.

A man convicted of the rape, anal sodomy, and murder of his mother-in-law wrote to his wife, the victim's daughter, that the homicide was just a "hump we've got [to get over] in our damn life." According to his grandmother, this man had been severely beaten and neglected in early childhood, had been forced to have oral sex with his alcoholic father, and had witnessed his parents having sex. Is it any wonder that the annihilation of a parent, even once removed, was simply constructed as a minor obstacle to marital intimacy?

Even absent prior sensitization attributable to very early maltreatment, emotionally distressing events of great magnitude or long duration may become desymbolized and incoherent in "peritraumatic dissociations" (Weiss & Marmar, 1997). The disruption of the ability to abstract these experiences underlies their tendency to be memorialized through primitive gestures or other overt indices like somatization, rather than through reflection and articulation. The paranoid projections that so often trigger violence may be an attempt to superimpose meaning on unorganized cognitive or affective "floaters" that become activated in the face of threat. They thrust agency on to the victim. One particularly vicious sex murderer in our files clarified his acts thusly: "A woman is hard to explain. I love women but this is not enjoyable. It's a problem because they are very sly. I will never fall in a trap again."

While in prison, he drew various pictures of knives with the caption "stuck in ladies (sic) neck several times," although he averred in another notation, "I just wanted people to be happy and content, like I wasn't." The file does not say much about the relationship of the man to his victim, only that she lived in his building and that he had previously tampered with her cable television connection. Found in her apartment, she was bound at ankle and wrist, beaten and stabbed. He denied killing her, but not to carrying out the binding and sexual attack (semen was found on her buttocks). He claimed that the victim had initiated the assault, that she had charged at him and he had to "throw something over her face and hit her back." From there on, things must have deteriorated, although the perpetrator claimed not to remember them.

One wonders whose face really was shrouded in that interaction. Offenders often attack the eyes of their victims (as Matias Reyes did), or achieve a functional blindness, like the attacker just described. It is an index of paranoia, yes, and a register of shame (Gilligan, 1996): Do not see who I am and, more locally, do not see what I am about to do. If victim and assailant are blind as well as mute, neither party can confirm or deny the violence.

THE EXPRESSIVE LOGIC OF CRIMINALITY

Robert Hare has dedicated his professional life to the empirical examination of criminal psychopathy. He has called attention to the contradictory, largely illogical, nature of psychopaths' self-assertions and the disconnection between their dispassionate words and the awful gravity of the acts those words describe. By measuring prison inmates' reaction times in word tests[8] and their physiological responses to emotionally charged language and pictures, Hare (1993) found a marked deficit in recognition and processing tasks for inmates who met his

---

[8]Administering associative word tests to criminals was, strangely enough, a specialty of Carl Gustav Jung, who hypothesized that offenders' delayed reaction times to emotionally charged words were attributable to memory gaps and misrecognitions. Jung believed that the gaps revealed an underlying complex organized around an extremely pained affective core (Costello, 2002). Jung's hypothesis is the exact *opposite* of what researchers today infer from similar data: that a percentage of criminals are slow to respond to high emotion words because, unlike "normals," they have *no* affective core.

criteria for psychopathy, as measured by the psychopathy checklist that he created. In addition, he observes through clinical anecdotes that the expressive repertoire of many criminals is limited to whatever talents for mimicry they possess. (Empty oratory is a strategy for fitting in; the simulation of affect in rhetorical discourse enables an illusion of humanity for both speaker and listener.) And Hare persuasively argues that a self-reflective inner monologue (of the kind his subjects' lack) is integral to the development of guilt and, consequently, of conscience. I could not agree more with Hare's observation that "psychopaths' thoughts and ideas are organized into rather small mental packages and [are] readily moved around" (p. 136). Hare imagines such rigid compartmentalization as genetically preordained, while I see it as a largely defensive operation that may have neurological, as well as psychological, origins.

For example, noting the inconsistency in statements like the ones I have referred to (e.g., Matias Reyes's statement that, despite his record of frenzied homicidal rage, "I am just not a violent person"), Hare, (1993), offering his own list of similar clinical anecdotes, opines that such thematic incongruence is indicative of an underlying deficiency in neural processing. He concludes that the inability to integrate two cognitions, or to couple a cognition with its appropriate affect, stems from a brain abnormality—a hemispheric chain of command gone awry, largely inborn. He hypothesizes that the ability to develop such complex emotions as anxiety and empathy is "provided in part by nature and possibly by some unknown biological influences on the developing fetus and neonate" (p. 173). Although acknowledging the possible psychological toll taken by maltreatment, Hare adamantly asserts that neither psychopathic behaviors, nor the language anomalies that accompany them, are caused by early childhood trauma.

While seconding Hare's observations about the linguistic poverty and emotional disconnection of many criminals, I think his findings raise questions and the possibility of alternate interpretations. Although it is likely that neural vulnerabilities predispose for many conditions, including violence, the *most* consistent finding of researchers and clinicians (Widom, 1989; Harlow, 1999; English et al., 2001)—and unfortunately the most often ignored—is the frequency of neglect and abuse in the backgrounds of violent offenders. It is primarily these pitiable experiences that sequester empathy and sense, and often render inaccessible the communicative forms that we equate with humanity. Yes, violent offenders "speak" to us in a different language. Yes, their internal dialogue is morbidly deficient. Yes, these deficiencies have neurological corollaries. But is the neuropathy independent of maltreatment, particularly at critical developmental junctures? The thesis that neuroanomalies in criminal subjects *precede* trauma has not been demonstrated persuasively enough to make the case, however there seems to be clinical evidence suggesting that the opposite premise deserves airing.

CASE EXAMPLES: THE ABSENCE OF SYMBOLIZATION

Work with violent offenders abused as children and the theory opposing Hare's is concretized quickly and dramatically: trauma warps interiority (and exteriority) in wholly demonstrable ways. Here, a child murderer—sexually assaulted for many years by an older brother (a formerly incarcerated incestuous pedophile, himself molested in childhood)—reflects on his most recent victims: "Those two little girls were my only meaningful playtime. I was obsessed with them emotionally. I loved them. I am very mad that they were taken from me."

In this story, symbolization is missing; the difference between an external object and an internalized one is blurred. Yet there is a real drive toward making a recognizable form from the miasmal fog. In the same way that people reassemble visual-perceptual incongruities to maintain cognitive consonance, traumatized persons attempt to realign new traumatic insignia with preexisting beliefs, wishes, fantasies, and elaborative schemes. In the killer's narrative, there is no incongruity—the most tolerable image of his own abuser is likely that of a loving brother. What seems most securely internalized, in this particular narrative moment at least, is the sense that his older brother focused on him, wanted him, *was only playing with him*. Through identification, the rapist-murderer can imagine himself as a lover of children, too. Children who are abused become other children, abused by someone else.

If the perverse, dissociative strategy of the abused child is to experience annihilation while pretending that it is happening to someone else, the dissociative strategy of the adult violent recidivist is to do it to someone else—to reify the initial, unsymbolized event. What Grand (2000) has described as the insistence by victims that abusive violation is not really *real* or is not really happening to *me*, for the criminal becomes the starting point of an exercise in reality swapping. By constructing an imaginary parallel universe that is ultimately authenticated through violent reenactment, the demands of the ego for consensual validation can be met without forfeiting defensive structure. What the child will not believe happened to him will, indeed, be made to happen to someone else, thus restoring the precarious balance between real and unreal that leaves the offender's sanity intact.

Let me return momentarily to the remarks that most plague me—the ones that disavow even the possibility of agency. They represent the interpellation of culpability by way of characterological reversal and so serve the same defensive master as the aforementioned reification of unsymbolized events. From my files:

> "I'm not that type of person. I would never hurt anybody" (The victim was bound and gagged. The baseball bat found on the bed was covered in blood, which had also sprayed the ceiling.)

> "I'm a peaceful person." (The victim was decapitated.)

> "I couldn't even picture myself doing it." (The victim was stabbed in both eyes, before a knife was plunged into her chest.)

"A negative statement says and doesn't say what is known and not known" (Litowitz, 1998), thus affirming that which is disavowed or dissociated. But insofar as the perpetrator's words also invent or define a personal truth within the context of intersubjective notions of morality, the utterance also voices conscience, however split off.

Sometimes an intrusive conscience performs CPR on a nearly dead victim or calls the police following a bestial attack. It was these kinds of discordant behaviors that, in my earliest interpretations of criminality, seemed indicative of alternate, fully formed personae. To borrow Thigpen and Cleckley's (1950) vernacular, popularized in the first mass market look at multiple personality disorder, *The Three Faces of Eve*: Joe Black raped and stole, Joe White called the cops. Like many other things with a nostalgic sheen, this interpretation wore thin with repeated use. To paraphrase Charcot (in Freud, 1893) theories come and go, but they do not stop facts from existing. The words spoken by perpetrators still ring. To wit:

In a failed assault on an underage acquaintance, a man asks his fleeing victim to "tell her mother, because what I did is bad." The offender's bounce from assaultiveness to requested punishment to loneliness is profound and is itself a compelling argument for the underlying dimensionality of emotional responses to one's own perpetration. Agency is the slippery deuce in a three-card monty game.

In another pedophilic sexual assault, concomitant to a break-in, the same offender disguised himself with a pillowcase, only to pull it off as the child was escaping. This spontaneously revealed to the girl his identity as a friend of her mother's. In yet another child molestation, he spanks, tickles, digitally penetrates, and hits a little girl in the head while calling her a stupid, dumb liar and then, returning her to her parents, warns the child that her parents won't appreciate that she has disobeyed him.

This man's escapades and his use of language were so regressed that I expected to find in the file evidence of stark cognitive dysfunction or developmental delay. I found neither; the child molester was simply operating in his behavioral-linguistic comfort zone, a place bereft of true syntaxic experience. I use the term syntaxic experience as Sullivan (1953) did, to imply a *profitable* employ of mutually agreed upon symbols that allow the discrimination between fantasy and reality, private and public, me and you. Conceivably, without syntaxic experience, there can be no relational mode because there is no linguistic currency to trade. Yet within the insistence that someone be punished (the perpetrator, or the victim) nests the idea of conscience, however abridged. Guilt may even have preceded wrongdoing, as Freud (1916) sagely hypothesized, because the criminal act invites punishment for one's imagined faults. Klein (1933), too, believed that guilt anticipates aggression in that "it is the excessive and overpowering cruelty of the superego" (p. 251), leading to persecutory anxiety, which engenders paranoia and ultimately triggers a retaliatory response.

In the double homicide eventually committed by the pedophile who "played" with the two little girls, the children were dressed and arranged in the attic crawlspace of the perpetrator's home, where they remained during at least one visit by homicide detectives. He never worked very hard to avoid detection, a performance of magical thinking common to offenders with significant histories of childhood trauma who so handily derealize and depersonalize criminal events.

Conveniently, this was his usual M.O.: assaulting those he knew, often under his own roof. Unsurprisingly, the small garden apartment he lived in as an adult mirrored the ambience of his childhood home, where an older brother had beaten and raped him many times in many different rooms. The reflection of the killer's own abuse is fractured but wholly discernible in his double murder. He killed the first child after a sexual assault and the second for being a silent witness. To the degree that the girls represented the conflation of self and others, the boy grown to predator managed to undo both complicity in and resistance to his own victimization, and to close forever the eyes of those who watched him suffer and did nothing.

REFLECTIONS

Every story has a back story. Writers craft subplots. Actors create imaginary worlds to dimensionalize to their characters. For the analytic dyad, the back story is made of transferential communications. A narrative is cold and dead without corresponding sponsors and shadows; that is why, when back stories are not articulated, we feel as if we are treading air. To the degree that stories cannot be told, will not be told, are not noticed, or deny mentalization, that is the degree to which they deanimate the main narrative or curve its direction in biased ways.

Therefore, I find it a particular necessity in this project to read between my own lines. You deserve to know, as best as I can relate it, how my own negotiations with aggression influenced the way that I chose or translated other people's narratives and the extent to which my own process says something more universal about people who encounter violent people, on purpose or by accident.

For example, while rereading an initial draft of this chapter, I had the disquieting feeling that my book was hiding somewhere in its footnotes. Every rereading made me wonder why so much of potential import was not elaborated in the main text— what exactly was I disavowing? When I reread only the footnotes, I saw how often my digressions house *my* aggressions. Whenever I was about to challenge the ideas of a more established colleague, I dissociated my thoughts from the formal manuscript. The footnotes were a kind of enactment: many people, after all, do not read the footnotes; you can risk aggressing there without comeuppance. Which reminds me to think about what attracts some of us to others of us who relegate violence to a psychic footnote rather than assimilating it into the main story.

There is symptom choice, victim choice, and—for those in clinical or research fields—population choice. Maybe it is not only violent actors who are locked in mortal embrace with intangible others who are vivified or annihilated through perpetration. Donnel Stern (2003) has made thinkable the idea that an analyst enacts the analysand's dissociation while he dissociates what the patient enacts. What does that say about the practitioner who does not happen upon murderers by chance, amongst an otherwise merely neurotic clientele, but who seeks out narratives of bracing, high aggression? Is there a predisposition in such a person toward aggressive complementarity?

I am often distracted from my work by those outside the cage: forensic practitioners and researchers who seem to reject the very idea that violent people deserve compassion. Do forensic researchers and clinicians withhold (in essence, a negative enactment) what their clients dissociate: empathy? As long as that angry communication is unformulated by the practitioner, its object has no hope of either integrating empathy or rage (and neither does its subject).

To put the discussion of countertransference reactions to offenders in a broader context, I began this chapter by saying how easy it seems for the public to dehumanize offenders by following the lead, unfortunately, of politicians, law enforcement personnel, and the medical establishment—who each promulgate their own version of bad seed theory. They are hunting monsters, fighting demons, stalking evil, and, most recently, staring into the eyes of neuro-biological mutants, as documented in myriad articles and books. (Depuet Schindchette, 2005; Hare, 1993; Harill, 2001; Morrison & Goldberg, 2004; Ressler & Schactman, 1992; Vronsky, 2004). It is this distancing that prevents us from assimilating aggression (our own and others') so that it is less likely to be acted upon.

The world-view of perpetrators is often filtered through "basic experiences of savage aggression from parental objects" (Kernberg, 1998, p. 376). The criminal justice system in many ways reenacts that original sadistic familial configuration (Gilligan, 1996), perhaps allowing us to recast recidivism as a special form of repetition compulsion. After all, prison recreates total dependence on an abusing caretaker: it becomes a literal embodiment of the masochistic cage.

Within correctional and mental health settings alike, it is basically believed that psychotherapeutic intervention with antisocial populations is totally unwarranted because its effectiveness is "practically zero" (Kernberg, 1998, p. 377). Little has been written about the *relational* context in which most criminals are evaluated or rehabbed; most programs eschew the idea of a criminal-corrector dyad that together make meaning. In correctional settings, all agency for failure redounds to the convict, who instinctively fulfils the correctional prophesy of intractable antisocialness. That is the back story for any article about why corrections does not correct. (It is time that someone invented relational/interpersonal forensic psychoanalysis.)

That unbridled aggression is the inevitable outcome of severely damaging early interpersonal relationships is an idea long acknowledged in some circles but rarely articulated publicly for fear of provoking the accusation of "excus-ing" the criminal. Thus most criminal justice policy initiatives never formulate remediations that take into account the need to facilitate an inmate's immediate and local ownership of his or her actions, much as Bromberg (2003) recom-mends an analyst do with any traumatized patient: "[Enable] a patient's here and now experience of [the analyst] to be felt as more and more relationally trustworthy, making it possible for [the analysand] to rely less and less auto-matically on dissociation as a proactive early warning system" (p. 562).

Rather, the few programs that exist are modeled on a "justice perspective" that attempts to teach democratic process and moral decision making to the incarcerated. Typically, inmates do very well in such programs while incarcer-ated (their scores on tests of moral reasoning rise precipitously), but they cannot maintain abstinence from criminality once released. "Graduates" of such programs inevitably recidivate. They have never had the opportunity to experience a real-time relationship that has affective potency but does not traumatize. So, thrown out into the world, they cannot regulate affective arousal any differently than they always did: through desymbolization and enactment. We really condemn people to their dissociative defenses every time we do not offer solace from the encroaching storms of retraumatization (Bromberg, 2003). To ignore or even reenact inmates' early traumas, as happens every day in the criminal justice system is, to borrow a prosecutorial term, truly *unconscionable*.

3

Criminals' Bad Luck[1]

Case One

The offender was a teenager who stalked, raped, and beat a 71-year-old women to death with a hammer. He then proceeded to her living room, where he grabbed a snack and watched a little television. At some point, the teenager performed CPR on the victim and even dialed 911 but hung up before the emergency operator answered. The offender was caught because he had made no attempt to retrieve a medical appointment card that had tumbled out of his pocket during the crime, even though he reported to officers that he had been aware of dropping it. The card gave his name and the location of the doctor's office where he would be at an appointed time, obviating the need for any high-level detective work to effect his capture.

As a child, the perpetrator had been physically abused by his mother, his sister, and an aunt—such children as he learn early the art of an uninhabited presence. Invisibility is both the salvation and the curse of the brutalized child: the wishes to be seen and yet not seen become defining poles of the abusive engagement. Given his history, this particular teenaged offender was probably used to hiding in plain sight. Leaving an appointment card at the scene of a murder you have just committed dares the police to restore your visibility. Even if the price of that recognition is execution, how familiar and comfortable it must feel. No surprise that homicide rates are highest in states that impose the death penalty (Baily, 1976; Lempert, 1983).

Case Two

Unable to find a prostitute, a young man decided to kidnap and sexually assault a little girl "just to try something different." In full view of the child's friends, the offender drove away with the child in a truck emblazoned with his employer's name. The truck, as the perpetrator knew, was fully outfitted with a satellite-

---

[1]At the turn of the 20th-century, psychologists labeled the tendency of offenders to betray their identity by leaving telltale clues at the scene of the crime, *Verbrecherpech*, or "criminals' bad luck" (Wulffen, 1926).

tracking device. He was located shortly, and eventually directed officers to the victim, whom he had left at a shopping center. She was terrified but still alive.

Case Three

A man strangles his next-door neighbor and successfully disposes of the body. Picked up months later on an unrelated, nonviolent charge, the man volunteers to police that he had lived next door to some murdered woman. Suspicious, the police check his vehicle. A rape kit (i.e., a bag rapists often carry that contains the tools they need to subdue their victims) is in the trunk. The rope used in the murder of the woman is lying on the front seat in full view. The man adamantly denies the killing and volunteers for a polygraph and DNA testing to prove his innocence. Both convincingly link him to the crime.

Case Four

An offender sexually assaulted his employer-victim before crushing her larynx and drowning her in the bathtub he had been hired to reglaze. He was convicted after offering to provide saliva and blood samples, which were later matched to DNA found at the crime scene. The killer explained that his semen had gotten inside the victim because he had had sex that morning with his girlfriend and then had surreptitiously taken a shower at his employer's house, in the tub where the she would, coincidentally, later be killed.

In this chapter I discuss the covert (and not so covert) ways offenders telegraph evidence of an extant conscience, however disengaged or disorganized it might be. Violence itself robustly testifies to the existence of an agentic murderous superego, inculcated by early punishments too heinous to signify semantically, so that instead the violence is dissociated and performed. In a dynamic replay of past abuses, the traumatized person moves between states of rage and victimacy, shame and guilt, injury and attempted reparation. Those who break the law often seek containment, censure, and approbation from outside "authorities," to whom they delegate moral agency when they can no longer handle the superego's volatile demands.

These observations comport with much in both classical and contemporary psychoanalytic theory. They stand, however, in opposition to the beliefs of several influential forensic clinicians and law enforcement agents who believe that many, if not most, violent, repetitive criminals perform their acts without conscience and with fully conscious intent. It is a position embraced by a criminal justice system only too eager to draw the moral boundary between "them" and "us" and to disavow its own capacity for aggression and moral detachment. The ramifications of this view for public policy—in areas of both child welfare and corrections—are enormous.

The violence done to children cleaves the ego and inaugurates the harshest, most punitive of defensive repertoires. My cases reveal how trauma is memorialized in the murderous superego, whose power derives from dissociated violence, both endured and perpetrated. My analyses concern the implications of the way that we construct our ideas about conscience not only on individuals, but also on wider social systems relevant to battered children and adult offenders.

FOLLOWING THE CRIMINAL TRAIL

Forensic diagnosticians have often conceptualized the obvious clues left by perpetrators as taunting confirmation of their grandiose sense of invulnerability, rather than as manifestations of conscience. (Indeed, as I leafed through forensic texts during my research, I was hard-pressed to find an indexed reference to either guilt or conscience that was not followed by ", lack of"). The air of immunity, the "catch-me-if-you-can" flirtation telegraphed by a crime scene trail is, in part, a smoke signal from the grandiose self. The message it attempts to convey differs from sender to sender. For offenders with a history of chronic parental maltreatment, grandiosity might be the discernible face of an introjected abuser in full omnipotence, "yet this is only a part of the story and commonly not a very useful insight" (Wurmser, 2003b, p. 227). More important, grandiosity might compensate for the offender's sense of existential invisibility, the "not-me" (Sullivan, 1953b), the "zero" (Yochelson & Samenow, 1976), the "nobody" (Guntrip, 1969), the "black hole" (Grotstein, 1990), or the unagentic self, perambulating an original traumatic injury[2].

Leaving clues to one's identity at the crime scene furthers four goals: recognition, punishment, containment, and restoration. Being sought by police signifies importance and desirability; being caught consensually validates one's existence. Moreover, by inviting capture, the offender tithes superego function over to an external authority who will offer the condemnation that an interior voice would normally provide were it not so split off[3]. Legal "authorities" contain the sexualized aggression that the criminal cannot control and provide a holding environment in developmental (Winnicott, 1965) as well as institutional (Foucault, 1977) ways. Consequently, restrictions are set on future behaviors—the cinematic wish "Somebody stop me before I kill again!" is fulfilled. These restraints are oddly relieving.

The imposition of a sentence terminates the anticipatory anxiety associated with impending verdicts, in much the same way that a severe parental thrashing ends the tension of conjuring its cruelty. (In reverie, most punishments meted out by the criminal justice system pale in comparison with the brutal assaults of childhood custodians unless, of course, the death penalty is invoked. It is in capital cases that abuse victims turned criminal may finally realize their childhood fantasies of being annihilated.) Finally, being punished perversely equates with love (Freud, 1919). Obedience to authority holds out the hope of salvation and resurrection; identity can be reconstituted without one's having to acknowledge the true source of anxiety or conflict as resting with distant others, more seminal and significant.

---

[2] I cannot resist the pictorial representation of this in my mind's eye as that of an unseen agent pushing trauma around in a baby carriage, or what used to be called a perambulator.

[3] Of course, many people make others their jailers—just in a more metaphoric sense. See Miller (2003) for an examination of the "natural tendency to externalize superego functions" so as to enliven a fantasy that punishment might be circumvented, controlled or contained (p. 5). Miller is particularly insightful on the analysis of transference phenomena in this realm.

ON NOTHINGNESS

The contribution of experiential "nothingness" to emotional dysfunction has been conceptualized in a variety of ways: as a cognitive appraisal of one's value (Yochelson & Samenow, 1976; Gilligan, 1996; Rhodes, 1999), as a voided, or avoided, self-state (Fairbairn, 1952; Sullivan, 1953; Laing, 1959; Balint, 1968; Guntrip, 1969; Ogden, 1989; Shengold, 1989), as a perceptual alienation from subjective agency (Sullivan, 1953; Winnicott, 1991; Fonagy, Gergely, Jurist, & Target, 2003), and as a neuropathological variant that drives risk-taking behavior (Raines, 1993).

In many violent offenders, there is a kind of emptiness, sometimes experienced as a profound loneliness[4] or intractable boredom. As discussed in the previous chapter, the internal world of such people may be insufficiently or erratically peopled, as maltreatment during childhood disrupts the ability to mentally hold and represent whole objects (Winnicott, 1958; Fonagy, Gergely, Jurist, & Target, 2002).

Each traumatic encounter within the claustrophobic dyad of brutal caretaker and injured child presents the same grim choice: either merge with the abusing object or sever the dyad completely. On one hand, to be fused with one's abuser offers the illusion of prediction and control, forestalls loneliness, and liberates one's own defensive aggression. Fairbairn (1952) called this bid for omnipotence in the face of helplessness, "the moral defense."

Developmentally, the price of such union is servitude to the internal state of the perpetrator. One is condemned to keep constant vigil in a persecutory surround populated with vicious "subjective objects"[5] that both anticipate and imitate the abuser. Joining is unpleasant, but, on the other hand, the dire cost of separating is a kind of existential cancellation.

In either dreadful scenario, there is no longer an autonomous self to be seen. Indeed, the failure of the adult to recognize the child's physical sovereignty initiates a phase of profound disgrace, toward the goal of defensively diminishing the impact of the trauma and, with it, the identity of the traumatized self:

> The expectation of being seen and understood as a feeling and thinking person, which is created by the attachment context, clashes violently with the brutalized person's objectification and dehumanization. Shame is a higher order derivative of pain [Fonagy, et al. 2002, p. 426].

> Soulblindness by the other creates massive shame in us: Our own being is as nothing, not worth being noticed. The eye expresses this contempt. Wherever massive denial rules, reality has to be riven: the doubleness of self and the world, the yes and the no [Wurmser, 2003a, p. 313].

---

[4] Richard Kuklinski—husband, father of two, killer of perhaps 200—told psychiatrist Park Dietz, "I am the loneliest man in the world," during a highly charged videotaped interview (HBO, 2003).

[5] By modifying "object" with the word subjective, Winnicott (1969) called attention to how the quality of internal representations of significant others may change in accordance with the idiosyncratic identification processes of the person internalizing them.

GETTING SEEN

The only ladder back to visibility and authentication for an abused child is through a partial introjection of the other, particularly the aggressive components that arouse libido. By the child's absorbing this dangerous mental representation, the idealized part of the caregiver can be split off, but preserved[6]. The external aggression, for all practical purposes "disappears"; the stripping of reality seeds the illusion of a more nurturing interaction than actually exists (Ferenczi, 1933). Rage against the abuser is then redirected inward against the cognitive processes that engender signification, keep reality intact, and facilitate intersubjective communication. Bion (1977) called these defensive maneuvers "attacks on linking," in that they prevent or dissolve meaningful connections among objects and ideas alike. When symbols are severed from their referents in this way, psychosis, of at least a transitory variety, ensues. Transitory psychosis may characterize the essential dissociative breaks that occur during acts of aggression. Bion understood the attacks to be fomented by persecutory objects, such as Klein (1933) had earlier proposed, and that I see as integral to violent perpetration:

> ... [T]here are elements that suggest the formation of a hostile, persecutory object, or agglomeration of objects, which expresses its hostility in a manner which is of great importance in producing the predominance of psychotic mechanisms in a patient; the characteristics with which I have already invested the agglomeration of persecutory objects have the quality of a primitive, even murderous, superego [p. 101].

Klein and Bion wrote of the *perception* that objects or part-objects were persecutory. I wish to underscore the degree to which internalized objects may be based on not so fanciful elaborations of abusive or neglectful caregivers. The strenuous superego spun around such deadly and death-defying objects indemnifies the ego against total dissolution. Undoubtedly, it does so by keeping rage in its most primitive, and self-sustaining, incarnation.

Splintered, internalized fury is experienced by the child as shame or guilt deserving of a punishment, a sentence whose imposition ultimately incurs still greater wrath. In adulthood, and particularly in violent criminality, these layers of dissociated rage may reappear as set-pieces that initiate sadomasochistic cycles in an interpersonal, rather than an intrapsychic, drama. The affective exchange of shame and guilt, or what Wurmser (2003a) has called the "archaic equation" of traumatogenic states (p. 311), becomes the template for a self-referential program of confused intentionality, both the perpetrator's (supposedly benign) and the victim's (allegedly provocative). Fonagy and his colleugues (2002) nicely summarize the ramifications of this, echoing the views of many established theorists within both traditional and contemporary analytic schools: "[T]he individual cannot evoke psychic experiences other than by enactment and provocation. Subjective states [] may be known mainly through creating them in another person" (p. 386).

---

[6] Fairbairn (1952) proposed that, to survive trauma, the infantile ego splinters into dissociated structures to process separately the idealized, the rejecting, and the exciting aspects of objects.

Once an actual crime is completed, guilt, humiliation, and rage are forcefully replayed in an institutional arena constructed by various forensic practitioners only too eager to supply the punishment that reactivates the cycle. This cycle differs theoretically, but not in its behavioral manifestations, from a classical view where the return of repressed rage eventuates in the replacement of shame with guilt, a development that Freud (1916) hypothesized drives the person to a position of "moral masochism" where he seeks punishment for the imagined crimes of childhood by committing real crimes as an adult.

Carveth (2001) a post-Kleinian, questions the Freudian construction by asserting that punishment-seeking is a "guilt-substitute" rather than a byproduct of guilt, a defensive way of avoiding the pain associated with *feeling* guilty. Carveth makes the case that someone screening the world from a paranoid-schizoid position cannot experience any guilt at all because to do so would automatically globalize one's "badness." Since such a person cannot tolerate the idea that good and bad might coexist, punishment-seeking is used to disarm any encroaching state that even suggests culpability:

> Freud's equation of the unconscious need for punishment with unconscious guilt has obscured the defensive function of unconscious self-torment and its role in the chronic evasion of mental suffering, depressive anxiety, guilt and remorse that must be confronted and contained in working through the depressive position [p. 14].

Shame, in this model, implies a narcissistic default to paranoid-schizoid splitting, which frees one from superego demands. Instead of guilt being a defense against shame, shame is a defense against the *consciousness* of guilt, a regression supposedly legitimated by a culture that disparages the civilizing function of conscience (Carveth, 2001). In Western justice systems, shame is rendered the refuge of a coward, and guilt the mantle of the mature, as if the two were not bound together with trauma's twine.

It seems to me that, given the affective diffusion that accompanies threats to one's integrity, shame and guilt are experientially indivisible. Susan B. Miller (1989), for example, calls attention to the interchangeability of these reactive states during childhood, particularly before the capacity for full recognition and articulation of feelings develops. She elaborates a developmental explanation, based on Erik Erikson's work, that imagines the shame-guilt sequence as structurally coalescing in an excessively punitive superego:

> Erikson's contribution is in pointing to a development through which flight from one of the specific affects associated with weakness, shame, may contribute to the hypertrophied development of an internal structure, the conscience, which in turn generates a second affect state, guilt [p. 234].

This line of thought is consistent with the views of biologically attuned researchers who emphasize that punishment-seeking may be a way of maintaining physiological equilibrium in the aftermath of traumatically imposed sensory disruptions (Herman & van der Kolk, 1987). In particular, trauma may influence the ability to discriminate stimuli and to muster appropriate levels of somatic arousal (van der Kolk, van der Hart, & Marmer, 1996). To restore order, external events are precipitated that can narrow focus and stimulate somatosensory domains—often in the form of imposed or received punishment, which can range from self-cutting to murder.

Arguably, then, not only are shame and guilt largely transposable, both are already nested within a punishment paradigm. Relationally speaking, intense shaming is, in itself, a conferral of guilt and a death sentence for identity. Thus, it may be phenomenologically inappropriate to insist on one or the other of these affective states doing much more than ephemerally dominating the interpretive landscape. The view of shame and guilt as mutually exclusive affective domains concords all too well with a justice system intent on eliciting stalwart displays of contrition, rather than potentially mitigating tales of childhood abuse, from those at its bar.

Penal institutions, mirroring the moral requirements of the societies in which they operate, now demand emotional productions from supplicants rather than reasoned arguments about their criminal culpability. Karstedt (2002), pointing out the difficulties of this stipulation, begins with the observation that remorse is invisible, is composed of numerous and sometimes conflicting elements, and is professed in a special relational configuration imposed by the criminal justice system. Working from a Kleinian perspective, British criminologist Alison Brown (2003) furthers the argument that, if the moral dictates of society are really to be internalized by offenders, the system should disavow emotional displays of shame and guilt as a legal barometer. From this perspective, if justice is to be truly "reparative," not only must injury be acknowledged but also *forgiveness* must be granted:

> Reparation moves the person away from the sense that they are the victims of the system's persecution and therefore have no choice but to retaliate. The transformation is one from sadistic to a regulatory superego (symbolized in the judge), and from enactment to symbolization [p. 428].

Carveth's (2001) observations about the defensive uses of punishment resonate for me in another way, perhaps different from what he intended. There are times when punishment-seeking *is* used to circumvent intolerable feelings, such as mounting tension or overwhelming remorse, but this remark probably speaks more to punishment's containing functions than to its value as a replacement for guilt.

HOLDING PENS

I have already discussed extensively the diffusive effects of child abuse both on the developing brain and on the nascent organization of personality. Organization is the key word here: people need an assimilative scheme that arranges percepts within reliable fields before they can accommodate novelty. The first mapmakers are our early caretakers: they take in our most disorganizing experiences and project them back to us in manageable and meaningful form (Bion, 1977). Caregivers metabolize our worst fears and our overwhelming arousal and return them to us, transformed by both forbearance and the buzz of their own anxieties. Reasonably healthy caregivers will mark the path of moderation, helping the child to navigate an emotional course that seems generally safe, with anxiety serving a mostly educative function (Sullivan, 1953). Pathological caregivers either cannot or will not perform this task—what they return to the child is nothingness or too-much-ness, a meaningless void or an obliterating anxiety. Each of these refractions distorts the burgeoning effort to symbolize, foreshortening the ability to self-navigate. Abused children, at a paradigmatic impasse, seem doomed to maplessly reconnoiter enemy territory, both within and outside.

If no adult is available to contain and process the child's turmoil in helpful ways, the child must intuit and demonstrate some system that can perform that function. Reorganization is facilitated in a number of ingenious ways, most of which begin with "isolating techniques" that delimit one's awareness of the circumstance in which they are mired (Sullivan, 1953b).

Compartmentalizing awful experiences is a way of containing their toxicity; splitting objects into their good and bad components halves their power. Dissimulating identity is a way of protecting the self and others from many varieties of affective contagion and engulfment. Coincident with splitting, "imaginary friends" may afford transitional experiences for the abused child. These include holding, soothing, and containment functions that adults have not provided (Klein, 1985; von Broembsen, 1986; Coleman, 1988; Bonne et al., 1999). (In my experience, imaginary friends of damaged kids are not always that friendly. I am put in mind of a violent predator whose childhood teddy bear, when raised to imaginary status, became persecutory and had to be destroyed.) Another way of looking at imaginary friends is that they are simple, reexternalized versions of subjectively transformed objects. Imaginary friends are similar to the "good-me," "bad-me," and "not-me" characters described by Sullivan (1953b), in that they may illustrate rudimentary personifications of the self on which later, more perceptually disconnected "personalities" are based (Fagan & McMahon, 1984; Trujillo et al., 1996). The encapsulation of segments of the personality into discrete entities creates the ultimate holding pen. It is method of containing violence until such time as one can get arrested and delegate that responsibility to another set of persons.

Clinical case

Sonny carried a diagnosis of psychosis not otherwise specified when he arrived at the hospital for a forensic evaluation. Like other men I had interviewed who claimed amnesia for their crimes, Sonny never denied the murder he was charged with committing: "They told me I stabbed him with a kitchen knife. I realized I did it, but I didn't know. I don't remember doing it."

Sonny had been hospitalized many times—for depression, anxiety, mania, hallucinations, suicidality, fugue. He had taken a long list of psychotropic drugs, but none had alleviated his symptoms. Sonny presented a puzzle: he had been graduated from a community college; he seemed a devoted family man. Yet his wife said that, in contrast with his usual "calm, polite" demeanor, Sonny at times became "a wild, different person who doesn't hear, doesn't respond." He had been telling doctors for years that his biggest fear was that he would lose control of his behavior. Now the murder had made his premonition come true.

According to his old hospital records, most of the doctors treating Sonny through the years believed that his symptoms stemmed from a 14-month stint in Vietnam, during which time Sonny's closest army buddy hung himself. Sonny was discharged after being hit in the face with a machete by an enemy soldier. Only in the course of my interviews with him did Sonny reveal that since childhood he had endured strange memory lapses and entrenched sub-narratives far antedating his wartime experiences. It is likely that traumas experienced in Vietnam merely reignited defensive responses honed during childhood (Grinker & Spiegel, 1963). Finally, when Sonny found himself in a situation that he perceived as threatening to his secure home life, he called on his "Protector" to obliterate the threat by committing a second-degree homicide. The killing was brutal, sudden, and, given the prior relationship of the fated dyad, inconceivable even to the man who had wielded the weapon.

For months, Sonny had been helping Bobby, a former neighbor, through a difficult time. One day Bobby asked if he might shower at Sonny's house, an arrangement that Sonny's wife confirmed would not have been out of the ordinary. Yet, arriving home to find Bobby there, Sonny became flushed and agitated, demanding to know what Bobby was doing in his home and insisting that he had not given his permission for the shower. Deaf to his own wife's pleas, Sonny grabbed a steak knife from the kitchen drawer and proceeded to stab Bobby, even as Bobby begged for his life on the grounds of their erstwhile agreement. The wife dialed 911, but Bobby was long dead when the police arrived. Sonny was dazed but compliant with the officers who arrested him.

Even before the murder, Sonny often lost time. Fifteen minutes here, twenty minutes there, sometimes he lost days:

I found myself in Jersey, camping out. I'd been gone for three days. It was me. I had a flashback, thinking I was back in Vietnam. I set up camp. I set up a perimeter and stayed there. I thought I was in enemy territory. Another time I found myself in Arthur Park in the Bronx. They said I was acting crazy.

He often relies on the accounts of others to supply the logical threads of his existence:

I'm not conscious. Other people tell me I've done things. They say I act like I'm in Vietnam. They say I get crazy, violent. One time I almost choked somebody, a kid.

I find things. I found a wallet in my dresser with money last Thanksgiving. I knew it wasn't mine. I found a gun in one of my boots. I turned that into the police.

Sometimes people come up and call me by other names. They say they know me from the streets, but I don't remember them.

Sonny's mother died when he was 10. He was left in the care of his abusive father, who "didn't tolerate nothing." Sonny was beaten with belts and extension cords and "punched in the face until I saw stars." His first "Protector" character ("I don't want to say his name") came when Sonny was six years old. At times this protector is perceived by Sonny as existing only inside his head, while at other times he is experienced as an independent entity.

Not infrequently, Sonny blames Bobby's murder on the Protector or fingers him as an accomplice. Alternately, he claims that the Protector only witnessed the murder: "He comes when I'm in physical danger. He came the night when I murdered somebody." Most interestingly, Sonny, like other dissociative men I have interviewed, spends a great deal of time trying to piece together the events of his life(lives). Sonny often plays the role of a detective trying to solve the murder to which he has already confessed: "I found some writing after the arrest. I had written on a piece of paper that I hadn't done what I was supposed to have done, but I knew who did it."

Sonny envisions his self-system as compartmentalized and controlled by others: "Junior is the strong part. He's a little kid, about 16 years old. He makes me laugh. There's also a baby part that wants to be alone."

When pressed for further details of the abuse he had endured at his father's hands, Sonny suggested that maybe Lawrence and Robert might remember. The memories, he said, were kept in a dark spot: "Lawrence and Robert watch over things. They don't want to share. If they do that, they would lose control of me."

Robert appears to embody Sonny's guilt and anger over abuse. Both self-abasing and vindictive toward others, he tempts Sonny toward suicide and contributes, along with a healing persona, to the refinement of Sonny's "Protector" narrative. Robert first appeared when Sonny was 10 years old, following his mother's death. "He talks about doing things right. When I do something wrong, he won't stop talking. He says 'You should know better. You ain't shit. You shouldn't be alive, you should not be alive. Kill yourself.'"

Lawrence, on the other hand, counsels Sonny to "straighten your life out. Go home, raise your kids, do things right." Sonny credits Lawrence with helping him to raise his daughters: a nurse, a teacher, and a servicewoman in the military. Lawrence works hard to purify Sonny.

Lawrence gives food to the homeless. He worked for the Church for over a year.

Lawrence cares about me. He tries to calm me down. Him and Robert get into arguments about me. Lawrence tells Robert to stop picking on me, to leave me alone.

Junior, Protector, and the Baby don't take over. Only Robert and Lawrence. When they argue, that's when I get bad headaches, or a pain in my stomach, or in the back of my head. A lot of times I have scratches and I don't know where I got them.

They control the moods. But Robert is more in control than Lawrence.

[Robert] came when my mother died. I didn't have no one. He started telling me what to do. In childhood and in Vietnam, where things were more confused. That's how things got started.

Subjectivity and Intention

The case of Sonny argues persuasively for the idea that, when basic danger situations (Freud, 1926) are reevoked during adulthood, a regressive dissociation is triggered that lands the person back at the site of the original splitting. Sonny's personal war began with the oedipal shame of his father's abuse and the guilt attending his mother's death (classical thought would put these as extenuations of the usual conditions for harsh superego formation). Sonny's internal war was recapitulated in the killings fields of southeast Asia. A "death constellation" (Hyatt-Williams, 1998) marshaled by maternal loss, paternal assault, and soldiering is a place where panic rules, where shame and guilt are so thickly layered as to be indistinguishable. If one is never quite sure who did what to whom, how can a moral dilemma be framed? As Grotstein (2001) puts it, "In primitive mental disorders one can see the rampant examples of mixed intentionalities—as if there were several different subjectivities within one personality, each with its own system of intentionality or motivation" (p. 580).

Sonny is not so much in a double-bind as in a double-pull of irreconcilable intentions. On one hand, he must be the best little boy in the world, the one with the most strenuously overworked superego: all good, all the time. This primitive superego functions to regulate affect (Wurmser, 2003b). It keeps threatening feelings at bay, shrinks them to less metastatic dimensions, or transmutes their character into ego-friendlier forms. But such absolute goodness as "Lawrence" embodies is one dimensional. Rigorous and inflexible, Lawrence's very perfectionism is a kind of internal sadism. Within this vigilant narrative, it is simply too dangerous to experience safety, comfort, or happiness lest it invite more terroristic threats: "[T]he inner judge, the archaic superego, has to prevent all pleasure. It shows itself the aforementioned doubleness—on the one side a very rigid inner authority, on the other side a large scale disregard for boundaries and limitations" (Wurmser, 2003a, p. 311).

For Sonny, another subnarrator, Robert, facilitates that narcissistic contempt through assault and, eventually, homicide:

Sonny: [Robert] has some aggressive behaviors. Sometimes he does it and other times he makes me do it. He hit someone in the head with a cane. They had to get stitches.

Like one time I got in a fight. I didn't want to. He gets in my head and takes control. It's hard for me not to do what he says. [The victim] and I were just talking. Then, Robert started arguing with him, "You think you're so smart" and so on. Me and him got into a fight. Robert punched him a couple of times and then he ran away. Robert just ran away.

Interviewer: Who did [the murder]?

Sonny: Robert. Sometimes he says he did it. I don't believe everything he says. But I'm not a violent person. I know something must have happened.

Trauma Redux

Offense is the other head of victimacy. To be seduced by one's own potential dangerousness is as intensely arousing as being in danger yourself. Crossing over from entertaining a violent action to its enactment will often trigger dissociation, even when dissociation has not itself precipitated violence (Porter et al., 2001). Henry (2004), for example, has documented dissociations in police officers who shot suspects during hot pursuit.[6] He found that during dissociation, the officers' normally operating signal anxiety ceases to function as an accurate early warning system. Any integrated assessment of future danger is undermined because the threat is unplugged from its current context and is infused with the shadows of earlier threats. Global paranoia and reactive aggression become a near-certain outcome—just as they do for a dissociating culprit. Research suggests that cataclysmic violence is often forgotten or transmogrified, even by people with no prior history of dissociation. Violence is the ultimate mind-altering drug.

Many violent people claim to have no memory of their assaultive or homicidal acts (O'Connell, 1960; Holcomb & Daniel, 1968 Bradford & Smith, 1979); these amnesias have been dubbed "red outs" in the forensic literature (Swihart, et al., 1999). During commission of a crime, proximity to a potential victim invokes an older, intensely stimulating trauma, along with the preconscious fear of the perpetrator's own capacity to inflict damage. Defying schematization, global arousal has uncontainable, terrifying dimensions. Fear is defended against through somatization, often in the form of sexual excitement and unmitigated rage. Defensive sexualization and aggression are then used to reestablish superego hegemony by projecting agency outside the self (into the victim) or beside the self (in a split-off identity) during assaultive enactments. Thus will offenders often claim that either the victim, or an incorporeal self, motivated their attacks.

Enacting rage momentarily keeps shame at bay. Aggression, though, triggers guilt (and more shame because the anticipation of retaliation is so mortifying), which must be exposed and punished by an externalized authority. The genesis of this dynamic looping in criminality was articulated by Melanie Klein (1933):

> [The child's] anxiety will serve to increase its own sadistic impulses by urging it to destroy those hostile objects so as to escape their onslaughts. The vicious circle is thus set up, in which the child's anxiety impels it to destroy its object, results in an increase of its own anxiety, and this once again urges it on against its object, and constitutes a psychological mechanism which, in my view, is at the bottom of antisocial and criminal tendencies in the individual. Thus we must assume that it is the excessive and overpowering cruelty of the superego, not the weakness or want of it, as is usually supposed, which is responsible for the behavior of asocial and criminal persons [p. 251].

Klein postulated that, as the child brought its internal image of the monsterous parents (fashioned by its own sadism) into line with the external reality of its relatively benign parents, the character of the superego would change. In normal development, the superego would modify its position as anxiety's chauffeur to being instead its gatekeeper by replacing reactive sadism with reparative concern. In situations where annihilation fears are reality based, however, this cannot happen.

---

[6] It would be interesting to know if officers with traumatic histories are more prone to dissociation and to the unreasonable use of force.

From Vigilant to Vigilante

> We might say that the symptom itself represents the locus of the performance
> of heroism. No wonder that one cannot give it up: that would release all by
> itself the whole flood of terror that one is trying to deny and overcome
> [Becker, 1973, p. 180].

Arthur Hyatt-Williams (1998), over 20 years' work with homicide offenders,
traced the arc from murderousness to murder through the lens of disturbed object
relations. He observed that violent persons both orbit and are orbited by a "death
constellation," which stems from early encounters where the child was likely
immobilized by terror or terrorized by immobility, often in relationship to abusing caretakers. Preoccupied with simultaneously disavowing and adopting the
dictates of the "murder-tolerating superego figure" (p. 35) that the caregiver represents, the child becomes immersed in murderous thoughts and impulses. He
kills the abuser over and over again in theory but, distracted by the constancy of
the threat to his bodily integrity, can never sufficiently attend to the work of
repairing those he has destroyed in fantasy. Like Sonny, instead of mourning his
imagined victims, the potential murderer continues a pathological identification
with his murdering object. As Klein (1935) wrote, "[T]he anxiety for himself is still
so strongly in operation he cannot endure the additional burden of anxieties for a
loved one" (p. 271). Later, in adulthood, when a confluence of imminently threatening events (imaginary or real) impinge on this mind presensitized to death ter-
rors, the ability to negotiate reality again collapses. Symbols are concretized,
people turn into their parts and, as Grotstein (1997b) has said, projected images
become the demonic "thing in itself," replete with agency and intention.

> Before the deed, conscious efforts—sometimes unconscious ones too—were
> designed and devoted to keeping the murderous encapsulations from action.
> Then something took place that broke loose the murderousness from its cor-
> doned off status so that the whole of the individual became devoted to enact-
> ing the murderous deed [Hyatt-Williams, 1998, p. 11].

Robert Jay Lifton (1983) has discussed the indelibility of what he calls the
"death imprint" in traumatic syndromes as being fueled as much by the guilt
of being ineffectual in one's efforts to prevent death as by the fear of death
itself. (One can see how easily "shame" might be substituted for "guilt" here.)
Think of all those that Sonny survived: his mother, his fellow soldiers, his best
friend. There was never enough mourning to assuage his feelings of triumph in
actual survival, much less in a fancied self-defense when he murdered Bobby.
When the work of mourning is incomplete, the job of reparation is crushing.

Reparation and Rapproachement

Such a surfeit of guilt as the offender demonstrates in his wish to be caught
(remember Sonny's docile surrender to police) leads to a highly ritualized
attempt to undo hate and to replace isolation with union. Police interrogation
techniques for eliciting admissions of criminal guilt rely, in fact, on this unspoken dynamic between confessor and confessant (Brooks, 2001).

Klein (1933) and Winnicott (1965) both hypothesized that the capacity for empathy could evolve only when one's parental objects survive their sadism and can accept restitution. The construct makes sense in relatively normal development. Both Klein and Winnicott addressed pathological adaptations as well, Klein with the notion that heightened anxiety and reactive sadism engender guilt that is persecutory and crippling rather than ameliorative. Winnicott, like Klein, refuted the popular idea that criminals have no sense of guilt and also attributed difficulties in controlling aggressive behavior to problems in the reparative phase of empathic development. According to Winnicott (1960), in cases where the caregiver cannot survive and forgive the child's aggression, residual anxiety is defended against with disintegration and splitting. A "false self" evolves, rooted in compliance with the caregiver's self-absorbed, disconfirming gestures. The false self is forced to live in an isolated and concrete world, too unsafe to play in. Rather than there being fantasy and complex symbolization there is only "imitation" (p. 147), which reminds us again of the mimicking facility of the so-called psychopaths described by Cleckley (1941), Meloy (1997a, b), Hare (1993), and others. Winnicott (1960) traced the origins of antisocial tendencies to childhood deprivation and articulated the idea that a person committing a crime is hoping that an external authority will provide the containing context that was not available to him in childhood. Winnicott's is another spin on the Freudian (1925) idea that guilt causes crime, rather than the other way around.

ASSERTING GUILT: PRIMEVAL FORMS

For what is "conscience"? On the evidence of language it is related to that of which one is 'most certainly conscious'. Indeed, in some languages the words for "conscience" and "conscious" can scarcely be distinguished [Freud, 1913, pp. 67–68].

Freud's tripartite structural model posited the superego as the agent of conscience, the place where guilt, manifested in remorse, resided. Freud's theory of moral genesis evolved over the years from the consideration of oedipal conflict (1923) to a broader view of the impact of social forces on the refinement of moral sensibility (1930).

Freud (1930) put forward that the repudiation of temptation in a person of conscience is virtually reflexive, where as knowledge of the origins of the anxious dread that trigger that automation is repressed. He conjectured that guilt-related anxiety arose from man's archaic desires to engage in incest, to kill, to defile the dead. Since the offender next described is three for three on these accounts, her story is a good point of departure for a further examination of conscience.

Police File

The victim had had multiple criminal arrests, but the perpetrator who killed him did not. In fact, Isabel had a valid pistol permit the night that she shot him, cleanly, just behind the right ear. And why wouldn't the authorities approve her gun registration? Her job record in the criminal justice system was unmarked by errors of judgment or attitude; indeed she had received only exemplary performance ratings during her lengthy employment.

Although a veteran of numerous other abusive domestic situations, Isabel insisted to police that her dead boyfriend had never hit her, although she offered that he had burglarized her house after their breakup and had many times raped her when he was drunk. Indeed, she had come to believe that only with "one of us dead" could she feel safe. She remembered pointing the gun at him and wishing that a guardian angel would still her trigger finger. "My hands were fighting me," she explained tearfully, by way of describing the sensorial dissociation of murderous intention. But later, in the police interrogation, she took a prideful responsibility for her acts, averring, "He never hit me. I just couldn't take it anymore, his lying and cheating and thieving. I thought about it for about 30 minutes (after he had passed out on the bed). It was meant to be fatal or I would have shot his foot off." (No doubt, the victim's feet were at least metaphorically where the shooter had aimed; the boyfriend had a history of stepping out on her, possibly reawakening earlier abandonment fears.)

The Interrogation

The crime scene photo showed a narrow cherry wood bed cushioning numerous stuffed animals. A princess phone and a photo of a horse stood on the bedside table. It was a strangely girlish room for a middle-aged civil servant, but, then, the psychiatric intake after her arrest described her as immature and easily frustrated, notwithstanding a high normal I.Q. Isabel's remorse appeared to the evaluator to be short lived, perhaps on the order of a narcissistic adolescent's. She told the defense team that, while dismembering her victim, she had pretended to be butchering a deer. When the steak knife could not penetrate bone, she switched to a meat cleaver.

Following the shooting, she had dragged the victim's body to the bathroom after checking his (lack of) breath in a hand held mirror. There she found herself driven literally to take apart the man who had forced his way into the apartment after she had changed the locks, who had so glibly taunted her with threatening phone calls at work, risking her perfect employee status. "He was still laughing at me and showing me who's boss. I couldn't take it; he had gone too far," she said by way of explaining to the police officer her need to diminish her victim once and for all: "I had to keep making him smaller and smaller." She undressed to do it, she said, so as not to ruin her clothes.

Finally, "physically and mentally exhausted" from the task of amputating her boyfriend's arms and legs, Isabel said, she took a nap before disposing of the body parts. She attended a family gathering that evening and, despite her anxiety, showed up on time for work the following morning.

Immediately following arrest, Isabel confessed the murder and dismemberment on videotape, aided detectives in the weapons discovery, and drew a map of the dump area. The victim's other body parts were found within 1200 feet of his torso, not withstanding the perpetrator's persistent memory that she had distributed them widely. Her uncoerced compliance with investigators and her good-girl demeanor during initial debriefing underscored the incongruity of her acts. Which part of her had been capable of such a violent reclamation of the self–other boundary? Maybe the part that devolved into cavalier commentary in later, more detailed iterations of the crime offered a clue. In many ways, the offhand descriptions of the murder/dismemberment/disposal seemed to echo the woman's bemused detachment from her own history of sexual abuse, which dated back to toddlerhood.

Family History

Isabel was the oldest in the family, a self-described fat tomboy, and a straight-A student who had received national honors. Her mother, eager for a more grown-up helper, made her daughter burn her security blanket when she turned 10. In adolescence, Isabel became both caretaker and disciplinarian for the younger ones and supplanted the mother in her siblings' affections. It was a role she had become accustomed to, having been her father's sexual companion since the age of three, a fact confirmed by her father but dismissed by the prosecution's psychiatrist as superfluous to any discussion of the defendant's psychological status. Although molestation had begun early, the psychiatrist reported, vaginal penetration did not begin until the defendant had already become sexually active at the age of 14, the implication being that this experience made the incest somehow less emotionally injurious. Since Isabel had remained close to her father following discovery by the family and the eventual cessation of abuse, and because she had never sought therapy over the issue, the psychiatrist's report concluded that the "sexual involvement with her father did not appear to have an overwhelmingly adverse effect on her." Her boyfriend-victim might have had a different assessment. In the criminal justice system, however, accountability is largely dissociated from internality, except in slightly modernized variants of the wild beast state.[7] "The culpabilization of madness" (Foucault, 1993) has reached full throttle.

The Mutilation of Objects

When profiling killers, forensic people make categorical distinctions between those who mutilate their victims for instrumental purposes, such as efficient disposal, and those whose goals are less mundane. FBI profilers have characterized non-instrumental mutilation as the "ritualistic expression of a sexual perversion" (Ressler, et al., 1986, p. 280), a theory at least partially substantiated by findings of masturbatory residue at mutilation crime scenes. Police contrast these offenders with the hypothesized opportunists, for whom mutilation is allegedly a rational calculation. However, a close examination of victim's bodies post mortem often reveals a level of gratuitous disfigurement unrelated to

---

[7]The English Common Law doctrine of the criminally guilty mind, first articulated in the 13th century, held that men could be held accountable for their crimes unless it could be determined that they possessed no more reason than a "wild beast." This standard went unchallenged until the 18th century, when Thomas Erskine persuaded a court that such total, raving insanity simply did not exist (Halttunen, 1998). The current standard for assessing legal culpability, when psychiatric issues are raised in court, is still quite narrow. The determination of guilt revolves around the single question of whether the defendant was cognitively capable of determining right from wrong at the time of the crime. Virtually all defendants, save the most floridly psychotic, know that they are doing wrong at some point in the offense. Thus, only the most wild of beasts pleading insanity are excused from criminal responsibility.

pragmatic aims, even in mutilations where efficiency is thought to be the defining goal, as in the case of the female perpetrator detailed above.

Even when there are no indications of ritualized postmortem violence or sexual catharsis, confessional stories hint at the intimate and symbolic nature of the decision to dissect, disembowel, or deface victims. To hear hitman Richard the "Iceman" Kuklinski wax philosophical to psychiatrist Park Dietz (HBO, 2003) about the relative virtues of Canoe cologne versus Vick's Vaporub as an olfactory block during mutilations is virtually to experience the way victims, even dead ones can suffocate their perpetrators. It doesn't get closer than this, although Kuklinski's recounting of a strangulation murder in which he noosed the victim and "used myself as the tree" (thus getting to feel the man die while spooning his back) is awfully competitive.

Postmortem mutilation occurs when rage is not satiated by murder but is aroused by it. I believe this to be true even when mutilation serves ancillary pragmatic goals. Isabel had to keep making her boyfriend smaller and smaller so that she could become bigger, omnipotent. For in addition to rage amok, there is fear unbridled—fear that the ever-powerful abuser can still hurt her, even though she has killed him.

Guilt forms but, instead of leading to mourning and concern, it leads to an even greater feeling of persecution. As regret grows, the victim seems to be rebuking the criminal, especially the partially perceived eyes that transmit blame and must be existed. The threatening symbol is concretized so that it seems agentic; only obliteration will suffice. Through mutilation, or other kinds of overkill, any chance that the abuser will revive is eliminated; the imagined persecutor is somehow deader than dead. Mutilation is the ultimate evidence of partialization; the victim is cut up to match the internal picture that the offender has of him: a tongue that scolds, hands that pinion and pilfer, feet that abandon, eyes that see all or naught.

Anxiety and Aggression

Whether pregenital, as in Klein's (1933) formulation of oral sadisim, oedipal, as in Freud's (1961) delineation of the sadistic superego, or developmentally unfixed, as in Sullivan's (1953b) notion of the "malevolent transformation" (p. 213), one's own aggression is so terrifying that it must be disowned and projected. In projection, essentially safe figures can radiate menace while ostensibly posing no real threat to psychic integrity.

In incestuous family dynamics, though, there is a fusion of the fantasied and the factual: a fusion that increases death-related anxieties exponentially (Stein, 2001). The wish to kill one's abuser in retaliation is fundamental to survival; it is as if only one player in the incestuous calamity can continue to exist. Such overpowering aggression, along with the anxiety it triggers, stays raw and undifferentiated; it resists the referential process that would give it meaning and measurement or place it on an autobiographical timeline (Sullivan, 1953; Bucci, 1997; Stolorow, 2003). With danger imminent, two kinds of death anxiety must be forfended: the dreadful knowledge that one will die during abuse, and the horrid desire to cause the death of the abuser.[8] As Isabel indicated, where threat collapses past and present, safety is achievable only "with one of us dead". However, if someone has never developed an intersubjective stance where the separateness of the other is recognized, victim and offender share agency (which must be destroyed). One is always destroying one's self.

Autochthony is a kind of self-reference, or the belief that one has precipitated events in the external world. Autochthony has important implications for the internalization of abusive experiences because the idea that one's self is the "first cause" of parental maltreatment is coextensive with a personal understanding of why trauma has occurred (Grotstein, 1997a). If the self cannot be held blame-worthy, then abuse is arbitrary and capricious, unstoppable. Thus, survival depends on the splitting off of the experience not only through dissociation, but also through autochthony: the deputizing of a "bad" agentic self to take respon-sibility for inviting abuse. Without this modification of agency, one would be "overwhelmed by [the] utter externality [of trauma]" (p. 408).

Mental organization, under such assault, would cede to psychosis. On the precipice of this chaos, felt agency for misdeeds (a.k.a. conscience and remorse) is constituted to (a) provide a stop-loss on psychic integrity and (b) maintain the illusion that abuse is controllable. With the assumption of the sadistic or seductive role, any perceptual separateness of object and subject founders. The metamorphopsis militates against the knowledge of the abuser's power and the immutability of traumatic engravings by displacing conscience, not forfeit-ing it. Children must consider themselves the primal agent of trauma until such time as they achieve recognition of the traumatizing object as existing outside themselves. Only then can they attribute an external causation for their woes, The vehicle that would transport agency is however, disabled by abuse, strand-ing intentionality, and guilt roadside.

The defensive dissociation of memories or affects associated with violence (both received and transmitted) simultaneously serves the wish to survive and disclaims the need to destroy. The bottomless shame of having allowed, on some primitive plane even having enjoyed, violation hastens the retreat of a victim identity while buttressing a malevolent identity. As malice escalates, aggression becomes muscular and overt. Guilt arises once the survivor of abuse feels that her life has been purchased at the cost of another (Lifton, 1976) but, in violent offend-ers, the feeling is actualized, as fantasied aggression jumps decades to find embodied victims (Stein, 2001). As Wurmser (2003a) has written about traumati-zation, "something concrete is [] sought that will give word and meaning to the unspeakable desperation and defend against the horror" (p. 311).

Wurmser is speaking of the incest victim's push toward self-punishment and retraumatization, a wish clearly discerned in the case of Isabel, the sexually abused civil servant who found a sexually battering partner in adulthood. However, the search for material equivalence in the here-and-now, in this authenticating of traumatic context, applies also to the ways that some abuse survivors punish and execute their own victims. By committing a homicide, the survivor is making crystal a memory of an occult murder, the murder of the

---

[8] When it comes to describing the emotional vortex of anxiety, perhaps no one, before or since, was as lucid a writer as Harry Stack Sullivan. By attaching words like awe, dread, loathing, and horror to primitive, parataxic experience, he tapped the otherwise autistic vein of trauma. Sullivan's (1963) description of some strains of childhood anxiety as consisting of a "paralyzing revulsion coupled with the desire to vomit" is simply unmatched (p. 316).

abusing parent. For example, recall the case of Sonny. For him the loss of the mother removed any safeguard against paternal abuse and likely vivified the most nightmarish of oedipal fantasies. Ashamed of driving away his mother and inviting the cruelties of his father, he was perhaps ashamed of his nascent symptoms of psychiatric illness as well. He was guilty about his sexual feelings toward his mother (which may have killed her) and his rage toward his father (which perhaps would kill him too). Later Sonny survives a war (by killing enemy soldiers) and outlives his best friend (who succumbs to a combination of depressive illness and wartime trauma). Killing Bobby is the culmination of Sonny's fantasized/realized capacity for murder.

The abusive interaction provokes intense anxiety: anxiety over one's own sadism and the imagined retaliation of the object of one's sadism. As Klein (1952) noted, in this malevolent interaction, violence is the only cathartic; "violence liberates anxiety" (p. 260). Moreover, since murdering the other and killing the self are synonymous, the killing takes care of guilt.

> Love is not absent in the criminal, but it is hidden and buried ... the criminal is now in the position of hating and persecuting his own loved object; as this is an intolerable position, all memory and consciousness of any love for any object must be suppressed. If there is nothing in the world but enemies, and that is how the criminal feels, his hate and destructiveness are, in his view, to a great extent justified—an attitude which relieves some of his unconscious feelings of guilt. Hate is often used as the most effective cover for love; but one must not forget that to the person who is under the continuous stress of persecution, the safety of his ego is the first and only consideration [p. 260].

Sonny protected his ego with a preemptive strike against a parental surrogate. Bobby, the murder victim, in that moment must have seemed to Sonny to be usurping his own masculine role vis-à-vis the female of the house, just as Sonny's father had once severed Sonny's relationship to his mother. Isabel finally succeeded in dismembering (with all the oedipal connotations of that word) her raping boyfriend, also a thinly veiled paternal surrogate. The violence of both Sonny and Isabel, without apparent motive, forgotten even as it was committed, seems to me evidence of the kind of primitive, dissociated sadism that Klein so well described.

The final illumination of rage—and consequent guilt—efficiently obscures shame, if only briefly (Lansky, 2003). Even in people with no history of overt maltreatment, shame–rage cycles may manifest in subtle ways along a broad range of human activities and interactions. In subjects less traumatized than those discussed in this volume, patterns may be made conscious through engagement and reflection. For the most severely traumatized, however, rage and shame tend to be serial states, too individually overpowering to be simultaneously apprehended. I believe that to be true for these particular victim-offenders.

REFLECTIONS

Unconscious subjectivity and agency are identical. Subjectivity is the other face of intentionality (Grotstein, 2001, p. 582).

Writing of his multiply traumatized patients, Wurmser (2003a) describes an archaic, despotic superego that provokes punishment in order to externalize the locus of shame and guilt. It thereby regulates the affects normally associated with those states. During abuse, helplessness, excitement, and hatred vie for affective dominance. But the incompatibility of various feelings or ideas—the conflict—is so paralyzing that affects and cognitions remain diffuse, unplugged from any organizing schema, and are inevitably resomatized (p. 25). Moral questions cannot take sentient form in a perceptual horizon fogged by this traumatic storm. Still, remorse, pity, grief, anguish, compassion—indeed the entire panoply of moral emotions—are demonstrated in the contradictions and contractions of criminal conduct: the teenager's attempt to revive his very dead victim (the rug underneath her head was saturated with blood and brain matter, according to police reports), the child molester's surveilled ride, the Vietnam veteran's out-of-character civilian murder, the law-abiding civil servant's very uncivil dismemberment of her beau.

The rest of us demonstrate similar contradictions and projections, in lesser forms, during the daily exercise of moral relativism. A cockroach crawling on the podium during a lecture will elicit students' hoots of "Kill it, Kill it," while a puppy mistakenly entering the classroom will seldom stir a demand for capital punishment (D. F. Sweedler, personal communication). If one of your young students kills the roach, that's maturity. (In fact if she feels excessively guilty about killing the bug, a therapy session is probably in order.) On the other hand, if the same student pulls the wings off flies, her action is a harbinger of perversity and, according to some criminologists, even a sign of impending homicidality. We socially approve some kinds of splitting because society cannot function without a certain level of aggression, and violence cannot be enacted without a certain amount of dissociation.

Such situational pathologizing has not gone unnoticed: Geoffrey White (2004) has suggested the inclusion in the *Diagnostic and Statistical Manual* of "political apathy disorder," defined as the lack of a social conscience. Like psychopaths, sufferers of the disorder have no subjective distress. Their actions are characterized by a pervasive pattern of failing to help those in need (e.g., the poor, the oppressed, the underprivileged) combined with overconsumption of the world's limited resources. Not surprisingly, White studies corporate power, trauma survival in the Third World, and the inaction of American Jews during World War II.

More germane to our discussion, for most of human history the world has allowed, even encouraged, the physical abuse and sexual use of children. We have largely, and quite adaptively, dissociated the real meanings of neglect and maltreatment; sometimes we have even promoted them as their opposites: discipline, education, or love.

We fancy the ones we hurt are the agents of their own mistreatment. Just as the prisons are full of pedophiles who tell you that little children seduced them, rapists who believe their victims wanted it, and killers who killed because of an imaginal disrespect on the part of their victims, so too are schools, houses, and churches filled with parents whose children "ask for" corporeal punishment or "need to be taught" about sex. Language is a vehicle for distortion, denial, and dissociation, just as Otto Rank (1941) and George Orwell (1949) suspected.

The clinical is cultural, to rework a vintage 1970s political adage, and vice-versa. For example, infanticide is most widespread where infant mortality from disease is highest because the chance that children will die young skewers attachment, promotes devaluation, and heightens death related anxieties: all are preconditions for increased aggression. As mentioned earlier, homicide rates are highest where the death penalty is most frequently invoked: capital punishment is most often applied where it is perceived as "just desserts" rather than as cold, premeditated killing. In fact, juries in capital cases must be "death qualified" to make sure that they have a view of killing that comports with this cultural dissociation. Lewis (1998), interviewing the executioner who had given the lethal injection to one of her pro bono patients, found a man similar in background and psychological instability to her executed patient. She closes her book about legal and illegal forms of violence by waxing philosophically that "society will always produce enough people who were so brutalized during their own childhoods, so muddle-headed and paranoid, that they are more than willing to perform the grisly jobs that other people would not dream of taking" (p. 284). The executioner, just like his charges, insisted (after 19 executions) that he had never killed anyone. In all likelihood, not dissociating the evidence of his own aggression would be psychologically fatal. As Adolf Bastian once wrote: "The double who catches sight of himself must die within a year" (quoted in Rank, 1941, p. 50). Even sooner, I would guess.

4

Maximum Perversion

When I was a forensic psychology student, there was probably no idea that I was exposed to more often than this one: the perpetrators of sex crimes, particularly serial sexual killers, were driven to commit their acts because their long-term indulgence in deviant sexual fantasizing no longer brought them erotic fulfillment. Tense with unsatisfied longings, perpetrators went and acted out their fantasies with unwilling victims.

From penile plethysmographs to Rorschachs, empirical studies had demonstrated that violent sexual predators embraced some rather creepy fantasies (Gacono & Meloy, 1994; Lalumiere et al., 2003). The perpetrators themselves often described, in nauseating detail, how their bizarre fantasies had formed a template for the crimes they eventually committed (Ressler & Douglas, 1989). To emphasize the soundness of their argument, researchers noted that offenders left ejaculate at the crime scene, or described using victim's belongings later to relive attacks as they masturbated. What more was needed? Indeed, there is abundant face validity for the argument that violent masturbatory fantasizing is a rehearsal for violent sexual activity.

No one in my classes seemed terribly disturbed by the fact that there were no control groups in those offender sexual fantasy studies, or that the little data collected on "normals" tended to show a not infrequent indulgence in fantasies of sexual dominance and submission, often quite aggressive (Crepault & Couture, 1980). In fact, a rare comparison study of juvenile sexual offenders showed them to have basically the same propensity toward deviant fantasies as did controls (Daleiden et al., 1998). All this probably comes as no surprise to psychoanalylsts, who have long explored the perverse details of their patients' dreams, daydreams, fantasies, and wishes.

The only empirical study (that I know of) comparing sadistic murderers[1] with healthy, nonoffender volunteers on a variety of measures, including those of sexual fantasy, found that a significant percentage of the noncriminal controls

---

[1]The sadistic murderers who constituted the offender group in this study were the same ones interviewed by Burgess and her (1986) colleagues in their study of sexual homicide, a study that is critiqued later in this chapter. Gray et al. (2003) did a secondary study of the Burgess data and conducted primary interviews with controls, recruited from a nonoffending population of college students.

engaged in sadistic fantasies and that the "high sadism" groups—offenders and nonoffenders—shared a number of etiological features (Gray et al., 2003). Adding their own findings to the batch of forensic literature that posits a connection between fantasy and perpetration, the authors assert that "available evidence *fails to support* any exclusive association between sadistic fantasy and sadistic murder" (p. 1020, italics, added).

The empirical inconsistencies, coupled with what I have learned during my own work with offenders regarding their dissociated histories of child maltreatment, leads me to question the linearity of the premise that sexually deviant fantasy—once it has somehow exhausted its physiological usefulness—blossoms into sexually deviant, criminal behavior. Deviant sexual fantasies are within everyone's purview; my interviews with violent felons suggest that it is not the perversion quotient of their sexual fantasies, but the underlying deviance of their internalized objects (and the sexualized images of attachment that spring up around them), that makes the interpersonal landscape so toxic. It is the tendency for symbolization processes to deteriorate rapidly in the face of perceived threat, coupled with this lust for symbiotic merger, that lays a foundation for the perverse, violent reenactment of unintegrated traumas. Thus, as Jessica Benjamin (1995) has noted, the concern should be not with sadistic fantasies per se, but with "the counterpoint between fantasy and recognition of otherness, especially the other's subjectivity" (p. 181).

Many forensic researchers seem not to recognize, or at least do not acknowledge, the wide phenomenological gulf between a person using fantasy toward defensive or cathartic ends and a more predatory daydreamer. The former engages the fantasy; the latter becomes an instrument of the fantasy and a catalyst for its reification. In fact, it is probably a misnomer to call this type of mental ideation fantasy as the term is used colloquially; it is more correctly regarded as a refraction of traumatic overstimulation, what Klein (1933) characterized as an annihilative–reparative "phantasy," or unconscious fantasy. The sadistic and ameliorative wishes embedded in these imaginings are largely dissociated from consciousness, whereas a more acceptable version, a sexualized elaboration of dissociated events, does rise to conscious awareness, or even preoccupation. The two kinds of fantasy—the unconscious, or dissociated, form and the intrusive, all too conscious one—combine to fuel enactments that are deadly derivatives of original traumas.

The focus of this chapter is on a conspicuous element of dissociation that is less theatrical than the overt presentations of divided consciousness that have so often captured the public imagination. Instead, I examine the tendency toward dissociative reverie: how it reveals itself in the offender, why it is so often primitively sexualized, what it signifies, and how it differs from (in fact is sometimes the very opposite of) what is usually called fantasy. I hope to reset the parameters of the fantasy argument and redefine its terms, in anticipation of inaugurating a different vision of why and how people aggress in a sexually depraved fashion. Whereas so many in the forensic field have concentrated on the criminogenic power of the paraphillic fantasy to transform dreamers into deviant actors, I suggest that it is the formative power of deviantized, preoedipal object relations, as well as the ensuing reliance on dissociative defenses (including obsessive rumination and quasi-delusional reverie), that determines who crosses the line from so-called fantasy into action.

Police File

Lester had spent years in several institutional settings following his mother's violent death. As an adult, he was convicted of multiple murders, all classified as sexual homicides. Lester particularized his M.O. for investigators; he included the fact that he had forced victims to pose for photographs (sometimes while wearing the underwear of previous victims) and had kept detailed records of his victims' age, virginal status, and the color of their rectal hair. He occasionally dug up their bodies and copulated with them again while thinking about the original crime. In a long and sometimes incoherent statement before sentencing, Lester derided his handling as a child in "the system" and claimed to have been sexually abused in many of his early foster placements.

Police File

Jermaine stalked an elderly woman and eventually made her acquaintance. The year before the stalking, he had sought counseling because he felt preoccupied with "wondering what a woman looks like" but he believed himself "cured" of this obsession at the time of the offense. He broke into the woman's house because he felt attracted to her large breasts but claimed to be too repulsed by her body odor to complete the rape. Medical evidence, however, suggested that both vaginal and anal penetration had taken place. Jermaine maintained that he remembered neither.

ATTACHMENT FANTASIES, ONCE REMOVED

A generally accepted theory in the forensic and criminological literature regards the ideational matrix of sexual fixation that drives sexual crimes. Most observers have attributed violent sex crimes to offenders' conscious dependence on sexualized, aggressive fantasies as the mainstays of a masturbatory repertoire (Burgess et al., 1986; Prentky et al., 1989; Ressler et al., 1992; Meloy, 2000; Schlesinger, 2000). Rather than using the term masturbatory in its strictly sexual sense, as criminal profilers do, I want to call attention to its other stimulating or satiating aspects. Particularly in people with a history of impaired objects relations, fantasy (even masturbation itself) may serve more of a self-soothing function than a sexual one, much like the rocking of an autistic child. In fact, given the phenomenology of not only masturbatory ideation, but the totality of sexual offenders' carnality, it is conceivable that their erotic ideation has little in common with what you or I would call sexual fantasy.

On close reading, the fantasies described often appear to be much more closely aligned with the magical remediation of disrupted attachments than with the satisfaction of erotic aims. With thorough inspection, the criminal manifestations of such ideas fit almost eerily with the stages of response experienced by toddlers who are suddenly separated from their caregivers: distress, anger, hopelessness, despair, and detachment (Bowlby, 1973). Predatory offenders often describe psychological conditions very close to those states during the days, hours, or moments leading up to their crimes: overwhelming tension, rage, futility, inevitability, and dissociation. The crimes themselves offer every indication that the offenders are attempting a perverse merger with their victims, one that either recapitulates the perversity of an earlier attachment gone awry or compensates for a bond that never existed.

For example, one police file related the story of a man who went out in search of his wife, with whom he had been fighting. He ended up at the house of his mother-in-law, whom he raped and then beat to death in a particularly animalistic fashion. In jailhouse letters to his wife he told numerous stories of her demise, none of which constituted a confession of his own participation. In one version, he told his wife of his actions after discovering her mother's supposedly already dead body: "I went to mom's side and gave her a kiss on the lips." In another, he claimed to have tried to save his mother-in-law from the humiliation of having been raped by a black man by masturbating and then manually depositing his own semen into her mouth, vagina, and anus. Then he claimed to have accidentally fallen on top of her, crushing her larynx! (This man, according to the accounts of numerous family members interviewed by law enforcement, had been neglected, beaten, and sexually abused by his father while he was growing up and had often witnessed sex between his parents.) His violation of this maternal/spousal stand-in and his fantastical confessions tell a tale of intense separation anxiety, unbridled rage, and desperate attempts at rapprochement, all nested within a web of magical thinking. The man later wrote to his wife from prison: "Come and take me home soon. I don't like this place no more." To my mind at least, his plea echoes the plaintive cry that his own mother never heard while Daddy was sodomizing him.

WHEN IS A FANTASY NOT A FANTASY?

In Alice Sebold's (1999) novelized account of losing her virginity to a rapist in Central Park, she tells how the attacker wanted her to kiss him goodbye following an ambush and a brutal physical attack. He told her she was beautiful, helped her on with her clothes, and parted from her with the words, "Nice knowing you, Alice. See you around some time" (pp. 20–22). Sebold acquiesced to her stranger-perpetrator's demands for intimacy; to save her own life, she even verbally reinforced his view that the encounter was romantic. This is not unlike the perceptions of many rapists—acquaintance *and* stranger—who treat their victims as if the two had been on a date, even in the aftermath of vicious assaults.

These perpetrators behave in a way that reifies their "fantasy" of consensual engagement. All too often, for male sex offenders, the script echoes their own experiences of early sexual abuse, encounters that they defended against by imagining themselves as the instigators, rather than the passive victims, of sexual activity. Some male offenders have told me how well their precocious manliness served them in attracting and bedding babysitters, aunts, neighbors, and stepmothers. "I did her," the offender often says, "when I was six." He dissociates a reality and elaborates an alternative truth. In adolescence or adulthood, he reenacts the scene with himself on top—imagined as lover, not rapist. The criminal enactment makes the elaboration an independent, demonstrable truth. Criminal profilers would call his a sexual fantasy based on a life experience, indulged from an early age, consciously honed and relied on for sexual stimulation, and reaching apotheosis in real time with real victims.

A psychoanalyst, though, should shift attention to how deeply the original elaboration guts reality and how the ensuing fantasy borders on delusion. As Donnel Stern (personal communication, 2005) has said, what deserves the name fantasy is something far more elastic and inventive than what these offenders mentalize:

> [A fantasy] expresses wishes that the fantasizer realizes are unfulfillable. [We] can tolerate having murderous fantasies because we know perfectly well they will never be enacted. That is the *sole* reason we can allow ourselves the pleasure we take in them. The distinction is between fantasies that go on in the transitional realm and those that come about when the transitional realm collapses into quotidian reality. (italics in original)

One man that I interviewed, Matty, had as a young adolescent been forced to have sex with his mother (his narrative appears in the next chapter). As an adult, Matty often became lost in reverie while looking at young women on the subway and subsequently fantasized that he would be invited to go home with them for sex. As it turned out, Matty was following women home and committing push-in rapes on their doorsteps, a version of events that became consciously embraced by Matty only when the police confronted him with evidence of the assaults. Until that time he remained convinced that he had only "dreamed" about the sexual encounters, which, in his imagination, were consensual. Remember Matias Reyes, who showered with his victims after raping them so as to reinforce the idea that they were truly a "couple"? In encounters so surreal, is it descriptively accurate to say that the perpetrator was acting out a conscious fantasy?

Following Robert Stoller's (1973) theoretical lead, I differentiate conscious fantasy from delusional or hallucinatory experience not by their contents or defensive functions (which may be identical) but by the way that what is inside one's head is expressed in the real day-to-day world. In his well-known analysis of the highly dissociative (and dually gendered) Mrs. G, Stoller remarked that, like Mrs. G, many women conceivably fantasize having a penis. Perhaps they have even elaborated the fantasy, as Mrs. G did, as an empowering bulwark against traumatic memories. But, wrote Stoller, a psychoanalyst would best acknowledge the difference between a woman who, no matter how intense her fantasy might be, nonetheless keeps intact a realistic body image based on real physical sensations and a woman who has so fully incorporated the penis into her identity that it has become as stable and as "essential a part of body ego [as the] nonhallucinated parts" (p. 23). A related distinction is made by McDougall (1972), who differentiates structural, or characterological, perversion from the occasional indulgence of perversion by more pedestrian personalities. She explicitly connects this "perverse structure" to a *lack* of integrative fantasy.

A similar case can be made for offenders whose so-called fantasies are really highly ritualized reenactments of early abuse scenarios that they keep returning to, as one might to the scene of a bad accident. For example, one convicted child rapist described to interrogating officers his "fantasy" (a memory, it turned out) of his brother anally sodomizing him. At three junctures of the interview, the offender represented this mental idea in three different ways: first, as a tool he consciously employs to reach orgasm while penetrating a little girl; then as an unwanted "flashback" that comes during a molestation and is triggered by his victim's tears. Finally, he described a ritualized elaboration of the real assault by his brother—during which his hands were sometimes bound—into a full-blown bondage scenario that he acts out with his own victims. To call these mentations fantasies is to miss something fundamental about their nature—to ignore the difference between a liberating flight of fancy and a perpetual enslavement to reality.

In a compelling empirical search for the relational antecedents of "fantasy proneness," Rhue and Lynn (1987) found that across all the age ranges they sampled the subjects most prone to fantasizing reported a greater frequency and severity of physical punishment, and a greater use of fantasy to block the pain of punishment, than did controls (p. 133). Of course, it makes intuitive sense that children isolated by their maltreatment would create compensatory worlds in which to sojourn. Here again, though, we need to extract more information about the nature of the so-called fantasies. How are people defining fantasy for themselves? Is it possible to determine whether people are discussing ideas that are creatively elaborated and volitionally conjured, intrusions that are engaged obsessively, or trancelike episodes of dissociated reverie?

It turns out that Rhue and Lynn's paper was inspired by Wilson and Barber's (1981) study of highly hypnotizable subjects who, in addition to describing themselves as heavily reliant on fantasy, reported experiencing hallucinations, somatic delusions, out-of-body events, and occasional difficulty differentiating fantasy from reality. Rhue and Lynn's subjects were not assessed on these variables, although the researchers report that their sample of college students may have represented a particularly high-functioning group of fantasizers whose manifest reality testing appeared to be intact. Only six of their 21 fantasy-prone subjects detailed egregious abuse at the hands of their caretakers; the remainder were self-described as merely having been punished harshly. Side by side, the Rhue and Lynn and the Wilson and Barber studies raise provocative questions about the continuum of punishment from severe to abusive and its connections to a continuum of fantasy, from the volitional and adaptive to the dissociated and potentially destructive.

I read files all the time wherein a perpetrator describes thoughts about the victim that seem to me to be obsessive, magical, or out and out psychotic ruminations. Then the interrogating officer or the evaluating psychiatrist chimes in with, "So this was your *fantasy* about her?" Ten times out of ten the perpetrator will affirm that what he describes was a fantasy, which then becomes the way the dialogue is transcribed in subsequent documents: for example, "The perpetrator admitted that he had violent fantasies about the victim." I do not think such thoughts qualify as fantasy in the strict sense; this is another point at which a small shift in definitional emphasis can substantially clarify a phenomenon. Perpetrators, particularly really young or extremely impaired ones, may be unable to distinguish between a fantasy and a recollection, or between the imaginary and the intrusive.

Sullivan (1953b) wrote, "The lonelier the child has been, the more striking may be the child's need of effort—need of continuous recall and foresight—to fix these distinctions between what, as we say, actually happened and what was part of fantasy process" (p. 225). Sullivan understood that a child who is sufficiently cared for will come to see reality as benign and can enjoy a playful fantasy of control over external objects, whereas a child who is not cared for appropriately will devolve into an "unreality" quite distinct from fantasy and play. Winnicott (1960) believed that the very process of symbolizing is born within the mother–child dyad's unspoken agreement to reify the child's illusion of omnipotence, thus promoting the cathexis of an acquiescing, but ultimately reparable, object. Absent this mutual confirmation of the child's power, wrote Winnicott, the playful, fantasizing self becomes protectively sequestered and a false, compliant, plagiarized self sets up shop. In the transformation, all that is fanciful is ruthlessly abridged. The indeterminacy of imagination gives way to the certainty of fundament; for the necessarily wary child, the concrete simply forms a safer precipice from which to view the world.

It is within this literalized context that the need for power and control comes to be forcefully dissociated and enacted rather than creatively imagined, as it is for less traumatized persons. "Rape fantasies," and even mild role-playing in the S&M arena, are common sexual currency for both genders (Hsu et al., 1994; Person et al., 1989; Rokach, Nutbrown & Nexhipi, 1989) and probably for all orientations. It is only through imaginative construction that destructiveness can be creatively integrated. As Stern (1997b) has said, dissociation is "the unwillingness to allow oneself freedom of thought" (p. 97). Unfortunately, for the potentially felonious, freedom of action is not similarly restricted.

FAILED FANTASIES

Fantasies allow one to alter painful realities in creative ways and to discharge libido endopsychically. Even for the average offspring of caring parents, reality can seem to be a bogeyman; the child uses fantasy to transcend the fear, pain, indignity, and overall confusion of real life (Bettleheim, 1989). The abused child, however, is trapped in a too harsh reality; the demand for anxious vigilance congests traditional psychological escape routes even as it sets up a parallel, covert system for the dissociation of historical truths.

Here, where the superego stringently imposes itself (see previous chapter), anxiety is neither expressed nor relieved in fantasized forms: it is instead discharged through violent performance (Lefer, 1984). For offenders, tensions find outlet mainly in offense; this is why offenders are apt to attribute what appear to be motiveless acts to an escalation of anxiety and to describe a feeling of wholesale relief (admittedly short-term) after the deeds are committed (Stein, 2002). Interestingly enough, forensic investigators often link this intensification of anxiety directly to the acceleration of violent fantasies; the investigators say that similar states of overwhelming tension are likely *not* experienced by daydreamers who do not act out their imaginative schemes, even as the researchers allow that there is no real control data on which to base this assumption (Schlesinger, 2000, p. 12).

Again, I would subtly shift the emphasis here from the content or frequency of violent sexualized imagery to its flat and perseverative character. It is this rutted quality that makes the violent sexual imagery of offenders ineffective in satiating desire; it is this that differentiates benign constructions from their malignant counterparts. In other words, it is probable that those who find relief in fantasy alone can do so because they are able to make the symbolic substitute of characters inside their heads vibrate sufficiently with detail and depth; they can therefore find catharsis in their imaginings. For many in the grip of perversion, on the other hand, fantasies fail. Litman (1997), for example, interviewed nine men involved in intense sadomasochistc activity and found that for none of them was violent fantasy sufficient to bring about orgasm; only actual bondage or pain brought climax. As Khan (1979) noted, the satisfaction of deviant desires is elusive both in fantasy and in reality:

> Just as the neurotic lives through his fantasies (conscious and unconscious), the pervert lives through his actions. This internal necessity *to act* makes the use of will and power imperative for the pervert . . .
>
> The pervert knows himself only through his victim's actualization of his intentions.[2] It is this which constitutes the essential poverty of the pervert's experience [pp. 208–209].

In a best case scenario, perverse fantasies can transmute anxiety and rage into pleasurable somatic events, particularly for people who find themselves able to use sexual fantasy as a prosocial adaptation to trauma.[3] Indeed, Meyers (1991) has observed that perverse masturbatory ideation seldom is acted out; she conjectures that the fantasies derive their erotic power from the very fact that they will never be publicly performed, exposing their host to danger or humiliation (p. 96). On the other hand, for a chronically abused child, an underdeveloped imagination and overdeveloped superego likely conspire to deracinate violent fantasies before they prove purgative. True, mental scenes of sexual retaliation may be mulled over, but this is not quite the same as an assuaging fantasy; it is more akin to the festering of a wound. These aggressive erotica quickly become the disavowed ideas that are later enacted.

Pye (1993) has described the persecutory nature of abused patients' memories as making imagination itself a "place of assault." Lacking the creative ability to fantasize richly, and experiencing his own imagination as intrusive and persecutory, an abused child who grows into a criminal actor cannot easily negotiate tension. Describing a noncriminal patient whose lapse into paranoia precipitated a psychotic, violent enactment, Blum (1991) puts it succinctly: *"The stabilizing function of the fantasy was lost . . . free aggression emerged rather than its sadomasochistic alloy"* (p. 448, italics added). Later, when Blum's patient recovered from the paranoid regression, his sadomasochistic fantasies returned.

Clinical observations of "murderous" (but not murdering) patients demonstrate that *the greater their ability to fantasize, the less likely that they will resort to actual violence.* The ability to use symbolic, fantasied representations of people

---

[2]Similarly, see Fonagy et al. (2002), Meloy (1997a), and Grand (2000).

[3]Much as been written about sexual fantasies that accrue from traumatic memory. Most writers have concentrated on the disabling sequelae of the fanatasies, such as guilt over experiencing pleasure in abuse (Davies & Frawley, 1994). Few have written about the defensive advantages in "using" trauma to reach orgasm. In its own pedestrian way, it is perhaps not unlike the mastery over trauma that is achievable through more creative sublimations, like writing poetry or painting.

and situations helps to purge anger and tamp fear, deflating tension. At the scene of the criminal opportunity, rather than forfeiting reality and becoming irreversibly concrete, the potential offender can imagine himself out of the assaultive action. Hyatt-Williams (1998) offers evidence of this very point: "I have encountered a significant number of instances in which there was a de-escalation, an increasing capacity to symbolize, and hence, no murder (p. 35). Hyatt-Williams does not go into detail about the nature of the shift from concrete to symbolic that occurred for these almost-offenders. It seems to me that, in addition to purging rage, at least part of the process of signifying and unplugging murderous intention would have to do with imagining a cause-and-effect relationship between actions and their consequences, a proactive function of cognitive rehearsal.

DIFFERENTIATING FANTASY FROM REALITY

For many trauma survivors, internal imagery stays pallid because it is always overshadowed by the specter of the real (Grotstein, 1995); they cannot make a conscious decision to ignore reality and liberate themselves from the domain of the flesh. Fonagy et al., (2002) describe as a kind of developmental arrest the inability of some trauma victims to enter an imaginative space where a fantasy's connection to reality can be safely severed "Indeed it is this very inadequacy in their capacity to represent aggression-related attachment ideation mentally that may place [traumatized individuals] at risk of violent acts in the context of intimate interpersonal relationships" (p. 344).

Shlomith Cohen (1989) pinpoints how, almost counterintuitively, the *diminution* of fantasy-making capacities, not their ascendancy, may presage major imbroglios with reality:

> In the activity of fantasizing there is evidence of the need and capacity to take an active position with regard to the laws and restrictions of the perceived reality, that is to exercise mental freedom from reality testing. This type of activity is by no means a sign of inadequate functioning of the ego or the higher mental functions. On the contrary, its absence is more alarming [p. 65].

Descriptions of the reverie of violent offenders abound in the forensic literature. Clinicians and police alike report mental contents more akin to borderline or psychotic thought than to what is conventionally considered fantasy, although with few exceptions they pretty much insist on labeling the imaginings "fantasy" (Burgess et al., 1986; Meloy, 1997, 1998; Schlesinger, 2000).

Layered with projections and fueled by alternating currents of magical omnipotence and delusional paranoia, perpetrators' imaginings quickly become nonvolitional. Their victim-objects are inseparable from earlier persecutory objects as well as from any subjective sense of self. When fantasy is nonvolitional in this way, it is not fantasy at all, but obsessive rumination. When fantasy is indistinguishable from reality in this way, it is not fantasy at all, but a quasi-delusion.

In the story of Matty, the multiple rapist mentioned earlier in this chapter, we find a man who constantly fantasized that he would follow women home from the subway and be invited into their houses for sex. He claimed that only when the police came to arrest him did he "realize" that he must have committed rape. Indeed, the only fantasy operating here may have been a superordinate one that allowed the perpetrator to delegate to violent subnarrators his failed negotiations with reverie and reality.[4]

BEWITCHED: THE SEXUALIZATION OF TRAUMA

Mental preoccupations develop in order to focus attention elsewhere, rather than on the fear and pain, or the anxiety, of impending threat. Because it is so strongly authorial, obsessive rumination reverses general powerlessness. You can see how this might work only too well in cases of maltreatment (sexual or otherwise) when a child can overattend to the stimulating dimension of the interaction as a bulwark against apprehending its assaultive aspects. If excitement is defensively sexualized,[5] traumatogenic arousal can be replaced with eroticism—even with a sense of oedipal victory—depending on the circumstances of the abuse. Thus preoccupied, the child is suavely[6] and dissociatively honing his capacity for perversion, all the while outrunning a greater traumatic implosion.

For many abused children, the connection between pain and sex is reinforced during adolescence, when violent fantasies can be used during masturbation to achieve orgasm. This use of violent imagery to achieve orgasm may fix the fantasy in a particularly intransigent way and disguise its more defensive functions. Blum (1991) articulates the physiological route traveled in the defensive response of sexualization:

> The very flooding of excitement may be used to disguise and control other sensations and affects which might be regarded as more threatening and painful.

> The sexual arousal or excitement at high intensity may also serve, perhaps on some psychophysiological level to diffuse aggression by a process of fusion and amalgamation, and by blending aggressive aims with erotic goals (pp. 445–446).

This process may be critical to the development of sadomasochistic fantasies, in which eroticization (in the form of seeing oneself as a desirable object) allows survivors of abuse to avoid malevolence toward needed others and the attachment context they provide (Howell, 1996, 1997).

---

[4]Gottlieb (1997) has written that an enabling fantasy of splitting and successive occupation operates in the background of all dissociative experience. This contrasts with a more contemporary view of dissociation that posits that it is actually the belief in psychic unity that is fanciful. Still, I think that Gottlieb has a point when he asserts that certain elaborations must evolve in order to sustain as rigidly compartmentalized a structure as we see in most violent actors; there must be a conscious commitment, as well as an unconscious predisposition, to split off violent performances.

[5]Abusive assaults may be defended against with sexualization, even when the nature of the actual assaults against which one is defending are already sexual. In evidence I offer the usual refrain of male inmates that were sexually assaulted in childhood that, even at an age as young as six, they themselves had played a predatory role in sexual interactions.

[6]Sullivan used the word "suavely" often in his writings, to describe the particularly seamless way in which dissociation operates. I can think of no better descriptor.

Even without overt sexualization, traumatized persons may create various "imaginary personifications" with which to couple; they become highly dependent on fantasy to fill insufficiencies in their real relationships (Sullivan, 1953, p. 223).

REGRESSION

Chasseguet-Smirgel (1991) has described perversion as a global rejection of genital reality in favor of anality, manifested in the blurring of distinctions between objects and among their parts. Kernberg (1992) has called attention to the pervert's need to destroy objects through segmentation and diffusion, thereby "analizing" them. It is difficult to discount this classical view, even if one is not a classicist, given that the distribution of activity in sex murders is weighted toward zonally regressed sexuality, such as anal rape, and is perpetrated across gender and generational lines with little concern about the victims' "suitability" in terms of conventional sexual dynamics. For example, many male sexual offenders are as likely to choose a child or an elderly person as a victim as they are an adult woman, even if their consensual relationships are along conventional lines and they have not demonstrated a previous paraphillic interest in a particular kind of sex partner. Rather than this being simply an opportunistic choice made when a "preferred" victim is unavailable, as has been suggested in the forensic literature (Knight & Prentky, 1990; Barbaree et al., 1994;), it appears to me to be characteristic of offenders' return to a diffusely organized, psychologically primitive state where self and objects are less individuated, allowing fantasies of merger with the mother to be maintained.

This return to a primitive state of diffuse organization seems particularly true when we look at the trajectory of violent serial sexual offenses, where criminals appear to become less choosy about whom they are assaulting over time (Guay et al., 2001). Simultaneously, they are also becoming more disorganized behaviorally, indicating a massive regression to earlier developmental stages. Even Ted Bundy, who was mythologized as a slick, magnetic, sociopathic murderer of lone attractive coeds, moved on to dual and multiple victims over the course of his increasingly frantic killings and capped his criminal career by raping and murdering 12-year-old Kimberly Leach. In Bundy's murders, "analization" and "zonal confusion" were not psychoanalytic metaphors: he was convicted partly on bite-mark impressions taken from his victims' buttocks and breasts. A hairspray bottle was found protruding from the body of one of the victims at the Chi Omega sorority house, where he manically attacked four girls in one of his last homicidal rampages.

FANTASY, FUSION, AND SEXUAL HOMICIDE

Much of the forensic literature has concentrated on paraphillic fantasy as a dry run for solitary rape-murder and serial sexual homicide (Burgess, et al., 1986; Prentky et al., 1989; Ressler et al., 1992; Meloy, 2000; Schlesinger, 2000). Despite overwhelming agreement among these authors that a preoccupation with sadistic or controlling sexual fantasies potentiates murder, only a few forensic clinicians (Meloy, 1997a; Lewis, 1998; Carlisle, 2000) have written about these ultimately realized fantasies as having been nurtured in the cradle of dissociated trauma. Meanwhile, the psychoanalytic literature has theoretically demonstrated a compelling link between dissociated trauma and some forms of sexual perpetration (Grand, 2000).

Former FBI profiler Robert Ressler and his colleagues (1992), largely responsible for the theoretical views that prevail in the forensic literature, strongly reject the idea that sexual violence is rooted primarily in childhood trauma. Rather, they believe that it stems from an overreliance on sexual and aggressive fantasies developed in response to various threats, only some of which may involve child maltreatment. The fantasies supposedly constitute a cognitive rehearsal for sexual murder, but, the theory goes, since repetition erodes the fantasies' masturbatory power over time, the person begins to seek out opportunities to act on them.

Sexual homicide, thus conceived, is an event driven largely by improperly regulated cognition, particularly if regulatory mechanisms are attenuated by environmental stresses (Burgess, et al., 1986; Ressler et al., 1992). The idea that trauma has little of importance to do with aggressive sexual fantasies and enactments is proffered by Ressler and his colleagues (1992) despite the fact that in their own study of 36 sexual murderers, *every single subject* had been severely maltreated or neglected in childhood, and not withstanding a separate study by their collaborator, Ann Burgess, in which she proposed a link between sexual abuse and sexual offending through the "cognitive operation" of "trauma learning" (Burgess, Hartman, & McCotmacky 1987, p. 1436). In this information-processing model, dissociation is conceptualized as the "encapsulation" of traumatic events, a definition that flirts with, but does not embrace, the full spectrum and weight of psychopathology entailed by severe dissociation.

In a more psychodynamic vein, Schlesinger (2001), an experienced forensic clinician, highlights both childhood maltreatment and eroticized maternal relationships by placing them at the top of his list of "ominous signs" dotting the road to sexual predation. Yet he concludes that what differentiates those who act out murderous sexual fantasies from those who do not is very likely "a drive to act out in order to relieve the inner discomforting feelings" produced by selected fantasies (p. 56). He notes that "the fantasy grows out of sexual sadism" (p. 56) but does not acknowledge the contribution of dissociated trauma to the development of either the fantasy's content or its extraordinary power to compel behavior. In fact, although conceding that gynocide for some killers is likely displaced matricide, Schlesinger adamantly rejects dissociation as the mechanism through which that sexual aggression is transjected. He insists that the offender "knows exactly what he is doing [and] can control his actions to a large extent" (p. 13). He reiterates Krafft-Ebing's astute observations about the driven quality of sexual murder as support for a compulsion theory of homicide: "[We] have concluded that those individuals who act out their sadistic fantasies do so because of a compulsion to act out" (Schlesinger, 2000, p. 12). Unfortunately, by relegating the stimulus for sexual homicide merely to an overwhelming, conscious urge to act out fantasies, he does not elucidate the roots of sadistic behaviors much differently than Krafft-Ebing (1886) did over a century ago, when he wrote:

What [the sadistic criminal] feels is, as a rule, only the impulse to cruel and violent treatment of the opposite sex, and the coloring of the idea of such acts with lustful feelings. Thus arises a powerful impulse to commit the imagined deeds [p. 57].

Contrast all this with the view that murder is not an event but a step in a very long, sometimes covert, internal process that begins in childhood and continues even after the homicide is committed (Gilligan, 1996). Gilligan's position acknowledges the resonant power of distal events, both in shaping proximate intrapsychic content and in drafting particular fantasied elaborations into active defensive service when other contextual cues for criminality are present. Since fantasies of sexual control and surrender through physical force are incredibly common in the general, nonoffending population (Leitenberg & Henning, 1995), and since sexual offenders fantasize about and engage in consensual sex at least as often as they seek out coercive sexual encounters (Marshall & Marshall, 2000), it seems equally if not more important to focus on factors that may so blur the fantasy–reality line for certain people as to deconstruct the fantasies themselves.

I have written elsewhere about the dissociative context in which many violent enactments occur (Stein, 2000, 2001, 2003). I have joined such writers as Grand (2000), (Lewis & Bard, 1991; Lewis et al., 1997), Meloy (1988), and Steinberg & Schnall (2000) in the opinion that dissociation is the default defensive position of the perpetrator, its probable genesis being the realization, and subsequent elaboration, of annihilative–reconstructive fantasies during terrifying scenes of actual abuse and neglect in childhood (Stein, 2001, 2003). However, I have had trouble imagining criminogenic traumata as going from wholly submerged to fully realized and projected to totally resubmerged, as the violence of dissociative offenders is sometimes characterized (Saks, 1997). Rather, my analyses of the narratives of violent criminals have underscored the delicate way in which conscious and unconscious forces parry each other for dominance in pre-, peri-, and postcrime mentation. Thus, I remain attuned to the conscious component(s) of criminal thought and activity and perceptive to the faint outlines of volatile selves that lurk in the corners of conscious awareness (Rank, 1971; Lifton, 1986).

Historically, forensic clinicians and criminal profilers, borrowing the paradigms of cognitive-behavioral psychology, have worked from a set of assumptions that see human behavior as largely conscious and rational, and fantasy materials as goal oriented, hedonic visualizations. Psychoanalysts have concentrated on unconscious motivations for behavior and the more symbolic modes through which needs and desires may be expressed, including in the creation and distribution of imagery in daydreams, night dreams, delusions, and ruminations, as well as more specifically sexual fantasies.

For an understanding of the role of fantasy in acts of criminal violence, I hope to demonstrate the utility of shouting politely across the theoretical divide. Unconsciousness is a leaky boat on the waters of consciousness; nowhere is the concept of "know(ing) *more* than one thinks he knows" (Ogden, 1989, p. 197, italics added)" more pertinent than in the analysis of human predation. Conversely, it is particularly important for a person perversely conjoined with a sexual object to maintain a state of dumbness because, to paraphrase Stoller (1985), "Insight is the death of (sexual) excitement" (p. 34). The insight to which Stoller referred is the knowledge that the actual aim of what he called erotic hostility is to undo humiliating, painful childhood traumas that threatened the development of core identity (Stoller, 1985, 1986).

The perverse sexual fantasies and performances that arise in response to the annihilating behavior of early caretakers are as much a barricade against anxiety and ego dissolution (Socarides, 1973) as they are a behavioral response to the stimulating aspects of mental and physical pain (Freud, 1919). The incipient fantasies, and their adult corollaries, are as much symbiotic as they are sexual. Violent sexual daydreams embrace without intimacy, risk engulfment (this supplies the excitement), evoke terror, and justify retaliatory violence. Given the nuclear power of the experiences from which such fevered dreams are derived, is it any wonder that some people cannot resist the temptation to revisit symbolically the scene of the original crime?

THE MURDER OF KIM STANDARD

[We] brutalized, traumatized, raped and strangled her with a piece of rope. [She] was convulsing and losing her bladder, then [we] disposed of her like so much garbage in a lake (from the confession of Alan Plethory).

I was invited to a friend's house. He pulled a knife on a gal. At that point everything went downhill. We ended up killing her. Why, I wish I knew, but we did, and I cannot change that (from the confession of Dave Justus).

Alan Plethory was an acquaintance of the victim, Kim Standard. That day they met in a bar where he made occasional repairs. He offered Standard a ride and the two, according to Plethory, proceeded to the house he shared with his wife, who was at work. Once home, he called his close buddy, Dave Justus, to ask that he come over with a six-pack of beer. (The two men had met in prison, where they were both serving time for sexual offenses. Later in their relationship, Dave had sex with Alan's wife, in her husband's presence.) The three drank for a considerable time and chatted amiably; Alan insists they spoke about group sex. At some point, Alan became concerned that his wife would return from work and not take kindly to an alien female presence in her house. Dave, too, was becoming anxious: he was scheduled to retrieve his child from day care.

Plethory later said that they decided to kidnap the girl because she refused to have sex with them. The men subdued Standard, undressed her, tied her hands and feet with rope and duct-taped her mouth, then put her in the trunk of Justus's car and drove off. When she managed to untie her hands and pop the trunk lid, they restrained her and drove instead to an isolated area. Plethory said he then watched Justus rape and strangle Standard but denied his own participation, other than to dump the body. Justus initially denied, but later admitted, the rape-murder. He said that together he and Plethory had strangled Kim with a rope and disposed of the body.

The young, divorced mother's decomposed body was found in a nearby lake, a circle of plasticized duct tape around her neck. There were wounds to Kim's hands and one breast, sharp perforations of her pelvis; her abdomen had been eviscerated. Blunt-force injuries ringed the upper body; her tongue had been severely lacerated. Kim Standard had been horrifically sexually violated, although neither assailant had penetrated her vaginally with his penis.

Were the men compulsively reenacting a traumatic sexual engagement from their own pasts? Little is known about Alan's childhood, but interviews with Dave's friends and family supply some provocative material. Justus's mother once told a friend that Dave always "licked the plate clean," a reference to his preference for cunnilingus, not his childhood eating habits. Justus's father sometimes tried to have sex with his son's friends' girlfriends; the house was filled with pornography, the parents sexually inappropriate in front of the children, and Dave was apparently introduced to sexual bondage techniques by his older brother. He later wrote of and shared his sexual fantasies—including having sex with a girl who had not yet developed pubic hair—with a married woman with whom he had an affair after his wife left him. His wife said that he liked rough sex and had once put a large knife to her throat during foreplay. Other sexual partners found him excessively brutal and disgustingly unclean. He took nude pictures of many of the women with whom he had consensual sex.

Lear suggests that rather than these repetitive engagements being viewed as driven (in the Freudian sense), they should be seen as "dramatic instances of mental self-disruption that are met with a repetitively failed attempt to lend meaning" (p. 89) to an event. Thus, violent sexuality may be an attempt not only to extinguish, or master, a timelessly recurring trauma (Herman, 1992; Shengold, 1999) but to find the logic of one's own catabolism through the destruction of others. We do not know if Justus and Plethory were sexually assaulted in childhood, but we can surmise that, at least in Justus's case, the sexual atmosphere in the home was deviant and, on some level, threatening to him as a young child, who likely responded by selectively attending to such overwhelming and invasive sexual stimuli.

The killers were apprehended in an attempt to flee the country. During interrogation, Alan offered scant information, most of it denying, or justifying, aspects of the crime. Dave, clearly shaken, provided a more detailed account of what had happened that day. Yet the narration of events by both men was retrieved from a place so stark and dreamlike that the stories seem, at times, more fanciful than real. In particular, the dissociated quality of Dave Justus's interaction with his victim appears stunning in its claustrophobic symbiosis. Where Alan projects, Dave adheres. Where Alan mentally flees, Dave virtually disappears.

THE JUSTUS-PLETHORY NARRATIVES

He and Kim were just talking when, Justus says, Alan Plethory emerged from the kitchen holding a butcher knife with a foot-long blade. He put the knife to Kim's throat and said, "This is a rape." According to Justus, she laughed and pushed Alan's hand away. Although there was no audible communication between the men, Justus says that he sensed that something was about to happen. Simply, somehow, Justus "found" himself undressing her. "She lifted up to help me take her pants off. She got down on the floor and said, 'If you're going to rape me, let's go out to the woods,' because she likes it there. Alan tossed me the rope and some duct tape. She let me tie her hands but said that the rope around her ankles hurt, so I brought her some socks to put on." She was hog-tied and put in the trunk of the car. "I said, 'Now what?' and Alan said 'Let's take her to your place.'"

Adhesion

Justus's communication is quite magical: his fancied communion with the victim and his wordless implementation of Plethory's wishes is remarkably seamless for what was, in essence, a very sloppily executed crime. In his story, the victim laughs ("Yes, I found that puzzling. We both did.") and even dictates the location where she will be violated. She assists in the stripping of her clothes and only tangentially objects to the roughness of the rope tying her ankles, whereupon Justus immediately cushions her feet. All agency seemingly redounds to the acquiescing Standard and the knife-wielding Plethory, who, in concert, create the parameters for the rape. Justus "only" binds the victim but is himself unbounded, already affectively leaking and leeching. It is as if Justus sees himself and Standard as working toward similar ends: she is pictured over and over as a cooperating, even giddy, partner in the assault. Justus, in the protective act of bringing her socks, engages in a magical reparation: untying and psychologically undoing; the retying now softened so that it is no longer experienced as an authentic binding anymore, the sadistic act is experienced as *not really real* (Grand, 2000). In this way, Justus rewrites himself as helper rather than a perpetrator.

The selective attention that served him in childhood is in abundant supply here. By not owning aspects of his own behavior (he simply *finds* himself in an abduction scene directed by his friend), and by disavowing the victim's fear (she *laughs* at butcher knives; she *prefers* to be raped in the woods), he spins a tale in which the victim has no claim to innocence, while he is already not guilty of a crime he has yet to commit.

Since, in this kind of adhesive state (Ogden, 1989; Mitrani, 1994), there is no sense of self as distinct from other, one cannot be the knowing agent of either active perpetration or active resistance. Instead, there is an imagined intimacy with the victim, Justus anticipating her comfort needs as Kim has anticipated his need to remove her garments. But the gratification of closeness will ultimately turn to the terror of engulfment (Socarides, 1973; Bach, 1991) that activates the murder. Whereas perceived separateness and felt agency might precipitate a view of one's objects as three dimensional and capable of being hurt (Ogden, 1989), here there is only a delusional transference that magnifes annihilation anxiety, and a reactive omnipotence that exacerbates sadistic retaliation (Meloy, 1997a).

Such pseudoidentifications as appear here between Justus and Standard reflect the need to devour and incorporate—a fanatasied symbiotic fusion most likely constructed in the absence of a need-gratifying object during the earliest stages of separation-individuation (Mahler, 1968; Socarides, 1973; Meltzer, 1975; Mitrani, 1994; Meloy, 1997a). As the most autistic-symbiotic aspects of the fantasy unfold in horrifying detail during the actual rape/murder/mutilation, Justus will be confronted with the terrifying, destructive magic of his own fantasies.

Justus is simultaneously engaged in an analogous identificatory process with his co-perpetrator. The communication between Plethory and Justus is wordless and seamless, and one senses that there are not even illusory boundaries between them. Justus's experience of Plethory's directives to truss and gag the victim unspool almost telepathically in this improvised—and impoverished—pathodrama. An autistic interface is effected, where objects are related to one another through what Ogden (1989) calls rhythmicity and sequencing, where experiences of "me-not-me" and "inside–outside" don't exist.

Plethory, inside Justus, dictates his actions while Justus, also an appendage of Plethory, makes the necessary arrangements for Standard's rape-murder. Although not even tacitly acknowledged, the homosexual overtones of their relationship (much of their sex lives appears to have involved sharing fantasies and then finding women who would agree to have sex with the two of them simultaneously) suggest an impairment in the development of masculine identification (Stoller, 1986), perhaps harkening back to an unsuccessful separation from the mother that was later compounded by castration anxiety during the oedipal phase (Socarides, 1973). If the inappropriate sexuality of the parents documented in Justus's life history is true, it is easy to understand the parental threat posed to the subject throughout his development.

Justus's adhesive orientation, coupled with his questionable gender identification, makes him especially vulnerable to seeking resonance with powerful male objects like Plethory. In the dynamic of sexual aggression, Justus follows Plethory's initiatives. As Meltzer (1975) has said in explicating Bick's autistic patients, this type of person bases his morality not on introjected objects that are precursors to superego, but on the imitation of others. It is a not uncommon trait in certain criminals to transmute in this way, to take on easily the form of the other. Such simulative ease points to a kind of "dissociative flexibility" (Meloy, 1997a, p. 143) and finds its most toxic home in the goodness of fit between two potentially violent psychopaths.

Projection

Unlike Dave's portrait of a submissive, even willing victim, Alan remembers Kim Standard as being boisterous and belligerent in the living room, obnoxious and excessively noisy: "I started getting paranoid because she was loud. She started saying that she was gonna yell rape. No one had touched her. We were seated fully clothed. We told her we were gonna tie her up and cover her face and she started to shut up a little more." Was there a conversation between him and Dave? "It was more than just a look 'cause we both . . . because of our backgrounds, the threat of someone crying rape . . . is pretty hard on a guy." She was bound. Gagged. They put her in the trunk, although she very nearly escaped. They drove to an out-of-the-way park.

Plethory seems to have had a much more conscious antagonism toward the victim than did Justus: Standard posed a real peril as well as a fanciful, projected one. I imagine that her initial response to Plethory's rape warning (if, indeed, she did "laugh") was excruciatingly dismissive, and diminishing. She must have seemed a potent, castrating witch with the power to send Alan back to jail, a threat to be neutralized at any cost. (The terror of returning to jail cannot be underestimated given the almost daily diet of assaults, rapes, robberies and more symbolic castrations (Gilligan, 1996) to which inmates are subjected). In response, Plethory proceeds to make Standard into "a controllable puppet" (Searles, 1960, p. 278), a hogtied symbol of all the dangerously unpredictable earlier objects he feared would dismember or dismantle him, and a stand-in for a previous victim whose testimony had sent Plethory to prison.

"Perverse people deal with their partners as if the others were not real people but rather puppets to be manipulated on the stage where the perversion is played. In the perverse act, one endlessly relives the traumatic or frustrating situation that started the process; but now the outcome is marvelous, not awful, for not only does one escape the threat, but also, finally, immense sensual gratification is attached to the consummation. The whole story, precisely constructed by each person to fit exactly his own painful experiences, lies hidden but available for study in the sexual fantasy of the perversion (Stoller, 1976, p. 105)."

Fusion

According to Justus, she emerged from the car trunk asking for beer and a cigarette. She wanted to know what was going to happen. Alan tied her up again and put her back in the trunk and continued driving. The two men never spoke of what they were doing. When they arrived at the new location, they removed Standard from the car and carried her to a more densely wooded area. Dave says that Kim requested something to lie on. He says that she then asked to be held: "I sat down next to her and she put her head on my shoulder. Alan went and got a floor mat from the car. Someone said, 'Now what?'" At this point, Dave says that Alan tried to penetrate the victim with his fist. "And I tried, too, because Alan wanted me to. She never said anything or cried." Then Alan found an old can, which he partially inserted into Kim's vagina. Justus found this strange and instead flipped her over and tried, unsuccessfully, to commit anal rape. When the investigator expressed surprise that the victim never screamed, whimpered, or cried during what must have been a very painful sexual assault, Dave ventured, amazingly, "Maybe she'd done it before."

The comment that "maybe she'd done it before" (referring to the vaginal penetration by fist and inanimate object, and the anal rape) is one of the more stunning pieces of criminal commentary I have come across. (It is reminiscent of the time a middle-aged man described to me how his four-year-old stepdaughter had seduced him.) Clearly, on a cognitive level, the words dovetail with observations that rapists tend to view their victims as sexually experienced and willing, sometimes even aggressively provocative (Marshall & Marshall, 2000). But I find the violative acts as well as the narration that selectively attends them suggestive of a level of fantasy more symbiotic than sexual.

It is a not uncommon feature of serial rape and sexual homicide to force large objects, including inanimate ones, into the victim's vagina. This activity has been examined mostly for its sadistic dimensions relative to a variety of behaviors coded on a "torture" axis in the criminal profiling literature (Dietz, Hazelwood & Warren, 1990; Stone 1998). Few have noted the rapists' almost childlike—even innocent—fascination with the proportions of the womb that is reflected in these acts, although Meloy (2000) does refer to the "curiosity" that often symbolically infuses certain aspects of sexual crimes, particularly genital mutilation (also a component of the Standard murder). The wish to "clear all obstacles that prevent a return to the intrauterine state" effaces the truth that the mother's internality is no longer accessible to the child. Adrift in the demanding world of genital sexuality, the only hope is to pervert the object he handles by transposing her erogenous zones (Chasseguet-Smirgel, 1991).

Plethory especially is concerned with how much, how many objects are needed to fill up a female container (his prior conviction was for raping a waitress with a bottle). In addition to the almost certain sense one gets that Plethory and Justus did not imagine their own penises sufficiently up to the task of filling a female (neither attempted penile penetration of Standard's vagina), the act seems a perverse attempt to create a missing birth tale.

The perpetrator's obsession with filling the womb is somehow synonymous with crawling back inside it and enacts a fantasy of symbiotic fusion. In this context, it is no accident that rapists most often attempt to fill the victim with varied detritus, having the vagina and uterus double as a garbage can. For them the act is a redux of the old adage: garbage in, garbage out.

Theoretically, a "good" mother makes the birth narrative a gift to her child. She satiates his phenomenal hunger with a monotonous retelling of how he got here (only she witnessed the birth, after all; he has no recoverable memory of it) In telling the tale, she confirms the child's existence as well as her pleasure in it. A bad or absent mother never validates the child's aliveness in any meaningful way. Through traumatic imposition, the abusing or abandoning mother may actually assist in the perceived *undoing* of birth. Searles's (1960) proposed stages of ego development have relevance to Plethory's inanimate extension of himself with the foraged can:

> 1) experiencing oneself as being alive, and therefore distinct from the inanimate things in the environment; 2) awareness of oneself as not only alive but human, and therefore distinct from the animate sector of the non-human environment (i.e. animals and plants); and 3) awareness of oneself as a living human individual, distinct from other human beings, including one's mother [pp. 43–44].

Plethory and Justus must get back inside to stem the tide of existential panic. But then they must pay the "consequences of retreating inside the maternal body" (Socarides, 1975, p. 434): the dreaded, irreversible loss of self. In this claustrophobic moment, only the destruction of the maternal symbol can reinstate separateness and restore homeostasis.

Dissociative Reverie

"Maybe she'd done it before." Of course, it was Dave Justus and Alan Plethory who had "done it before." Alan had already served time for a bizarre, brutal rape. Dave had abducted and sexually assaulted an adolescent girl at gunpoint with his friends. His wife had left him after charging that he had sexually abused their infant child.

Alan says that he walked back to the car to get the mat because he thought that Dave was "going to have sex with her and I didn't want to be there." He "stared off into space" but at some point turned and saw Dave Justus having sex with Kim, she on her belly. "I continued spacing out." When Alan eventually returned to the scene, both physically and mentally, Dave was kneeling beside the victim. She appeared dead. "I don't want to say [what I saw]." He helped carry the body back to the car. "I did not see one drop of blood anywhere. I didn't. I swear I do not see blood."

In Dave Justus's version of events, when the rape ended, it was Alan who picked up her head and put a rope around her neck. He handed one end to Dave and they both pulled. No words were exchanged.

> "She didn't make a noise. She didn't move."
> "How long did you do it?"
> "I didn't know. Time just seemed to take forever." She didn't struggle. She convulsed.
> "Everything seemed to take forever and then, too, it didn't take very long either. She convulsed and lost control of her bladder."

Dave tried to find the pulse on her neck, and then Alan untied her hands. They drove to a convenience store to purchase soda and candy; Kim Standard's body was in the trunk. Dave called his wife to say that he would not be able to pick up their child from daycare, after all.

Afterwards

Justus and Plethory headed out to a river to dispose of the body, but the car got stuck within sight of the shoreline and Justus went to get help. He walked to town—a considerable distance—and flagged down a police officer, who helped him to make assistance calls.

It is not uncommon for criminals to tempt capture in this way. Is this a guilty conscience lacing its own trap (Freud, 1916)? Or is it merely diagnostic evidence of a grand and brazen psychopathy (Millon et al., 1998) that convinces its host of his own invulnerability? Perhaps Justus could ask an officer for help unencumbered by any real fear of arrest because the memory of the murder was successfully converted to a kind of unreality, a conscious unconsciousness that many violent offenders articulate as "waking dreams" (Stein, 2003).

"I kept walking, kept expecting her to walk out on the pavement anytime. Kind of stupid, huh?" The investigator asks if Justus thinks that Standard was going to come after him. He admits, "I wouldn't blame her." When Dave returned to the beach, Alan Plethory had already disposed of the body. Most of the victim's personal effects were discarded, although Justus kept Kim's running shoes, as well as a soiled piece of her clothing, perhaps as mementos to aid him in reliving the crime, perhaps as trophies to signify his triumph over this threatening object.

Although her pelvic and abdominal region had been gutted, both men denied knowing the origin of Standard's wounds. Justus conjectured that Plethory had mutilated the body in the hours when Justus had sought help for their disabled automobile. Plethory claimed not to have seen any wounds: "I don't know of any damage. It frightens me 'cause I don't. I don't remember anything like that. I don't want to picture it. I do not remember seeing a single drop of blood anywhere. It's scary to think. I . . . I can't picture Dave doing anything . . . I don't want . . ." (At this point the investigator reminds Alan of the other horrible things he has seen Dave Justus do.) "Everything I saw, I told you, I swear I did not see any blood. I know I did not see any blood."

Plethory and Justus have each accused the other of the pelvic evisceration of Kim Standard, and the forensic evidence cannot decisively assign blame. Interestingly, it is in discussions of mutilation that criminal profilers do accept the gravity of sexual trauma histories. They find that "undisclosed and unresolved early sexual abuse may be a contributing factor in the stimulation of bizarre, sexual, sadistic behavior characterized in a subclassification of mutilators" (Ressler et al., 1986).

Indeed. The ritual components of a sexual mutilation conceivably constitute a scream for purification in the face of one's own perceived defilement at the hands of early caretakers.

exemption from defilement is not produced in any total and direct action, it is always signified in partial, substitutive, and abbreviated signs: burning, removing, spitting out, covering up, burying. Each of these acts marks out a ceremonial space, within which none of them exhausts its significance in an immediate and, so to speak, literal usefulness. They are acts which stand for a total action addressed to a person taken as an undivided whole. Hence, defilement, insofar as it is the "object" of ritual suppression, is itself a symbol of evil [Ricoeur, 1967, p. 35].

Discussion

The fantasies of the perpetrators have been inferred through an analysis of their words and deeds. I remind you that I have never met Plethory and Justus. Of course, even in cases where a direct assessment of subjects' fantasies can be made, there is little guarantee of the veracity of the information given. The reports of deviant fantasies given by offenders following arrest are particularly questionable, given the secondary gain to be realized by defendants whose accounts appear bizarre, disorganized, or psychotic.

Forensic clinicians are often left to draw conclusions about the use of fantasy from projective tools like the Rorschach, or they must rely on penile plethysmograph data to ascertain the connection between thought and arousal in perpetrators (Meloy, 2000). But even if we find that sexual offenders are aroused by so-called deviant material, or resort to it with greater frequency than do "normals" (neither idea ever having been even close to being documented conclusively), we still know us little about why certain men or women, unlike others with similar fantasies, end up acting out the most violent and perverse aspects of their inner dramas.

Most motivational models of violent sexual behavior posit that a number of conditions tend to adhere for active offenders. Among those conditions are poor social circumstances, psychopathic personality, autonomic dysregulation, cognitive dysfunction, a history of abuse, and deviant arousal patterns. Of these, particular emphasis has been placed on the role of paraphillic fantasy, consciously modeled, as a cognitive rehearsal for violent sexual crime. Listen to the most eminent of criminological theorists:

Whereas psychological motives for violent behavior are usually conceptualized in the literature as having roots beginning with trauma, insult, and/or overstimulation in early childhood, our thesis is different. We hypothesize that these men are motivated to murder by their way of thinking (Burgess et al., 1986, p. 257).

"Murderers are consciously aware of the central role of fantasy in their lives and their preference for fantasy over reality.... Such thinking becomes an important component in the maintenance of sexually aggressive violent behavior" [Burgess et al., 1986, p. 258].

Indeed, over the years, a virtual cottage industry has arisen among cognitive behaviorists who treat the fantasies of deviants as the independent variable in the equation, attempting through aversive techniques to change the fantasies and hence the dependent variable of behavior. The long-term effectiveness of these interventions has not been clearly demonstrated (Leitenberg & Henning, 1995).

Psychoanalysts, on the other hand, have most often treated paraphillic fantasy as an effect, rather than a cause, of conduct. Some, however, taking an intermediate position, see fantasy as both a derivative and a determinant of behavior. (For a review of both the behavioral and psychoanalytic literature, see Abel & Blanchard, 1974.) The latter position seems the most fruitful avenue of discovery on the subject.

Robert Stoller believed that the wish to harm may be the organizing factor for all sexual excitement.

[T]he details of the script underlying [sexual] excitement are meant to reproduce and repair the precise traumas and frustrations-debasements-of childhood; and so we can expect to find hidden in the script the history of the person's psychic life [Stoller, 1986, p. 13].

The hostility in perversion takes form in a fantasy of revenge hidden in the actions that make up the perversion and serves to convert childhood trauma to adult triumph [Stoller, 1985, p. 8].

Expanding the Freudian perspective dictating that *everyone* has suffered and repressed trauma (and thus possesses the raw material for perversion), Stoller (1976) hypothesized that the character of paraphillic fantasy stems, *"not from some generalized state of oedipal alarm"* but from the fact that "in childhood, one was *truly* threatened with a danger to one's sexuality.... This trauma was very severe ... it was prolonged too far, or else hit too suddenly, *or when one was too young for adequate defense* (pp. 118–119, italics added).

Not all traumas are created equal. Preoedipal annihilation fears that are realized rather than simply imagined, because the caregiver brutally abuses or chronically neglects, form the basis for a dissociative adaptation that exponentially magnifies the destructive power of ensuing elaborations. Stoller believed, as do I, that it is in the very potency (and early timing) of the experience igniting the perverse and vengeful fantasy that the propensity for violent enactment can be found.

A very high percentage of violent offenders have horrific histories of maltreatment at caretakers' hands, and clinical evidence suggests that much of this early trauma has been dissociated (Stein, 2001, 2003; Lewis & Bard, 1991; Lewis et al., 1997; Lewis, 1998; Saks, 1997). The manner in which early, prelinguistic experiences of defilement become embellished and internalized should be of great interest to forensic clinicians, precisely because the experiences so often find their ultimate representation in the graphic reproduction of evil, to borrow an evocative phrase from psychoanalyst Sue Grand (2000).

In my work with offenders of all stripes, I have found this to be largely true: that violent thoughts and deeds are primarily a reparative response to the enduring trauma of perceived annihilation in early childhood, whether trauma took predominantly sexual or physical forms (Stein, 2001, 2003). Often, even the purely physical violence that is expressed in crimes has symbolic sexual components (see Schlesinger & Revitch, 1997, for a review of findings in this area), just as a good deal of sexual offense conveys conflicts not directly sexual. As Silverstein (1994) has observed, aggressive daydreams are essentially a way of reasserting one's power in relationship to exceptionally oppressive, or sadistic, parents. Sexually aggressive fantasies especially, because they signify union, express both the terror of separation from, and the terror of engulfment by, early objects who set up a suffocating entanglement with the child. The more legitimately terrifying the actual interactions on which the fantasies are based, the greater the likelihood that a terror-inspiring resolution will be attempted. The abduction and rape of Kim Standard demonstrates the perpetrators' need for symbiotic fusion. Her murder and mutilation communicated the need to sever those same haunting ties.

REFLECTIONS

As spotted with dissociative amnesia as many criminal accounts are, acts of violent perpetration are not easily reconstructed. But a close analysis of the so-called fantasies of perpetrators suggests that, in elaborating the stimulation of initially dissociated traumata, a powerless child can generate a compartmentalized dream of sufficiency, which gives him or her a way of staying intact. Carlisle (2000), commenting on the inner lives of serial killers, says:

> Intensely painful memories and deep emptiness can lead to intensely experienced fantasies, which over time take on a greater and greater degree of reality. When a person is totally absorbed in a fantasy, he dissociates everything around him.

> Over time, the person may turn to this pseudoexistence with increasing frequency when he feels stress, depression, or emptiness. This leads to a dual identity, one ... associated with reality ... and the other the secret identity in which he is able to manifest the power and control he would like over others [p. 109].

Interestingly, although Ressler et al. (1992), strongly opine that "men murder because of the way they *think*" (p. 272, italics added), even they admit that cognitive content may be structured by early trauma. In fact, belying their own argument that it is primarily the conscious dedication to fantasied themes (and

not experiences of child abuse, neglect, or trauma) that allows offenders to perform and retrospectively justify rape and murder, the authors' own article is
heavy with examples of the horrific traumas suffered by their subjects in early
childhood. Indeed, Ressler and his colleagues do not mention any examples of
subjects who engaged in sadistic sexualized fantasies who were *not* traumatized in childhood. Even worthier of mention, they repeatedly cite examples
given by subjects that detail the peculiar excessiveness and intensity of their
own daydreams, even during preadolescence.

It seems, then, that it is not only the content of the fantasy, but the constant
resort to deep reverie in times of stress that indicates psychopathology, probably of a dissociative nature. Inside the sexual imagination, both agency and
identity blur (Malone, 1996), making dissociative fantasy the logical retreat for
people whose boundaries are eternally compromised. In the case of Plethory
and Justus, the crime committed, the fantasies that partially engendered it, and
the trauma(s) being elaborated in its service are all intermittently dissociated.
Thus, the acts of rape and murder *are* practiced, but not in the logical, goal-
oriented manner alluded to by forensic clinicians and criminal profilers. There
is no "felicity calculus" (Bentham, 1791) informing these kinds of violent
forays, as neatly as that theoretical premise might comport with the cognitive-
behavioral paradigms adopted by most researchers of criminal activity. I quote
Sullivan (1956):

> [W]hen we see a person moving through life with a striking type of selective
> inattention, like the boy who everyday had sadistic fantasies. . . we are justi-
> fied in assuming something like this: that if we had a full record of this boy's
> sadistic fantasies, day by day, we would see in this record certain continued
> stories, certain elaborations, and so on, which would literally represent a
> development of the skill, detail and refinement of his sadistic fantasies.
> There would be a growth in refinement and increased specificity of the
> impulse to injure innocent bystanders. . . . So we have to assume that such
> things as dissociation—which go on quite suavely, but entirely exterior to the
> personal awareness of the creature that is showing them—also become elab-
> orated and refined. Thus what may start out as a rather clumsy dissociated
> activity may finally become a performance which is strikingly and exquisitely
> refined—in the sense of showing a vast amount of experience—even though
> the person is blissfully unaware of it [pp. 69–70].

The criminal profilers are largely correct about the uses of fantasy, although
they may be highlighting the wrong words. It is not the overreliance on *deviant
fantasies*, but the *overreliance* on deviant fantasies that should sound the first
warning bell, because it signals an inability to negotiate lived experiences of
closeness and threat. Second, rather than viewing the fantasies themselves as
totally volitional visualizations, I would recognize that imaginative material
also occurs as borderline delusional phenomena that mix, not only sex and
aggression, but shame and grandiosity, violent separation, and symbiotic
fusion. Third, and most important, such dependency on dissociative reverie
can usually be traced back to startling, perverse traumata that become elaborated and reenacted in the service of saving one soul, dreadfully and irrevoca-
bly, at the price of another.

Psychoanalysts are beginning to understand just how often the story of the maltreated child is the story of the violent perpetrator is the story of the maltreated child. Around it goes, as attested to in both the empirical and clinical literature (Widom, 1989; Lewis, 1992, 1998; Lewis et al., 1997; Grand, 2000). It is therefore imperative that those who work with very violent persons acquaint themselves with the psychoanalytic understanding of malignant dissociation, characterized by Sue Grand (2000) as the process that enables victims of massive trauma to transcend metaphorically the loneliness of annihilation by inflicting it on another person.

Dissociated traumatic experiences fuel the repetitive fantasies of union (both consensual and not) that cohere the internal world of the victim-perpetrator. The elaboration of these asyntaxic events lend shape and meaning to personal narratives and trigger a variety of enactments, only a very few of which are criminal. Depression, suicidality, compulsive sexuality, pathological lying— even serial monogamy—can be understood, depending on the patient, as autonarrative extensions of a traumatic manuscript. Often it is the intractability of these kinds of enactments that most frustrates psychoanalysts, precisely because the early experiences on which they are based seem so split off and inaccessible. According to Bromberg (1998), it may be that "trauma and dissociation breed in *every* human being discontinuous realities that are not amenable to interpretation" (p. 259). Dissociated self-states may appear most fossilized when trauma was especially early, particularly perverse, or simply unrelenting (Stein, 2000, 2001, 2003).

Where repetitive fantasies and behaviors are at issue, there is much that can be gleaned from the study of dangerous persons through the lens of dissociation. The inability to learn from experience, the inevitable return to destructive behaviors, and the lack of expressive remorse so emblematic of the aggressive criminal are seen across a wide spectrum of psychopathologies. Understood within the framework of dissociation, the immutability of certain behavioral patterns reflects a *lack* of conflict regarding those behaviors (Bromberg, 1998) precisely because the actors are inextricably mired in a particular division of the self-system, a certain subnarration that so closely resonates with their experience of the world that competing subnarratives of sorrow or generativity, among others, cannot be foregrounded. Contorting the narrative into inflexible, but familiar, forms lends coherence to the storyline even as it obfuscates other narrative voices (Stern, 1997b). This narrative construction becomes painfully obvious in the case of serial offenders, whose crimes can seem like one long, monosyllabic howl.

When the trauma-dissociation paradigm is imposed on the study of violence, perpetration is placed along a fathomable continuum of human interaction rather than in the "beyond" to which it is usually exiled. Indeed, investigations of the "criminally insane," the "stone cold psychopath," and other "evil seeds" have been unnecessarily set off from the study of less virulent psychic forms, despite the long standing arguments of such theorists as Robert Jay Lifton (1986) that these outliers, however alien they may seem, have much to teach us about the range of human adaptation to titanic threats.

5

Dreaming While Awake

In a short yarn by Ray Bradbury (1948) a 13-year-old boy named Charles is stricken with a fever or, more accurately, becomes possessed of a fevered dream. Alone in his room, the boy watches in mute horror as each infected appendage becomes somehow not his own, a hot and alien presence in his sickbed. The boy is being murdered, piecemeal, by some opportunistic disease but, uncannily, the outer body sustains, so that no one can know he is dying. The boy's mother wipes his brow with scant fret; the doctor mollifies his panic with sugar pills.

In his fear and frustration, Charles's hands rise to choke his own neck; the doctor advises strapping them until the fever passes. As his parents sleep, the fever razes Charles to nothing. Writhing in terror, the boy watches as his body is "reproduced . . . in feverish duplicate" (p. 22).

By the time the doctor arrives the next morning, the lad seems completely normal, at least to others' approving eyes. Charles hugs and kisses his parents (although he does not recognize his own name), and pumps the hand of the doctor ebulliently. In the night, from the fever, he has become an omnipotent, evil replica of his former self. The youngster knows that the touch of his hand now conveys a delayed but certain death. The boy is all malicious intent—and as eager as he has ever been—as he bounds upstairs to pet the family canary.

The following is excerpted from my interview with a man convicted of robbery and then transferred to the hospital for a psychiatric evaluation:

One day after school, my mom chased me into the room and got on top of me. I was 12, no, younger. Maybe eight. After, I was screaming. The veins were hurting. It wasn't right.

It's like someone's awake and I'm asleep. I have to wake up by breaking a window and I don't want to. I space out for a few days. I just start daydreaming. My conscience tells me to do something to that lady.

I followed women home from the subway five or six times. I never raped them because they opened the door and got undressed. I can't see, I'm in a daze. One day the cops knock on my door and accuse me of rape. I said that

I didn't rape them. Then the memories came back and I knew I was in trouble. That's when I just died.

Now I came back.

—Matty, 36 years old

THE ESTRANGED SELF

I hope that Harry Stack Sullivan sprang to mind as you read the Bradbury tale and the excerpted interview with Matty. Both remind me of Sullivan's (1953b) idea of the "malevolent transformation" in juvenile development and the retributive justice that severely traumatized—perhaps we should start calling them "evilized"—children seek. Like Charles and Matty, Sullivan's hypothetical adolescent suffers a cleavage of self rooted in the uncanny emotions accompanying physical pain. In Charles's case, the source is organic, a mysterious fever. Matty, a convicted felon, also suffers a mutation of consciousness. His pain has an exogenous origin: sexual abuse by his mother.

Sullivan argued quite explicitly that most pain experienced by a child is a result of corporeal punishments imposed by authority figures. He suggested that, insofar as the parents' brutal acts seemed random, the child's predictive capacities would be degraded. If sufficient fear and anxiety accompanyed the pain, he imagined, cause-and-effect thinking might be demolished entirely. "[Severe anxiety has] the effect of a blow on the head. Thus, one has very little data on which to work in the future—we might almost say that there is nothing in particular to be elaborated into information and foresight" (p. 205).

Sullivan did not know how prescient his neurologic metaphor was; the debilitating social sequelae of chronic maltreatment are now presumed to have physiological, as well as psychological, roots (van der Kolk, 1996). Whatever combination of factors contribute to the cognitive-affective data void that Sullivan described, it has certainly been observed, both clinically and empirically, that child abuse dulls the perceptive capacities of its victims, making it likely that salient environmental prompts for behavior will be ignored or misinterpreted (Fonagy et al., 2002). It is as if someone had pressed the mute button during those early confounding anxiety exchanges and forever disabled the connections among what is intuited, what actually happens, and what is apprehended.

Because how the child acts in the abusive context has little effect on parental responses, all the child can do is to cast about aimlessly, hoping to hit on an action that will successfully reduce his or her pain and anxiety. Most children will eventually find a few strategies that work. Some might become adroit at sweet-talking their way out of punishments; some will simply zone out; others will find, as they age, an increased ability to physically intimidate their parents. (Many of the incarcerated men I spoke with indicated that abuse ended when they were able to retaliate physically, especially if the abuser was the mother or another female

---

[1]Sullivan's (1953b) term for a child's acquisition and sly use of propitiatory, rationalizing, or deceptive language that protects the self from a parental infliction of anxiety or pain.

caregiver.) By both art and artifice, pain and anxiety are successfully dodged. Whether through charming, manipulative "verbalisms"[1] (hello, fledgling psychopathy), autistic withdrawal (trance states), or more complex aggressive constructions that become personified aspects of the self (incipient identity disorder), the caregiver's brutality is subverted, or the victim's mental attention is diverted, from difficult encounters. In each case, what is attended to is something outside the actual event; a dissociative shift has occurred.

In Sullivan's (1953) model, not only the experience but also the part of one's self having the experience are dissociated. Stepping into the breach is a "dramatization," a consistently successful enactment that replaces authentic intersubjective contact. Dramatizations, over time, may become highly durable, inter-relational tools; there is not *necessarily* a pathological edge to such enactments. In cases where youthful circumstances have been particularly grievous, however, constant repetition entrenches "as if" performances so firmly that rather than being an expression of character, each dramatization achieves a characterological status of its own:

> These dramatizations tend to become what I could safely call sub-personifications. The roles [acted out] are organized to the degree that we can properly call them personae; they are often multiple, and each one later on will be found equally entitled to be called I [p. 209].

The degree of dissociative rigidity and the muscularity of ensuing personifications vary depending on how deeply and frequently deceptive the abused person has needed to be to cover up supposed "violations" of parental authority (pp. 208–209). One could assume a correlation between the level of what each child perceives as necessary concealment of his or her activities, which may actually be quite benign, and the severity of parental responses to those activities. Hence, personifications fostered in a particularly abusive surround will be more likely to appear as autonomous, "as if," entities.

What makes child abuse so identity rending? The compartmentalization of cognition and affect, both building blocks of personality, proceeds not only from the overwhelming nature of interpersonal ordeal (van der Kolk, Mcfarlane, & Weisaeth, 1996), nor exclusively from the intrapsychic elaboration of precedent traumas (Freud, 1905), nor entirely from the idiosyncratic meanings ascribed to disturbing events (Shengold, 1989). Clearly, each of these operations plays a role in psychological and behavioral outcomes, just as they do in cases of less shattering trauma. But child abuse is a special kind of trauma that wraps its tentacles like a stingray, forever dragging its prey backward through a tsunami of undifferentiated terror. Applying Sullivan's language again, we may say that, in a significant number of these extreme cases, simple dissociation has *failed*. Mere inattention, and even the more powerful forms of somnolent detachment that characterize traumatic dissociation in general, have not sufficiently protected the person from the perception that death is imminent. The resort is to full-fledged personifications of the self that can aggressively engage as well as deflect the trauma, while remaining too primitively organized for symbol-making. Instead, the personification is itself the symbol of an unnatural disaster. Not all traumas are created equal, and neither is their symptomatological expression.

A CLINICAL EXAMPLE

Crew was one of the more paranoid inmates on the prison ward. One day the 20-year-old hit a ward nurse because he felt that "she was going to bite me." Crew claimed that he had trusted no one since childhood, when even "a stuffed teddy bear seemed real and I had to break it." The medical chart indicated that Crew sometimes became rigid, almost catatonic, but when I asked him about his family he seemed oddly relaxed. His speech was fluid and lucid:

> My dad hit me with a garrison belt. He beat us for little things, like bad report cards. One time I ate the report card to avoid the beating. Lots of times. It was intense pain like you can't even imagine—everything you can think up. We had to stand on rice or kneel on a grater. He tied my brother and me up.
>
> My stepfather started doing me when I was seven. You think that I like laying on the floor bleeding from both ends? He took pictures, porno shots, when I was like 12, 13, or 14.
>
> I dreamed I saw people with gunshot wounds. I was a little kid that was driven to see things I shouldn't see. People falling. People can't get up. Stepbrothers. They fall for trying to say an untruth.
>
> I don't know what's real now. I lost hours. Not just hours, years. A lot of childhood. Too much childhood.
>
> He thought he was making men but he was making robots.

Crew became a "robot" when threatened; he exhibited signs of catatonia and had been diagnosed as schizophrenic. He also managed to dissociate that which would rightly haunt him. Huge segments of Crew's childhood were missing, as were portions of his adulthood: he knew neither why he was arrested (drug possession) nor how he ended up at the hospital. He was, however, willing when pressed to confabulate answers to both of these questions, which made his narrative seem candid until further investigation proved it false. No wonder that, in addition to being labeled schizophrenic, Crew was considered by the staff to be an inveterate liar. No wonder that, when he talked about a boyish "Vinnie" who shared his body, it was taken as further evidence of both schizophrenia and malingering, depending on who was doing the diagnosing.

TRAUMA AND PRE-TRAUMA

Research has found that the cumulative effects of psychiatric and neurological disorder, when combined with experiences of abuse, are more likely to produce dissociation than is a history of maltreatment alone. In my study of hospitalized inmates (Stein, 2000), which correlated pathological dissociation with "underlying" psychiatric or neurological vulnerabilities, I abstracted that responses to trauma were likely shaped and intensified by mental illness, that mental illness was exacerbated by traumatic experiences, or both. While acknowledging that neurological dysfunction could be a byproduct of head injuries sustained during abusive episodes, I largely assumed at the time that most neurological and psychiatric problems were organic, predating trauma, and, if anything, functioned as catalysts for the parental frustration and rage that triggered maltreatment. That supposition may very well be true. However, more recent studies of the brain suggest that interpersonal experiences may play a significant role in the development, as well as the amelioration, of mental and psychiatric disorder. We may not always know what came first (Reiser, 1984; Pardes, 1986; Grady, 1988; Freidman, 2002; Wade, 2005).

In the context of un/awareness, the most basic neural endowment (Damasio, 1999),[2] coupled with the natural progression of interpersonal events in childhood, will lead to transitory lapses of attention, circumscribed dissociations, enactments that are reinforced through successful repetition. All these are within the range of normal reaction and presume exposure to a garden variety of threatening events, all of which might be called traumatic, in its most liberal definition. On the other hand, unrelenting exposure to catastrophe, especially in early development, reshapes the psychic and the neural landscape, preparing lacunae into which much relevant experience[3] will eventually collapse. Early, ongoing abuse augurs just this type of developmental failure.

If the most serious abuse transmogrifies mental structure, as well as content, it becomes impossible to operationalize variables that are unique to each sphere. Although I for a long time was convinced that child abuse wreaks the most havoc in a person rendered particularly vulnerable by virtue of other contaminative conditions, I have come around to considering the chicken-and-egg possibility that the most hellishly abused suffer multiple injuries that affect evolving neural systems as well the material that is encoded within them. Thus may much vulnerability—formerly considered antecedent to severe dissociation—actually be posttraumatic phenomena.

ANNIHILATION REALIZED

Melanie Klein (1921) hypothesized that the fear of being obliterated was universal. An infant must initially protect itself from starvation, suffocation, lunacy, and, ultimately, psychic deconstruction. Later, the child will struggle to remain intact despite the threatened loss of body parts (phallic equivalents), body products (feces), and loved objects (caregivers). These struggles, we are reminded by Klein, occur even under optimal developmental circumstances. What happens when childhood trauma arises not from imagined scenarios of parental abandonment and sadism, but from the very real persecutory actions of caretakers?

> My father beat my mother and me. He hit her with an iron cord, sometimes a pan. He hit me with everything: a belt buckle, his hand, an extension cord. During beatings I was so scared—I just wanted it to be over.

---

[2]Damasio (1999) posits a neurosensory domain that gathers the raw material, or potential content, for mental imagery (these are housed in the more primitive sensory and limbic cortices) and a "dispositional space," in the higher cortices, where the processing into images can take place.

[3]Discussing the less optimal uses of dissociation, Sullivan (1956) opined "The thing that determines whether [the suspension of conscious awareness] is done well or ill, from the standpoint of long range results for the person, is how smoothly the control of awareness excludes the irrelevant and includes the relevant" (p. 43).

He used to tie me up and leave me in the closet for the KKK. He said that I was too black.

Once he slit the dog's throat and left me in the closet with him for three hours. He told me, "I'll do the same to you."

—McClean, age 30 (convicted of armed robbery)

In cases like McClean's, a fault seems to form in the very foundation of self because of the pervasive sense of dread (E. Balint, 1963; M. Balint, 1968). Chances are that, even prior to abuse, the entire relationship in which the trauma eventually becomes embedded is itself so lacking in nourishment as to constitute a massive threat to survival. Breuer and Freud (1893-1895) posited this idea of "partial trauma" to account for the cumulative, presensitizing effects that multiple petite traumas might have on the defensive system. Krystal (1988) has called attention to the way that the resulting "ego strain" likely makes one more vulnerable to acute trauma, if it should occur.

The convict McClean says that early on he had trouble distinguishing fantasy from reality because "my mother lied to me all the time." Here, the dynamic landscape is laced with mines. The mother's fabrications and denials support the boy's disavowals of what has happened to him within the family; her oscillating organization of reality becomes a template for his own fragmentation.

Myriad moments of neglect and trauma, coupled with the distorted sense of reality proffered by parents, likely sensitize children like McClean to the antic-ipation of danger and embed a tendency toward, if you will, an "aggravated" dissociative response. Not simply a selective inattention to threatening stimuli, aggravated dissociation is characterized by a level of autistic withdrawal that mimics trance and necessitates subsequent confabulation. For someone thus sensitized, everyday life feels "relentlessly traumatic" (Atwood, Orange, & Stolorow, 2002). Real life is rejected and replaced by elaborate refutations of reality. The self is replicated in safer space or as a less vulnerable target. This is how McClean described his frame of mind during his father's beatings:

I used to think, "I'm laying dead on the ground." I'd be happy. I could close my eyes and make myself go across the street.

I felt nothing. Dead. I couldn't think right. I was so scared, my fear just stopped.

I could be across the street now. You just program yourself.

Shengold (1989) has dramatically termed the chronic overstimulation of child abuse, alternating as it does with emotional deprivation, "soul murder." Again and again during interviews offenders seemed to be without viscera, "soul-less," in both the anthropological and the spiritual meaning of the word. McClean, like many of the inmates, appeared simultaneously dead and alive. His imitation of death may have been in the service of survival, but it wavered perilously near the precipice of real annihilation.

The vicious circle around meaning is something like this: Perceiving a vari-ety of external situations and inner images as deadly, he cannot permit him-self to feel. Equating such feeling with further threat, he wards it off via both mimetic deadness (including conversions) and explosive but superficial emotional outbursts, for there is also a deep fear of being "stilled" [Lifton, 1983, pp. 205–206].

Unfortunately, for McClean the "emotional outbursts" he produced to counteract death were not always superficial. At the time of our meeting, McClean had been arrested more than 26 times. His list of offenses included assault, robbery, and kidnapping. He is currently serving a life sentence for armed robbery.

ATTRIBUTIONS OF AGENCY

External agents are created inside our heads all the time, whether they are the imaginary friends of childhood or the powerful deities of religious life (Wegner, 2002). In psychoanalysis, the very idea that we internalize significant objects takes for granted that agency may reside in forms other than the first person. Most forms of even the simplest self-reflection will incorporate the disparate viewpoints of imaginary foes and friends. Because of this dynamic peopling, imaginative constructions naturally invoke dialogic relationships among made-up speakers whose conversations have a rich affective subtext (Hermans, 1999).[4] Contradictory positions among imagined voices may be reconciled, be integrated, or remain adversarial.

Not only can we facilely imagine that agentic entities exist, we can intuit their reactions in a variety of circumstances, including how they might perceive and relate to our own behaviors. As long as a person retains the awareness that fantasied people or situations are imaginary, everything is fine. But for some people that line may become blurred. In a literary example, in Kafka's (1912) short story "The Judgment," the protagonist commits suicide at what he believes is his powerful father's behest, although in actuality the father is quite physically enfeebled and mentally deranged. The story can be interpreted as an illustration of how rage at one's parent, and the subsequent guilt over that anger, is projected onto a retaliatory agent when, indeed, the castigator really exists inside the protagonist's head, in the form of a punitive superego. My own work with offenders maltreated in childhood has generated myriad examples of how reality can easily become subordinate to hypervivid fantasies of both annihilation and heroic rescue.

During intensely imagined episodes there may be a breakdown in the processing of reality cues. Wegner (2002) offers the example that when we are deep inside a [nocturnal] dream "everything *seems* real" (p. 230), which may cause upon awakening at least a momentary confusion about what actually happened and what was only dreamed. Virtual agents, whether appearing in nighttime dreams or dreamlike states, can seem quite real, too, especially when they are readily recognizable and emotionally familiar. Wegner cites as the third source of the transformation from imagined agent to believed-in agent the incorporation of the belief that agents are uncontrollable: "The observation that an

---

[4]Hermans (1992) distinguishes between such normal, garden-variety multiplicity and pathological forms of splitting by calling attention to the relative paucity of dialogic relationship among narrators in the latter. Hermans concept his is similar to Bromberg's (1998) idea that functional dissociation involves a negotiation between self-states, while pathological dissociation forfeits compromise in favor of self-preservation.

imaginary agent does not respond to our conscious will, then, is a cue that the agent is real. It is also a cue, however, that the agent is not the self" (p. 235).

Wegner has likened the development of what he calls "virtual agency" or "virtual authorship" to the more common forms of projection I discussed in earlier chapters, where actors make attribution errors about the intentions of real people with whom they come in contact. Common examples of criminal projection are the rapist who feels sexually taunted or seduced by his victim and the batterer whose jealous rage is blamed on his wife's imagined infidelities.

In Wegner's schema, a dissociated identity is a kind of extreme projection. To lay his scheme on a Sullivanian model of the mind, we would say that mental contents, instead of being projected outward, stay cloistered within the self-system and are instead "projected" onto other "I"s. In the cross-current, not only self-initiated actions, but also their ownership, are wrongly assigned to the dissociated parts of subjectivity. What endures is a kind of categorical error that forfeits both agency and experience.[5]

The misattribution of authorship within the self-system is sometimes supported by the psychological minimization of events external to it, so that perceived agency is made less burdensome. Unconscious dissociations are also scaffolded by conscious activities that superficially nullify reality, exemplified by a killer who wrapped his victim's long hair around her slit throat so as to hide the evidence of his crime from himself. According to his confession, doing so allowed him to remain at the crime site with his victim for a while and watch television. The scene evokes Jon Mills (2003), in full Lacanian jacket, addressing the dissociative leap from knowing to not knowing. The example, like so much about actual violence, makes shockingly literal the psychoanalytic metaphor that "paranoiac knowledge is not merely fear of the unknown, it is a trepidation of knowing a particular truth that the subject may find horrific" (p. 41).

That quote is particularly apt given Mills's digressions regarding structural aggressivity. He argues that persecutory internalized objects become fragmented (mirroring the splitting of the ego[6]) and projected, their perceived goal—in the mind of the paranoid—being an assault on the integrity of one's own body. The imaginary twinship of victim/perpetrator, illustrated by the man who watched T.V. with a nearly decapitated corpse disguised as a viewing partner, calls attention to the ricocheting nature of the offender's projections. As soon as he "splits" his victim by cutting her throat, he mends her; as soon as he severs their relationship through murder, he reconstitutes it—by making her alive again. Mills might say that the killer's dissociated fantasy of wholeness was as applicable to him as it was to her, or that merger and separation are not mutually exclusive states. That merger and separation are not only exclusive is particularly true if one accepts the idea that the perceived location of agency for early trauma—*and hence its reenactment*—fluctuates because the young child

---

[5]Sullivan (1953b) discussed a similar process in the genesis of the hallucinatory experience in schizophrenia where, he said "what is dissociated is represented in awareness by some group of ideas or thoughts which are marked uncannily with utter foreignness-they have nothing to do with oneself" (p. 361).

[6]Mills (2003) uses the term ego in a more Lacanian than Freudian sense, as an illusion of control synonymous with a socially constructed self, rather than as an executive apparatus (p. 33). As I use "ego" here, though, I do not think that difference matters much.

appreciates neither the separateness nor the intentionality of the threatening person (Grotstein, 1997a). In fact, an abused child in the autochthonous[7] stage may truly deposit perceived agency for the violence he has endured into dissociated parts of subjectivity, later to be called forth in violent enactments.

As Stern (1997a) has noted, abused children, having disowned annihilative experiences, necessarily construct personality both in, and from, a phenomenal void. Under such circumstances, experience—and its linguistic extension, explicative narrative—is cadaverous, truly emptied of self. To survive, a parallel story must be articulated, consciously and unconsciously, that makes sense of original trauma and the defensive operations that they have engendered. In the most pathological of adaptations, dissociators vivify phantasmagoria to tell their tales. Indulging false selves allows them to maintain attachment to primary care-givers at the relatively small cost of altering their identity.

PERSONIFICATION AND SUBNARRATION

Sullivan (1953b) conceived of the self-system as an organization of learning experiences created to avoid or minimize anxiety. The nascent system is built on the "personifications" of significant others (usually the mother, but not exclusively so) into a "good," or nurturing, entity and a "bad," or overture-rebuffing, entity. These secondary personifications of the good and bad caregiver form the basis for the rudimentary self-personae of "good me," "bad me," and "not-me." "Good me" helps to birth a healthy ego-ideal; it accrues from equal measures of maternal consistency and unconditional warmth. "Bad me", is formed along a gradient of anxiety—the perception that one's needs will be ignored or even punished and that all attempts at need satisfaction will be thwarted. "Not-me," unlike the other personifications, stands distinctly apart from the growing perception of one's physical integrity. In fact, "not-me" is birthed under conditions of such extreme threat (real or perceived) that it cannot incorporate without risking eradication. This disconnected persona, in the healthy adult, might hold paralyzing fears never owned up to, or murderous rage never realized. It emerges in our dreams and parapraxes and sometimes in destructive life choices. Under stress it might even trigger minor dissociative episodes.

For most people, "good me" and "bad me" fuse as the developmental process moves forward. However, when anxiety and terror cannot be removed, destroyed, neutralized, or differentially managed by the young child (as would be the case with ongoing physical or sexual abuse), it must be "ignored." Thus, a particularly potent adaptation in the face of ongoing terror is to dissociate experiences that threaten to stimulate what Sullivan (1953b) called "uncanny emotions": awe, dread, horror, and loathing. The dissociative person's seeming apathy in the face of horrors both endured and perpetrated (what is often noted as inappropriate affect in the abused child or a lack of remorse in the violent criminal) is actually a form of what Sullivan would call "somnolent detachment"

---

[7]The term autochthony refers to the referential psychology of a primitively developed self. At early developmental stages, we may create the other as an illusory object whom we control rather than appreciating its autonomous power to act (Fairbairn, 1940; Grotstein, 1997a). This is a fancy way of explaining the sensation or belief that one has induced one's own trauma.

(p. 55). The detachment arises from a sense of total powerlessness. When feelings of impotence are chronic, such selective inattention can be activated at the slightest hint of anxiety. The sleepwalker is literally not himself a good deal of the time.

Thus, "not-me," the cornerstone of dissociative process, is a primitive character, infused with dread, incapable of corporeality. "Not-me" becomes acquainted with reality through experiences suffused with intense, unremitting anxiety. As accurate learning cannot take place in such threatening circumstances (imagine learning your multiplication tables with a gun to your head, as one man I spoke with had), the perception of reality is both unreal and unrealistic. Moreover, because the meting out of abusive punishments is arbitrary and capricious, the caretaker personification on which "not-me" is based is itself inconsistent and nonsensical. Therefore, the actions of the "not-me" persona are not founded on an understanding of cause and effect. The dissociated self exhibits only the "rationality" of the dreamer; "not-me" speaks in a private language and behaves in symbolic equivalents. For most of us this dissociated self is evinced only in nightmares or is recognized only in Ray Bradbury stories. For an unlucky few, "not-me" is a walking, talking parallel self.

Meloy (1997a) notes that perpetrators often control the criminal environment and interaction in a way that facilitates dissociative disjunction. For example, Meloy has observed that, by curtailing eye contact and dialogue, sexual predators can handily derealize both the victim and the brutal scenario. Perpetrators can continue to perceive their victims as "two-dimensional, perceptually flat, stereotyped objects" (p. 154). This consciously assisted dissociation later is used to support the perpetrator's contention that it all happened in a dream (such as Matty's narrative at the beginning of this chapter). Thus, an offender's real tendency to dissociate undergirds the fanciful elaboration of events that effectively nullifies his culpability.

PLURAL STATES

When Sullivan (1953b), called dissociation "a prolonged state of dreaming while awake" (p. 323), he intuited the systemic shutdown that occurs in the face of trauma. Dissociation is the ultimate tool devised by the self to avoid recognition of one's own powerlessness to confront a massive assault on physical or psychic integrity. Much as an infant will suddenly fall asleep when its crying brings no relief from hunger, chill, or pain, a child schooled in the successful resolution of terror or anxiety through selective inattention to the fear-arousing circumstance will likewise find comfort in sleep.

> My father tied me to a chin-up bar. I was whipped with a skinny leather belt with a small buckle. I got welts, scars. I was naked except for my underwear. I was just a little penguin. From seven to about ten [years old]. He didn't mean to beat me. It made me a man.
>
> I can make my heart stop beating since I'm real small. Go ahead—get a stethoscope. Put me in a bathtub and cover it up real good. I bet I'll survive. Put three grenades under my bed. The bed will blow up, but I won't.
>
> You know, I'm still sleeping, but I'm listening to you.
>
> —Coates, age 36 (convicted of assaulting a police officer)

Far from being a static experience, the dissociator's "sleep" (sometimes referred to as self-hypnosis) is actually a dynamic process of vigilant awareness. Shengold (1989), for instance, tells of a patient traumatized in childhood who could block out perception and emotion while remaining hyperattuned to reality. That person's dissociative sleep served a number of purposes. First, autohypnosis may function as a psychological aide to survival, much like a wild animal's "playing dead" occasionally outwits potential predators (Laing, 1959; Becker, 1973; Lifton, 1983). Second, "ignoring" the traumatic experience may provide a mechanism whereby painful material can be automatically "erased" from conscious awareness. Third, the total passivity that such feigned inertia implies allows one to avoid responsibility for having "provoked" the attack, as can be seen in the following narrative.

> My brother trapped me in the attic and [we were fighting]. My mother made my brother go to his room and she beat him with a strap. She beat my brother's weenie with a belt until it bled. But when she beat me it was like "Johnny" took the beating [Johnny is the subject's imaginary companion].
>
> —Wesley, age 25 (convicted of fraud)

Fourth, dissociative sleep lets one remain blind to the identity of the villain, particularly useful if the perpetrator is a much-needed caretaker.

> I have no memories of my mother. I can't remember her name. I draw a blank. (The subject lived with his mother for the first 12 years of his life, After which she abandoned the family.)
>
> —Steadman, age 37 (charged with grand larceny)

> I think so, but I don't remember [about the molestation]. A building on the East Side. Maybe I was five or six. It was a person inside the family. I don't know.
>
> —Fredo, age 29 (admits a double homicide)

Finally, autohypnosis grants one the opportunity to indulge the compulsion to repeat the original trauma in its terrifying as well as its seductive aspects, a phenomenon that Shengold (1989) calls autofacilitation. It is important for clinicians working with formerly abused clients to note that in this blind, compulsive reenactment—the evidentiary residue of what Bromberg (1998) has called a "timeless, traumatic past", dissociator may play perpetrator instead of victim (van der Kolk, Mcfarlane, & Weisaeth 1996). In either case, playing victim or perpetrator, the drama unfolds while the actor sleeps. And vividly dreams. This offender referred to the multiple stabbings of his numerous juvenile victims:

> It was like I was following a technical manual. I knew what happened when I woke up but I did not know if it happened for real or was imagined.

Another man, a veteran of at least two prior *voluntary* psychiatric hospitalizations, sliced his victim's throat and calmly walked away. Lonnie was apprehended moments later by the police, to whom he confided, "I just can't get along. I want to go to jail for life." The correctional system obliged.

He experienced his violent act this way:

> I saw it on T.V. I saw the fact that I was driving with her. I saw the fact that I just reached out and stuck her and picked her eyes out.

In another case, Jake, a man convicted of three spectacularly brutal kidnap-homicides averred that all his victims had had "serene," "easy," "peaceful" deaths. Although freely admitting the murders and saying that he was glad to get locked up because "the potential was there" for additional murders, he insisted that he had never tried to hurt anyone. It seems that in the sphere of traumatic knowledge, dissociation allows certain stories to be sidelined in favor of other stories, toward the end of preserving some illusion of "good me" and characterological unity. It is the ultimate expression of paradoxical knowledge—freely offered by myriad *confessed* rapists, pedophiles, and murderers—to swear that they would never hurt a fly.

PERSONAE NON GRATAE

McClean, to whom you were introduced earlier, told me that he had "a body living inside my body" that helped him to endure difficult or dangerous circumstances. There must have been many such frightening moments in childhood, given the almost psychotic rages to which his father was prone. As a child, McClean began his own violent enactments:

> [I'd] get angry and throw chairs thinking about my father. I used to hit [people] as if they were my father, but I didn't know that.

At age 15, McClean was involved in a fight that resulted in the death of another teenager. He experiences neither his own injury nor his part in the murder:

> He stabbed me in the arm. I didn't know I had a knife in my arm. I was looking at the guy and it was like a dream.

McClean went on to describe several different imaginary characters that handled different situations for him:

> I can talk to the other person inside. I can become the big guy. The bigger, stronger one is the good one. The bad one has no patience. Flame came first, then Robinson, Manny, Fence, and Eagle. Then Lori, who makes me feel five years old.

Some men I have interviewed acknowledge that their alternate selves house emotions or perform tasks that they themselves are incapable of feeling or doing. They speak of vicious, uncontrollable invented personas who protect the self from real or imagined harm.

Shorna can set fires and sacrifice animals, but Barka is the violent one. Barka comes when I have to defend myself. I have to recede, he's stronger.

—Andrew, age 25, convicted of arson

Andrew had named the entities within. He experienced them as powerful individuals living inside his body. On the other hand, Nick, whose father was a violent drunk, housed his rage in a separate space without naming it. He explained that "only the part of me with a deep voice wants to decapitate people." Like Andrew's Barka, Nick's disembodied avenger could not always be contained. Nick had been picked up while roaming the streets of the Bronx and indiscriminately firing an automatic weapon. Asked about his actions, he related that he had just "flipped" following the death of his young daughter from meningitis. "It really wasn't planned. I had just finished crying. I needed a shoulder to lean on." Despite numerous incidents of violence, including attacking a ward nurse at the hospital and trying to kill his girlfriend by pushing her out of the window ("the guardrail saved her"), Nick described himself as "by nature, a passive person." This characterization seemed incongruous, unimaginable. Then one day an extremely suicidal inmate, Frank, who had privately been nicknamed The Weatherman (for the odd metereological expertise he had exhibited while in a dissociated state) begged to be taken to his "therapist," who turned out to be Nick. I watched Nick for nearly 10 minutes as he quietly and lovingly counseled Frank the Weatherman about hope and hanging on, before returning to the phone call he had abruptly ended when he was informed that Frank the Weatherman needed him. Nick had confided in me earlier in the day, "All of a sudden, I flip. Bang! I want to know how it feels to kill someone." It was hard to tell who was the "real" Nick. In fact, they both were. Although Nick did not seem to house individual "personalities" with historical continuity, that is, he did not fit the criteria for a diagnosis of dissociative identify disorder, he exemplified the extreme and unreconcilable multiplicity of selves so often seen in adults abused as children.

Interestingly, when asked to what degree these dissociative offenders perceived their rejected aspects to be parts of themselves, the men I spoke with were usually quite adamant that they were not at all aspects but distinct, autonomous entities. Extremely dissociative persons described their "other" parts as differently gendered, of other races, cultures, or ethnicities. But even those who were only moderately dissociative, like Nick, had a hard time accepting the idea that the violent, or passive, or even the spiritual sides of themselves were manifestations of a single psyche.

Hermie, who "don't make no noise when I cry [because] when my father beat me, if I cry out, he hit me harder, until blood came out," describes himself as "a lot of little people made out of sticks." He is in prison for armed robbery, but his memory of the crime is spotty. At times he imagines that he may have killed his victim (in actuality, no shots were fired). Before beginning his interview, I had to have Hermie sign a second consent form because he had signed the first as Juan Baez but then could not remember doing so, claiming, "I never signed Juan Baez for me." During the interview I surmised that Hermie sometimes blacks out and becomes Juan who, it seems, is pulled out of his violent persona only by other people's crying.

I blacked out and started hitting my girl. She started crying. I saw and I said, "Oh my God." I don't know why I hit her. One time when my brother walked by I stabbed him with a pencil. When I came back to me I saw my brother crying. I don't remember why I did it.

Even confronted with the incontrovertible evidence of his own actions, Hermie simply refused to acknowledge that he could have been the one to perform them: "I am just not a person who likes to hurt people." Unbending, Hermie was resolute. The firmness of his proclamations made me realize the extent of his psychic division.

Juan is *not* me. No, no, no, no, no.

I understood that no brief therapeutic conversation was likely to unify that which was so cleaved.

CONTROLLING THE BODY

Laing (1959) described many of his patients as "ontologically insecure," concerned mainly with preserving, rather than fulfilling, the self. As we know from interviews with abused children, in the aftermath of physical and sexual maltreatment there is a heightened concern with survival, a preoccupation with "being" over "becoming." Barbara Marcus (1989), whose clinical work has been with incest victims, has suggested that there is a disruption in the normal developmental sequence that facilitates individuation and mature ego functioning. She tells us that the process of separation-individuation requires, initially, that the child be able to establish the illusion of control over the caretaker. Secondarily, the process requires the capacity of the parents to (a) relinquish control over the child's body and (b) encourage mental, as well as physical, autonomy of the child. In abusive relationships, these requisite conditions are notably absent. Because the child's needs are subjugated to parental desires (for sex, physical dominance, or both) mastery over the self, vis-a-vis the internalization of the caretaking role, is never attained.

Worse than the rape even was that my father wouldn't let me take a shower after.

—Fredo, age 29 (admits a double homicide)

My mother locked me in the closet. She said, "Are you going to pee?" I cried, "No mommy, no mommy." I was afraid but it stopped me from peeing on myself. I wouldn't call it punishment.

—Alan, age 44 (charged with drug possession)

My mom to this day washes me. I cover here (subject cups his genitals) but she does it. She wants me that much, as her baby.

—Shane, age 23 (charged with burglary)

Clearly, many of the natural weapons that children can enlist to fight annihilation fears are rendered impotent in the face of such parental control. Children like Hermie and Alan cannot discharge anxiety by screaming, crying out, or wetting themselves, for fear of inviting greater punishment. Children may even be physically restrained, like Crew, to the extent that they cannot attempt any motoric discharge of tension. If indeed abuse is perpetrated with the tacit approval or even the participation of several family members, there may be no other benign adults around to act as transitional other-than-abuser objects. This last was true for almost all the abused inmates with whom I spoke. Abuse was regularly perpetrated by multiple family members: children had no safe harbor from the storm.

When abuse is sexual in nature, anxieties are compounded and thus magnified. Particularly in an incestuous relationship, anxiety that would normally be neutralized as the oedipal struggle is resolved, instead is exacerbated. By having, sex with a biological parent, the child wins a victory of sorts by having apparently supplanted the adult partner in the caregiver's affections (Diamond, 1989). Thus, rather than coming to the realization that one can never possess a parent romantically, the opposite conclusion is reached, intensifying both confusion and guilt.

With any type of sexual molestation, the body may confound psychological defenses because it experiences as pleasurable events deemed inappropriate by the conscious mind. In this painful betrayal, even the body's own reflexive arousal triggers annihilation fears. Sexual fantasies of union with the caregiver, rather than being repressed, are expressed, bequeathing shame and self-recrimination (Diamond, 1989). Ultimately, one's own flesh, rather than forming a protective barrier against stimulus onslaught, yields to, and may even embrace, the trauma. The traumatic scene may be reenacted again and again with the original perpetrator or a stand-in (Herman, 1992). Even the body cannot be trusted. The physical self must be banished.

My mother would pick me up out of the crib and get sexual feelings. She would put me on her stomach and it was like an orgasm.

They said I pounded the wall. Did I do that? Where was that? My memory is like a spider web. It's like waking up in a nightmare. I can't trace back the steps.

—Lenny, age 35 (convicted of attempted matricide)

James Gilligan (1996), a psychoanalytically trained psychiatrist who headed Bridgewater State Hospital, a maximum-security hospital for the criminally insane, calls shame, which often stems from early maltreatment,"the primary or ultimate cause of all violence." Gilligan observes that "the purpose of violence is to diminish the intensity of shame and replace it as far as possible with its opposite, pride . . . a man only kills another when he is, as he sees it, fighting to save himself, his own self—when he feels he is in danger of experiencing . . . 'the death of the self' unless he engages in violence" (pp. 100–102). Gilligan's clinical observations certainly dovetail with my own, namely, that in the garbled syntax of the perpetrator, violence is felt to be an act of both rescue and redemption.

I was nine and she [the babysitter] said she had something good for me to taste. It went on for about six months. She abused me but I liked it. I would have a quasi-orgasm with her. I didn't feel my pain.

—Lawrence, age 50 (charged with drug possession)

Just as early trauma must be disavowed because it does not comport with already elaborated organizing schemas (Stern, 1997a), perpetration is both disowned and rescripted to preserve the "good me". Sadistic ("not-me") personifications are projected onto the victim (Meloy, 1997b), whose threat must then be neutralized. In this death dance, only the victim's annihilation reconstitutes the idealized self. Grand (2000) speculates that not just malignancy, but vacuity itself, is projected onto the victim so that the perpetrator may finally share the isolating traumatic moment of execution with another human being.

Thus, in response to chronic abuse there is first a split between psyche and soma; the child self divorces the victim's body. One can then allow the body to be wounded or even destroyed with diminished threat to the "psychic nucleus," M. L. von Franz's (1964) apt term for the seat of self-organization (Jung et al., 1964). An example would be the rather common dissociative experience of seeing oneself floating above a dangerous scenario and witnessing the violation of one's body as if viewing a movie; no affect is expressed and none is gained. For some people this is a dissociative moment, a temporary dislocation. For others, particularly if abuse occured prior to the development of object and self-constancy, it may be the fissure that portends the chasm. Since it is the body that provides a sense of oneness, wholeness, and continuity over time, to disconnect from it is tantamount to death. As Laing (1959) eloquently reminds us: "To have no body is to be nobody"(p. 111).

> I feel strange. I used to say, "I know I'm in here." I see myself inside my body looking out.
>
> —Saber, age 35 (charged with petty larceny)

THE THREE FACES OF ADAM

Although Chris Costner Sizemore, the pseudonymous "Eve" of Thigpen and Cleckley's classic case of study of multiple personality (see Sizemore & Pittilo, 1977), had by her own admission over 20 separate embodied narratives, the doctors saw fit to distill them to their essential "good me" (Eve White), "bad me" (Eve Black), and "not-me" (Jane) qualities. Similarly, the narratives of the offenders that I interviewed tended to fall into stereotypic molds; they were often caricatures of certain "types" whose enactments mirrored standard literary or cinematic plot devices. This is not an uncommon finding among those who work with highly dissociative people (Dell & Eisenhower, 1990; Barrett, 1994). The three most common narrators and their story arcs are (1) a petrified child for whom the future was, to quote Albright (1994), "like the past, nothing more than a state of uninterrupted amnesia" (p. 23); (2) a "protector" character, rapidly cycling between attitudes of fusion with—and violent cleavage from—his victim/objects; and (3) a spiritualist, or sage, who offers reparation for the catastrophic excesses of the other narrators (Stein, 2000).

Petrifaction: The Lost Narrative

Immobility, or frozenness, in response to trauma is akin to feigning death in dangerous environs—it allows the victimized child to titrate abusive episodes and facilitates psychological numbing, a way of psychologically marginalizing the experience of bodily threat (Lifton, 1983). Laing (1959) observed that, in situations where more normal processes of depersonalization proved insufficient to protect psychic integrity, the complete "[foregoing of] one's autonomy becomes the means to secretly safeguarding it." He termed this condition petrification and noted that "to turn oneself into stone becomes a way of not being turned into stone by someone else" (p. 51).

Coates, whom I mentioned earlier, was convicted of assaulting a police officer. He insisted that he had been able to "stop his heart from beating" during abuse. Many of my research subjects shared that they had become "disappeared" during maltreatment. Andrew, an arsonist, simply "detached" while being sodomized, at age four and a half, by his grandfather.

Because experience is turned away from, one consequence of petrifaction may be amnesia for what occurred. The abused person's juvenile aspect can even become freeze-framed at the developmental juncture where abuse began. Andrew, for instance, maintains a five-year-old narrator who bears witness to his maltreatment. Wesley, in this time for fraud but carrying a history of brutal assaults, has preserved, in the left side of his head, the character of ten-year-old Jamie.

> [Jamie] does not write—he just makes up songs and rhymes. When my father banged my head, he made me laugh.

Wesley, interestingly enough, engages in much head banging—his own—on the ward. He says that he bangs his head to dislodge his father.

Crew, the paranoid, assaultive drug abuser we already met, introduced a boyish narrator to explain the dynamics of his self-system:

> We share the same body. We have the same experiences. [During abuse] I helped him out.

Another violent offender, usually quite grandiose, shared that

> I'm 36 years old, but only in my body. I think the baby's coming out [now]. I bring him in my pocket.

A murderer, Ezra, described those he imagined present at the scene when his father picked him up by the neck and tried to kill him. As near as I can guess, he is here describing himself in the third person:

> Oh, *the Boy* was there, too. *He* passed away.

Ludwig (1983) has speculated that such "sham deaths" have great species-survival value. The isolation of traumatic experiences acts to conserve physiological and psychological resources, thus allowing children to better defend against future violations.

Putrefaction: The Vengeful Narrative

To treat others with concern and respect one must be capable of empathic response. Empathy involves identification with others, but abused children tend to maintain egocentric views (Barahal, Waterman, & Matin, 1981), or they incline toward identification only with aggressors (Wilber, 1985). Of course, the caretakers of abused children are themselves egocentric, unempathetic, inconsistent, incapable of responding to their children's distress cues, and often overtly hostile (Straker & Jacobson, 1981). Hence, it is not surprising that maltreated children have difficulty interpreting emotional cues in others (Barahal et al., 1981). In fact, their response to distress in others can be quite bizarre. For example, Main and George (1985) found that abused toddlers, when confronted with a crying or panic-stricken agemate, responded with fear, anger, threats, or physical attacks. Not a single abused toddler in their sample responded with concern, or a helping behavior, to a crying or frightened peer. Howes and Espinoza (1985) observed children in both free play and structured situations and also found that abused children responded aggressively to playmates in distress. Moreover, they evidenced no remorse in the aftermath of their hurtful behavior. Their reactions are strikingly similar to those of adult predators.

While petrifaction suggests a paralysis that mimics death, putrefaction underscores the degree to which the traumatized person retains and reflects the "death imprint" (Lifton, 1983) left by abuse, the injury that the petrified self has so conveniently forgotten. It is this aggressive narrator that survives to avenge the trauma.

One unrepentant rapist, for example, requested a cigarette during our interview, only to extinguish it on his wrist as proof of his imperviousness to pain and his general invulnerability. In a subsequent session, the same man insisted on being tied to a chair and sedated lest he lose control and strike me during the interview (during this meeting, the subject reported being tied to a tree during his father's frequent physical assaults). He reenacted the paralyzing effect of his abuse by insisting on being manacled. He both welcomes and rejects punishment by burning himself but feeling nothing. The part of him that invites pain also blithely inflicts it: only in this inviolate persona does the man brag about the rapes he has committed. In this way, childhood abuse—his Kleinian "death equivalent"—is embodied and reenacted through sadistic behavior.

The avenging subnarrative is self-aggrandizing. One can cheat the death dealers, triumph over the death threat, erase the death imprint left by child abuse. The frightening childhood is mastered with a power grab; by reenacting the suffering with oneself as perpetrator, one's prior annihilation is magically reversed, and far more demonstrably than it is during mere fantasies of parricide. Presumably, the more violent the act, the more authenticated the role reversal.

Purification: The Redemptive Narrative

Dennis Rader really surprised the members of the church, where he had just been elected council president, when he was arrested as the notorious BTK (for "bind, torture, kill"), a serial murderer who had evaded capture for years while serving as a local law enforcement agent. Prolific sex slayer John Wayne Gacy clowned for disadvantaged children in his spare time. As mentioned earlier, Ted Bundy, when he was not busy raping and disfiguring coeds, did volunteer work at a Seattle crisis clinic. Every few years the papers report yet another homicidal "angel of mercy" who, under cloak of medical licensure, is repeatedly reviving patients that he or she has furtively poisoned or unplugged from life support. One incredibly assaultive inmate I interviewed used the name Mr. Whiteman when involved with a healing ministry at an Assembly of God church. Another violent recidivist, a rapist, told me of a "healer" side who wanted "only to love everybody." (Apparently, as we can see from his rap sheet, they were "loved" whether they wanted to be or not.)

Most of us achieve sufficient unification of our good and bad selves that we can "stand in the spaces" between them and appreciate the conflict their opposite natures engender, but severely traumatized people find such reconciliation elusive (Bromberg, 1998). Shengold (1989) views the vertical splitting of consciousness in child abuse as beginning with a neurotic delusion of the rescuing parent. The absolute need for a good parent is, at first, compartmentalized as a mere fantasy-image. While children from reasonably loving homes usually come to accept that a parent can be nurturing and rejecting, by turns, the maltreated child tends to keep contradictory aspects of an abusing parent segregated from one another. For abused children, these fantasized partial objects—on whom later personifications of the self will be based—anticipate a more pathological disengagement from the overarching self system.

In aggressive persons, the nurturing aspect of personality may at times assert itself as convincingly as the more destructive elements can. I have spoken to many offenders, and read the accounts of many others, who insist they are peaceful, nonviolent, Godloving and law abiding, much like the idealized "good" parent who was supposed to protect them from the (one and the same) "bad" parent who perpetrated, or tolerated, abuse. The imaginary beneficent caretaker evolves into a living, breathing corrective for the avenging narrator. By performing good works, or by policing aspects of the self that would inflict punishment on others, this aspect of the self tries to purify the child soiled by physical or sexual abuse.

For Becker (1973) the concept of heroism is a refusal to accept mortality. Heroism embodies not only a meeting with death, but a return from its embrace. In this light, the production of a "healer" character may be understood as a particularly muscular counterweight to endured or enacted violence.

For example, one violent, dissociative inmate on the prison ward sometimes described himself as an old, blind priest (interestingly, many dissociators have "blind" personas reminiscent of the hysterically blind patients seen by Freud) whose duties included caring for a "baby" inside the subject and offering pastoral counseling to other inmates. He insisted that he could heal physical ills through a laying on of hands. The performance of this ritual seemed to undo his shame over having been a victim and his guilt over having been a perpetrator. It was as transparent and clichéd a script as a clinician is likely to encounter, but one that exteriorizes trauma with an undeniably palpable punch.

Lifton (1983) asserts that the imagery of death (separation, disintegration, stasis) is always wedded to complementary images of life (connection, integrity, movement). Even in abuse scenarios we see the simultaneous appearance of each kind of imagery. During abuse, there is both the loss of the protector/nurturer and the connection-possession of the parent through a sexualized union (even abusive encounters that are not explicitly sexual in nature may become highly eroticized because of the intense physiological arousal that accompanies the aggressive physical intimacy of a beating). In actual sexual molestation, the child may be in equal parts reviled and aroused, simultaneously anesthetized and orgasmic, the last representing both a physiological betrayal and a robust affirmation of life.

SCRIPTED IMPROVISATIONS AND VIOLENT FINALES

Reflecting on the connections between forensic and dramatic oratory, Enders (1999) observes that "truth" (at least in theater and in the law) is established histrionically. Memory, she continues, is merely the honing of this invention into recognizable forms, until the created illusion reaches an acceptable approximation of the real. At rhetorical climax (a legal summation or a theatrical finale), an enactment spectacularizes the reified, turning memory into both memorandum and memorial:

> Delivered illusions of truth may then be reconsigned to memory as factual, spawning a vicious, logical circle . . . delivered performances then provide the material for future inventions, which in turn generate future mnemonic images, which in turn generate future verisimilar deliveries in an eternal hermeneutic circle of violence [p. 117].

A similar, albeit less extreme, theory of pseudomemory and enactment undergirds social-constructivist approaches to autobiographies, or self-narratives, where presentations of the self are seen as attempts at a rhetorical resolution for moral uncertainty (Sarbin, 1989). In such an accounting, narratives are reified metaphors that imbricate and infuse memory: "Once we develop a workable narrative 'theory' about how the Self developed, we are prepared to shape even our flashbulb fragments of its history in congruence with it" (Bruner, 1994, p. 46).

Contemporary psychoanalytic formulations echo this understanding of narrative composition and dynamism, appreciating memory as largely inferential and co-constructed rather than idiosyncratically fixed (Schafer, 1980; Stern, 1997a). Insofar as language schematizes memory, and memory constitutes subjectivity, the self seems to be basically dialogic, even in its non-verbal lexis. Stern (1997a) for instance, avers that phenomena cannot even "attain the status of [] experience" unless they are linguistically accessible (p. 14). Thus, even those "uncanny" events marked by awe, dread, loathing and horror (Sullivan, 1953b)—including traumas that are apprehended asyntaxically—end up being known (and expressed) "in relation to experience that already has some degree of linguistic structure" (Zeddies, 2002, p. 11). Conceivably, trauma itself may have the effect of coagulating meaning, thereby thwarting a finer articulation of experiences and forcing narrative expression into stereotypic molds (Stern, 1997b, p. 134).

Memories can exist only in synthesis with the narrative account that contextualizes them. Since it is the primary job of the self to bring conflicting aspects into a meaningful (and consensually validated) configuration (McAdams, 2003), and since our understanding of self necessarily involves the ascription of intentionality, agentic inventions must arise to explain why one was victimized and why one chooses to victimize others. These narrative creations—repositories of fear, anger, shame and guilt—are, in their turn, experienced as endogenous parts of the self that behave compulsively yet exactly according to script. Just as Enders (1999) observed in the oratorical traditions of medieval theater, invention impassions action and reifies memory, spawning the rhetoric of cruelty and compensation that constitutes violence.

Robert Knox Denton (1995), recounting the narratives of Semai men who had committed homicide while in a dissociated state that the Malaysians call *blnuul bhib*, writes:

The stories seemed affectless and detached. They had no undertones at all that I could detect: no remorse, no humor, no irony or gloating, no self-justification or apology. The narrator would look off into space or down at the floor in what seemed like contemplation of a distant object. One would not have known that the narrator was involved, except that he used the first person plural.

This rhetoric, unlike irony, does not protect narrators from the emotions they felt; instead, it reenacts their emotional emptiness (pp. 225–226).

TIME WAITS

The essence of meaningless is when lived experience seems to be driven by no form other than brute sequence (Mattingly, 1998, p. 47)

Martin Heidigger (1927) saw the phenomenology of time as the underpinning of the human experience. The men whose acts are detailed here seem exempted from humanity in this realm. The disconnection from temporality, the inability to perceive and schematize time in educative ways, is the starting point for a cascade of retardations, neural and relational, that foment the "crisis in symbolization" (Bucci, 1997) that invites dissociation and enactment.

Heidigger (1927) spoke of the "ecstatical unity of temporarlity," the notion that our continuity as selves pivots on the ability to inhabit the three dimensions of time simultaneously, thus imbuing present-day experience with both historical meaning and intentionality. His analysis suggests that identity feels to us authentic insofar as it is time laden, folding perception, meaning, desire, and anticipation into a present accordingly thickened by those imaginings. The seamless and unconscious joining of past, present, and future is how people create the "existential now" of contemporary identity (Ricoeur, 1980).

In addition to the variety of defensive deployments triggered by ongoing maltreatment, child abuse may crack the chronograph that laces temporal dimensions into meaningful spheres. Like little boys in Neverland, maltreated children are characteristically frozen. Where childhood identity is inchoate, adult identity is not imaginable.

[The self can emerge only] with the ally of time. Traumatic experience kills off that ally. The victimized child self cannot be shucked off, refashioned or brought forward because, without the concept of time, none of these actions are possible. It's the loss of time as a tool that's problematic here, not just the traumatizing event [Susan Waggoner, personal communication, 2003].

Fenichel (1945) wrote movingly about the reassuring power of time in affirming both sanity and control. After all, if ongoing experience is not anchored in time, one has no dependable referent for contemporary realities. Where time stops, reality is dreamlike: listen to the narratives of crime that unfold in slow, surreal motion. If time stops, agency is forfeited: laws are violated by disembodied facsimiles, not me. When time stops, interpersonal engagements become an endless repetition of nebulous, earlier injuries that provoke retaliatory aggression. So, while past, present, and future uncoil with alarming intrusiveness during violent enactments, their shared condition is one of jagged segregation, not the faultless fusion of temporality that Heidigger (1928) envisioned. During enactments, each temporal element is an occluding system rather than a bridge-able vantage point from which to symbolize the other dimensions.

Consider this blitz attack in a parking lot. The police file records the shooter as a not unfamiliar type of perpetrator: a Caucasian male virgin, still living with his mother. He and his victim had worked for the same company before he was fired for inappropriate interactions with customers. At first, he told police that his mark was "too liberal" and "a feminist"; he wondered if perhaps she had had romantic designs on him. He "guessed" that his motive was hate. "I'm not a knife person, I wouldn't strangle someone. *My problem was people*" (he reiterated this assertion many times). He claimed to have died when he was 14.

Later he came to believe that his victim was alive and well, that the whole thing had been staged. "She kept absorbing [the gunshots] like she was super-human or something."That is what led him to insist that the scene had been fixed, that the girl was only faking her death. Remember, after all, it was he who had died at the age of 14—the subjective shooter did not exist. Once again, it was all a fever dream, where corpses walk and dead men tell the tales.

Offenders like that are usually diagnosed as paranoid schizophrenic. Laing's (1959) contribution to the discussion of nihilistic delusions in schizoid and schizophrenic states, such as this offender had, related the discontinuity of the temporal self to death anxieties: "The self dreads to become alive and real because in doing so the risk of annihilation is potentiated" (p. 109).

Ontological repudiation triggers what Laing regarded as a death loop, a need to murder the other that ends up backfiring. This boomerang effect may explain the offender's need—like that of many others profiled in this book—to reanimate his victim in some way. This particular killer was more adamant than most that his victim's death was bogus, but it is not uncommon, in my experience, for per-petrators to wonder if their victim's are "really" dead. Sometimes this doubt leads to episodes of what criminal profilers call "overkill." While overkill is gen-erally chalked up to a surfeit of rage, it has seemed to me in many instances to be occasioned by a surplus of annihilation anxiety—the fear that the victim would rise vindictively to avenge the attack, as in so many low budget horror movies.

> The more one attempts to preserve one's autonomy and identity by nullify-ing the specific human individuality of the other, the more it is felt to be nec-essary to continue to do so, because with each denial of the other person's ontological status, one's own ontological security is decreased, the threat to the self from the other is potentiated and hence has to be even more desper-ately negated [Laing, 1959 p. 52].

Laing's description is as good an alternative explanation for overkill as I have heard.

MEANING FROM NOTHINGNESS

[Narrative sequence] goes nowhere without its doppelganger, or shadow, causality (Kermode, 1980, p. 83)

Schafer (1980) has noted that no one offers up an invariant version of his or her life. Through interrogation, reflection, and reweaving, one's multiple narratives might eventually coalesce to capture the sweep, or even distill the essence, of a life, but life stories sure don't start out that way. For everyone, but most achingly for a traumatized child, reason must be imposed on the illogic of personal events. This can best be accomplished by a dispassionate narrator of events, who can add sequence and meaning to life experience, while creating an interpersonal space between the self and the audience hearing the story, an audience that consensually validates the false self in ways similar to the original maltreating caretakers. The narrating self creates "a role enactment that fits the perceived requirements of his or her moral career," loosely based on stereotypical characters and prototypical plots, as a strategic validation of moral decision making [Sarbin, 1989, p. 194].

Those who create imaginary agents to express dissociated traumas are not only supplying story, but also assigning sequence and meaning to formerly inexplicable events. Whereas their own traumatic history lacks a rational plot, a clear villain, a diachronic anchor, the dissociator's created subnarrator "emplots" the story, giving it meaning, cogency, and a timeline that confers the illusion of causality (Sarbin, 1989). By distorting, condensing, and confabulating facts, one's story becomes both universal and cautionary, inflating meaning beyond its traumatic parameters.

According to Mattingly (1998) narratives are created not simply to communicate what happened, but to place events in a context that allows one to take "a moral perspective on past events" (p. 29). Nowhere does this explanation resonate more powerfully than in the case of victim-perpetrators, who feel a defensive obligation to protect both their abusers and their own wounded selves from mortification. Each narration/fictive persona becomes a thesis or argument to explain and justify the prologue—abuse—and the denouement— a violent offense.

As Mattingly proposes, real-life narrators, like their literary counterparts, perch above the story, supplying an authoritative perspective, in narrating backwards so that the conclusion will seem inevitable:

> The narrator begins at the end of his organization of the story, though he is likely to tell it, more or less, from the beginning, creating Barthes' "chronological illusion" ... the story's structure exists because the narrator knows where to start, knows what to include and exclude, knows how to weight and evaluate and connect the events he recounts, all because he knows where he will stop [p. 38].

In an adroit defensive reworking, temporal fission—the traumatically imposed sundering of past, present, and future—sequentializes narrative, creating the impression of causality. One narrative might lead from the conclusion "I murdered someone" to the prologue "My mother only beat me when I was bad"; another narrative might work backward from "I'd never hurt anyone" to amnesia for maltreatment, and so forth. As Sullivan (1956) noted about dissociative processes, it is no surprise that the ersatz memories informing flawed explanations assert themselves so effortlessly (p. 174). Explanatory tales, and the role enactments that constitute them, are rehearsed in the interpersonal arena, from childhood on, until they are smooth as silk. Practice makes perfect.

Ricouer (1980) observed that the essence of repetition may be that, in reaching back, we generate a fanciful vision of grasping our potential: this time I will get it right, change the future and, with a new ending, be able to rewrite the past. "Acting out is a form of remembering" (Schafer, 1980, p. 38) but narrativizing enactments, as dissociators do, enables the distortion that presages—not a happy ending but one that makes sense in the wider context of brutal experience.

REFLECTIONS

While some forensic clinicians have called attention to the ubiquity of dissociation among offenders (Meloy, 1997a; Lewis & Bard, 1991; Lewis et al., 1997 Steinberg & Schnall, 2000) others working with criminals doubt the credibility of dissociative diagnoses. Schlesinger (2000), for example, says that

> descriptions by the offender of "another personality taking over" are not indications of multiple personality disorder or dissociation. The serial offender knows exactly what he is doing; he can control his actions to a large extent, but he chooses not to because he seeks relief from the state of tension he is in [p. 13].

Although I disagree with the breadth of the assumption, Schlesinger's comment astutely picks up on the conscious facilitation of dissociation: the way that offenders may purposefully use trance to bypass threat, both as a way to avoid annihilation-in-the-moment and to erase their own culpability in the aftermath of criminal behavior. The habitual resorting to dissociative processing is eased by the blurring of self and other boundaries (Meloy, 1997a)" that virtually defines violent perpetrators, whether or not they experience actual amnesias or discrete changes in personality.

As Ferenczi (1927) inferred from his work with dissociative patients, the seeds of dissociated personification are sowed in the soil of identification with two-faced, hypocritical abusers. Dramatic personas may be nurtured through ongoing, often quite conscious, deception. This mix of unconscious and conscious elements is, in part, what has made it so difficult for the criminal justice system to dismiss intentionality—a prerequisite for most findings of criminal guilt—in cases where the defendant claims to have dissociated identities rather than straightforward amnesia for the crime. After all, *someone* did buy the weapon, find the opportunity, and elude the police. Accordingly, some time in the 19th century, legal formulations of responsibility began to separate states of "unconsciousness" (e.g., amnesia, sleepwalking) from those of "double consciousness," although the change in the medicolegal designation from disorders of consciousness to disorders of personality did not happen until the 1970s (Eigen, 2003). In his wonderful account of criminal cases of "mental absence" from the Old Bailey trial records, Eigen notes the importance of the legal modification: "This is no idle philosophical query. If the second state is merely a state of unconsciousness, the forensic construction of a person—an intentional being who chooses to engage in action—is profoundly challenged" (p. 22).

In other words, the recognition of unintegrated states of consciousness has made it *less* likely that defendants will be exonerated on claims of multiplicity, since even second (or third, or fourth) selves can be conceived of as intentional agents in this formulation, whereas "unconscious" automatons can not.

Dissociative identity disorder and its progenitor, multiple personality disorder, are two diagnostic monikers that unfortunately have obfuscated more than they have clarified, particularly in the criminal justice world. Overall, it the clinical tendency to reify the personas of dissociative person has overwhelmed rational discourse about dissociation. This is especially so with regard to forensic evaluations that make Jekyll and Hyde the standard for mitigation. I have always liked Nancy McWilliams (1994) characterization of dissociative identity disorder as not very different from anorexia nervosa, in which the frail victim of self-imposed starvation insists that the image in the mirror is obese. The public (clinicians included) never treats that perception of self as independently "true" the way we do the multiple consciousnesses of dissociative identity disorder patients, even though their symptoms may be part of the same somatosensory continuum.

It is my strong sense that the current psychiatric taxonomy encourages clinicians to reify the imaginary constructs of their dissociating patients in a way that stimulates neither good treatment nor solid theory. The *DSM* criteria for diagnoses of dissociation, calling as they do for the existence of discrete identities with separate consciousnesses, can be met only in the most metaphorical sense.

For the inmates that I interviewed, the line separating conscious from unconscious material—and narrative voices from one another—was porous, even where the subjective perception was one of staunch division. Affect and experience leaked both horizontally and vertically. In this regard, I am drawn to Lifton's (1986) theory of doubling, which calls attention to the opposing, or shadow, selves that straddle consciousness and may become uninhibited under extreme stress.

Doubling theory focuses on the "holistic function of the self" (p. 420); the basic human need to replace psychological chaos with cogency, and division with wholeness. This is an important addition to the more classical analytic formulations of splitting (Breuer & Freud, 1893–1895; Klein, 1921) and dissociation (Ellenberger, 1970), which perhaps explain the initial traumatic moment better than they do the facilitative role of the dissociative defenses in the proliferation of violence.

Given the incompleteness of their psychic forms, it is only logical that the criminals I spoke with attempted to author a more cohesive self-narrative. Indeed, in some ways, their false selves had less in common with true personality constructs, which have far greater depth and complexity, than with the reconstitutive stories that we all make up about ourselves. On the other hand, considering the dire circumstances under which many criminal narratives are birthed and serialized, the destructive trajectory of the plotline becomes fathomable, if not inevitable.

6

Conclusion

Consciousness, Culpability, and Control

Evangelical preachers and criminal profilers paint strikingly comparable monsters and demons (Ressler & Schactman, 1992). Medical doctors wax poetic about the time when we "will be able to isolate genes that [underlie] constant murderous violence" and use brain imaging techniques for the preventive identification of certain killers (Morrison & Goldberg, 2004). *The New York Times* (Carey, 2005) leads its science section with an article about using "evil" as a diagnostic marker (yes, psychologist Michael Stone has created a scale!) for offenders who commit particularly "breathtaking" murders. The otherworldly connotations deliver us backward to a time when crimes were believed to be acts of magic performed "by ghostly hand [rather] than by flesh and blood" human beings (Reik, 1945). It has become increasingly acceptable in supposedly scientific circles to treat criminal violence as a manifestation of something anomalous, even nonhuman. In truth, violence represents the extreme of behaviors that are all too human.

Stone's 22-item checklist, called The Gradations of Evil Scale, is arranged, according to its designer, "in ascending degree of inhumanity." It is based on Stone's reading of 278 biographies of murderers (Millon et al., 1998), an admittedly un-representative, but nonetheless fascinating, sample of the population of aggressors. Despite Stone's championing an unenlightened taxonomy of violent behavior, he insightfully ends his article by asserting that a history of child abuse is exceedingly common in the most violent of evil people (the figure he cites is 75%) and that such wickedness might best be vanquished through early intervention with abusive families and through parenting education for potential procreators (p. 354). This has been my point, exactly. Sadly, though, by proposing "evil" as a diagnostic category, Stone does what so many highly respected forensic people do (and what grown-ups maltreated as children also do): they acknowledge the source of the problem and then quickly change the subject.

SHADES OF AGGRESSION

Many students of crime have concentrated on the hypothesized line that divides conformity from deviance, but I have been impressed by the continuum of behaviors that straddle that reified boundary. Law breaking seems to me part of a spectrum that includes completely legal forms of manipulation, corruption, and risk taking, as well as specifically outlawed acts like drunk driving or date rape. To relocate Sullivan's (1953a) thoughts on mental illness to the cells in which I practice, there is nothing exceptional about the most earth-shattering violence: "these processes are exactly of a piece with processes we [each] manifest sometime every twenty-four hours" (p. 7). Aggressive acts differ in magnitude, not essence; the same security operations that adaptively titrate survival processes in one person or situation may become disproportionately active in another.

Even the most extreme and horrific behaviors, like suicide bombing, amplify common human struggles with pain, anger, and loneliness that the messenger ultimately could not convey in a more conventional or prosocial way. Like the criminal narratives detailed in this book, interviews with potential and failed suicide bombers have noted disabling fears of annihilation and abandonment (Lachker, 2002), unstable internality (Volkan, 2002), and disturbed identity patterns (Volkan, 2002). Lloyd Demause (2002) has speculated that the rampant cruelty, sexual abuse, and mutilation of children in many countries have birthed a generation ripe for exploitation by enigmatic father figures who help abuse victims channel their dissociated rage toward political ends. If that is so, the political is surely very personal.

OF MEANS AND ENDS

Criminal profilers often speak of "instrumental" versus "expressive" violence; these labels are intended to differentiate persons who aggress with a specific hedonic goal in mind from those supposedly propelled by impulse or insanity. This too is a false dichotomy. Based on the concept of the felicity calculus (Bentham, 1791), wherein humans always seek to maximize their own pleasure at as minimal a cost as possible, the key assumption is that the majority of wrongdoers consider the likely consequences of their acts and make rational, conscious choices about how to behave. As Gilligan (1996) has remarked, the only problem with the "rational self-interest" theory of crime is that *it's totally wrong* (p. 84, italics added). My scrutiny of crime scenes and criminal narratives bears out that the majority of offenders operate somewhere between repetition compulsion and dissociated enactment, most of the time, with only a peripheral nod to the good or ill products of their acts, even as concerns their own safety or freedom. Far from being a measured performance, violence is usually delivered unprocessed and raw, often in the same box in which it arrived during earliest development. This is what gives criminal acts what detectives call a signature: the imprint of the child's earliest derogation and the defensive rituals devised to obviate it. Crime is mostly ceremony, not cerebration.

FROM DISSOCIATION TO ENACTMENT
AND BACK AGAIN

This is not to saying that most violence is random or purposeless. All violence, like the majority of non-physical aggression, has a very definite aim: attenuating a perceived threat to the person committing it (Gilligan, 1996; Hyatt-Williams, 1998). The nature of the threat may be quite real, as in victim-precipitated homicides (Wolfgang, 1958), or it may be imagined to varying degrees, as in the case of substance-facilitated assaults, street muggings (Lejeune, 1977),[1] and homicides with no apparent motive (Satten et al., 1960; Holcomb & Daniel, 1988; Stone, 1993).

The response to a perceived threat goes like this. A person feels vaguely imperiled and casts about for the source of danger. Menace is projected outward and becomes embodied in a particular object. The possibility of annihilation now overshadows any thought of pleasure or punishment later. If this level of dread stays inside, deep depression, psychosis, or suicide may result. Only when impending danger is successfully externalized can it be forcefully contained and potentially eradicated.

In attack repertoires, intrapsychic control is exerted through mental precursors to ambush behaviors: intrusive thoughts, dream states, rumination, stalking, or hunting for prey. It is these dissociated, delusional, or obsessive resistances that are often misinterpreted by profilers as conscious, willful fantasies. Indeed, there may be some occasional, rudimentary fantasies, but these are potentially constructive rather than destructive: actual fantasies tend to familiarize one with potential ends, *out* of which the prospective offender can then opt, especially if the fantasy has been rich enough to provide catharsis. Dissociated reverie, to the contrary, is little more than a gnawing unthought.[2] What is dissociated is almost destined to produce an enactment, if only to make it thinkable.

Sometimes ambush activities go on for years and forestall actual violence, as the potential offender remains too defensively paralyzed to execute a criminal game plan. Such paralysis apparently caused lengthy intermissions between homicidal binges for serial killer Dennis Rader (BTK), whose obsessionalism kept him from killing until the various pieces of what he referred to as his "projects" were perfectly assembled. The punctilious search for an ideal victim, location, and method matched his most zealous performances as a "control officer" in his small community, where he sometimes measured blades of grass to make certain that homeowners were in compliance with local law. In cases like his, obsessiveness and paranoid hypervigilance may work to keep compulsive episodes of violence at bay for a time, but they also provide surreptitious mental practice for what is to come. This is not a conscious rehearsal, as the profiling literature argues (Burgess et al, 1986); it is a demonstration of how sadistic preoccupations can contribute to final performances that seem very polished, even though they go on largely outside a person's awareness (Sullivan, 1956).

---

[1] In a fascinating set of interviews with men who have commited street robberies, (Lejeune, (1977), the author documents the degree to which muggers are terrified of their potential victims.

[2] I use the term unthought here to mean what is known but what has not been mentally processed through the level of symbolic representation because of trauma, not as Bollas (1987) defined it to designate an essential receptive quality in preverbal children.

Unfortunately, abstinence from aggression is usually short lived. For persons on enactment's edge, interpersonal triggers for hostility are in continuous abundant supply. Sooner or later, someone or something in the environment, perceived as threatening, will precipitate a counter-offensive or a displaced attack. Once the threat is eclipsed by brutal action, the perpetrator's internal terror subsides, and a more intact identity state can reassert itself. The act of violence itself may be totally forgotten. This can be as true for soldiers and police officers as it is for criminal offenders (Bourke, 1999; Rivard et al., 2002; Henry, 2004).

Are all acts of violence completely forgotten? Of course not, and most perpetrators are not so pathologically dissociated that they have developed full-fledged alternate personae to do their criminal bidding. For most aggressors, hostile actions are at least partially conscious, as are many memories of early trauma. But an absence of the most extreme pathology should not undermine discussion of the place that dissociation and enactment hold in cruel performances.

Dissociation as a response to personal disaster is both an intrinsic fail-safe—like your computer's operating system automatically shutting down a program that might crash it—and a learned technique for manipulating incoming data. For example, certain murderers work hard to stage pre- and post-crime scenarios in ways that enable the depersonalization of self and victim. In this, stagging the victim-perpetrator uses a natural[3] capacity for dissociation—which has been honed to exquisite effectiveness in earlier traumas—in an almost willful way. The actor has learned which situational dynamics best induce trance, or automatism, or the kind of split between cognition and affect that can facilitate a successful aggressive performance, and calls them into play.

In cases where identity has developed around a particularly aphasic nucleus of impotence, as occurs in highly abusive homes, attempts to reset the system and restore a powerful identity are more agitated and inevitable. Sometimes an "extra self" that incorporates the enactment in a marginally conscious way, often with an exaggerated sense of self-worth, is formed. The extra self, as I understand Sullivan (1953a), is located in the dissociated part of personality, the part that did not make it into the self dynamism. For people who need to attend to a constant threat of devaluation, the part that is extraneous is often the part that feels worthy or entitled. This part asserts itself in enactment and may insert itself into consciousness when it is validated by significant others in the person's interpersonal field. Such validation is often forthcoming for violence that is supported by a social network of one's peers, violence that is defined as preemptory or that confirms one's gender or status within a larger group. When violence is consensually validated, and therefore personally validating, the act itself is less likely to be forgotten (in fact, it is usually remembered in hyperrealistic relief). Although technically remembered, it is bereft of the affective context that would impart a meaning beyond its empirical outline.

Even for the majority of us who experience everyday imbroglios as relatively manageable, some threats are attended to in aggressive performances that skirt

---

[3]Natural to all of us, not only the victim-perpetrator.

consciousness. Responding to internal tension by verbally besting a competitor, or catcalling a young girl on the street, are pedestrian examples of assault in the service of psychic cohesion. In these ordinary events, although there is no amnesia, there is a degree of disavowal, usually in the form of insistence that the victim deserved—or may have secretly enjoyed—the attack, or even in a denial that the attack was injurious at all.

Techniques of depersonalization and derealization, as they weave aggressive engagements, are unconscious catalysts and conscious strategies to facilitate enactments. (For example, in my experience it has been less the case that a man killed because he was drunk than that he drank in order to facilitate his disso-ciated stance from the hómicide he—consciously or unconsciously—wished to commit. The same is probably true when a single man picks up an intimidating woman in a bar; "liquid courage" is the cultural synonym for dissociated enact-ment.) Partial ownership provides the guilty pleasure in such acts, but partial dissociation virtually guarantees their mindless repetition.

The fluctuating consciousness of one's acts has been termed doubling by Lifton (1986), who uses the concept to explicate human participation in the mechanized forms of dehumanization that pave the road to totalitarianism, cult worship, and genocide. The term doubling draws attention to the plurality of awareness as opposed to its division, and to the ways that people and events can be actively made to disappear, as opposed to merely not being attended to. In the scenarios that Lifton discusses, agency is not completely disavowed—because there is knowledge and memory for events—but it is always exceedingly distorted. This is a common offender profile, as well as being the modus operandi of many people working in a criminal justice system that so aggressively contains and corrects them.

FROM EMPATHY TO SELF-CONTROL AND BACK AGAIN

The internal coordination of schemas that inhibit violence—like attachment and empathy—are fragile in humans. This is a fact attested to by the indecency of so much of our general social interaction, yet one that is often ignored in the urgency to place the criminal's unfeeling attitude in sharpest relief. There is cer-tainly no shortage of reflection about attachment and empathy in texts about criminals. Everyone seems quite clear that they don't have or want any, although there is plenty of argument about why that might be so.

We think of empathy as the ability to resonate with another person's fear, or pain, or grief, or even delight, and to tailor our reactions accordingly. Empathy is the basis of affective communication. Sullivan (1953a) used the term to describe the emotional contagion in reasonably consonant caregiver–infant dyads; empathy has to do with the way the caregiver interprets and satisfies the baby's most basic needs. In the process, the caregiver organizes and labels diffuse sensations for the infant and transmits cultural norms about their expression. It is this empathic sense that forms the template for transitional objects or experiences that can offer the child, and later the adult, solace in the absence of a significant nurturing adult. In other words, self-composure is antecedent to self-control. Under ordinary circumstances, transitional experi-ence can smooth the progression from external comforting to self-regulation and provide a space where internal and external reality can peacefully coexist (Winnicott, 1965).

When the somatic interdependency of parent and child is violated because of abandonment or abuse, there is no translation from the physiological realm to the affective one. Sensations in the child's body have no epiphenomenal extension. Instead of interpreting a somatic event in emotional terms (my blood is boiling, I am enraged; I'm shaking like a leaf, I am terrified) the psyche, well, just pays it no mind. Physical sensations may intensify or abate, but coincident affects are isolated. During subsequent traumas, powerful emotions may come to be registered as emanating from other people, who are then perceived as the causative agents of one's internal distress. As Richards (1998) observed, "It is impossible for these infants and children to tolerate (let alone incorporate) the emotional and evaluative reality of their parents and others, which is perceived as being intrusively and ruthlessly imposed upon them, almost from the beginning of life" (p. 75). Ultimately, the only way to regulate one's own internal state is through those imagined gate crashers (Krystal, 1980, p. 319). Lachmann (2000) has noted that, when development is marked by substantial trauma, victimizing others may become a regulatory and reparative act: discharged aggression results in the conversion from a tension state to one of satisfaction, a transformation that could not take place in the earlier traumatic context (p. 141). The singular concern with forcefully imposing one's will on another person undermines the use of people and things as transitional phenomena, to say the least, and impedes progress toward an empathic stance of one's own, unless one is referring to the "dark empathy" of intuiting another's defenselessness (p. 11).

Remember the offender whose transitional object, his teddy bear, became so menacing that it had to be destroyed? For some children, like that one, the only transitional objects are the split-off portions of the child's own self, imaginary friends that become agentic repositories of vile or virtuous intent and that can become the persecutory, commanding voices of self and other destruction. Unlike the facilitating environs described by Winnicott (1965), in this rough locale there is no easy transit into, or out of, the various modes of being that stand in relationship to objects and the appraisal of reality. In its most extreme manifestation, rather than being an interchangeable vantage point for positive action or imagination, each self-state is mired in a particular persecutory construction of the world that seems immutable. The stage is thus set for a kind of conditioned dissociativity, where both overstimulation and deprivation can be avoided, but at the cost of all that falls in between. In chronic trauma, the most alienated part of subjectivity is the most strenuously and continuously exercised. Under stress it emerges, seeks, and destroys.

AGENCY: THE UNSEEN HAND

There is a visible and invisible world. That is why people get hurt.

—an inmate explaining his crimes to me

Countless victim-perpetrators live with the oxymoronic sense that their real selves are obscured by invisible ones who commit violence. This is how strongly the "not-me" aspect of subjectivity is perceived as authorial. "Not-me" personifications arise from interpersonal experiences of unadulterated anxiety and reappear in subsequent situations that evoke a similar "absolute tension" (Sullivan, 1953b, p. 45), yet the relational context in which agency and control over one's actions are born tends to be particularly marginalized in discussions about crime.

Many otherwise progressive thinkers have bought into the popular rhetoric about child abuse and crime and have called posttraumatic stress and dissociation the "trendy alibis" of our era (Radwin, 1991). For example, well-known defense attorney, Alan Dershowitz (1995), penned a book of inflammatory title,[4] which challenges the idea that childhood maltreatment or adult trauma should provide mitigation in the courtroom. Margaret Hagen (1997) has excoriated Harvard researchers Bessel van der Kolk and Judith Herman for providing forensic practitioners, whom she calls "whores of the court," with the ammunition to challenge defendants' culpability on the grounds of posttraumatic symptoms of abuse, including dissociation.

Having spent a few years evaluating youngsters on a child and adolescent psychiatric ward, I have observed that everyone feels sorry for an abused child—until he bites someone. Then suddenly they want him tried in adult court. I find fascinating the point at which the pitied become a pariah in the eyes of the body politic.

The legal uproar is unwarranted. Contemporary courts have largely rejected the idea that dissociation so violates the necessary conditions for consciousness and volition that *mens rea* cannot exist (*Ohio v. Grimsley*, 1982; *Kirkland v. State*, 1983). Amnesia itself presents no bar to competence (*State v. Badger*, 1988), and even when the court has acknowledged that there is adequate evidence for a determination of dissociative identity disorder (DID) neither the defendant's competence nor his sanity is necessarily impugned (*State v. Darnell*, 1984; *State v. Rodrigues*, 1980). Unlike the infamous Billy Milligan (Keyes, 1981), who was acquitted of multiple rapes on the basis of his dissociative pathology, the majority of defendants who register such claims have been unsuccessful in pressing them. Of course, many defendants who probably could do so never lodge DID defenses or even submit evidence of child abuse as a mitigating factor for their violence. In fact, many offenders prefer to go to prison or the death chamber rather than make public the truth of their upbringing or reveal their mental instability (Lewis, 1998).

Far from providing a "get out of jail free card," child abuse and pathological dissociation are largely overlooked. Remember, Stone (1998) said that in upward of 75% of the homicide cases he had reviewed there was childhood mistreatment of the worst kind. The vast majority of the 64 men I interviewed in my initial research had been abused. Not one had been diagnosed with a dissociative disorder, although at least 14 were severely dissociative, and many more bordered on being so.

Recognition of the centrality of childhood maltreatment and defensive dissociation in violent criminality is problematical for the forensic field on legal, medical, and psychological fronts. First, to uphold vigorously the social contract, we have to exempt from it as few people as possible, which is why the

[4] Dershowits, A. (1995). *The abuse excuse: Cop outs, sob stories, and other evasions of responsibility.* NY: Little, Brown.

legal system must have the narrowest possible interpretation of justification and excuse standards. Frankly, allowing evidence of child abuse to be entered into the record for violent defendants could potentially raise the issue of mitigation in over three quarters of cases, a moral debacle that the courts would rather avoid. Second, for psychiatrists, conceding the seminal influence of child maltreatment on adult violence seriously challenges agendas focused on biological determinism on the research side and the potential efficacy of pharmacological interventions on the treatment end. Finally, in the field of psychology, researchers and clinicians may, as Goldsmith, Barlow, and Freyd (2004) have warned, fear opening up the additional lines of inquiry and analysis that trauma investigations and therapies require. Acknowledging trauma means acknowledging the role of interpersonal relationships in the production and persistence of aggression, a connection that casts its Jungian shadow over every therapist–offender dyad (Maruna, Matravers, & King, 2004).

CLINICIAN, HEAL THYSELF

Repeat offenders engender a kind of hopelessness among the populace, among their political representatives, and even (perhaps especially) among those who are charged with evaluating them and recommending appropriate dispositions.

Strong reactions to criminals include the pressure to evacuate the aggression that offenders deposit inside one, a need to compete with the criminal in aggressive displays of masculinity (for male practitioners) or feigned imperviousness to threat (for female practitioners), and grappling with superego control of one's own aggressive and sexual impulses as they are stirred by the aggressive offender (Hyatt-Williams, 1998, p. 259). Lacking appropriate supervision in correctional settings, where caseloads are often overwhelming, many clinicians fail to acknowledge fully their own countertransferential envy, rage, and arousal. This is particularly true in therapeutic settings geared toward behavior modification, where supervisors themselves may eschew discussion of the unconscious dynamics between inmates and treatment providers or reject wholesale the impact of early abuse.

The dissociation of such powerful affects, and the grandiose posturing that likely disjoins them, sometimes cause clinicians in forensic settings to over-identify with police, the prosecution, and correctional personnel. Indeed, rare is the clinician who has shared with me a cherished memory of something human, touching, and compelling about the inmates they have evaluated.[5] On the contrary, the most cherished mementos of many forensic practitioners I have worked with are the prison banners, baseball caps, and handshake photo-ops with prison staff collected in the course of various prisoner evaluations. There is nothing evil, or even counterintuitive, about this identification: it is safe and highly gratifying to stand shoulder to shoulder with perceived heroes and to internalize their moral and material authority. On the other hand, to engage the offender as a person risks the possibility of wholesale contamination.

---

[5]My earliest mentor, Dr. Dorothy Lewis, and her closest colleague, Catherine A. Yeager, were notable exceptions.

In literature, criminals are usually allegorized as scum, dirt, feces; even their play is foul (Duncan, 1994). Whose side would you rather be on?

The practitioner is first introduced to a prisoner's paranoia, rage, hatred, and sadism by reading the police or court records of the offenders deed(s). It is best, however, to regard these records skeptically, as they reflect the same biases as any other narrative report. In any case, they tell little about the offender's perspective on the deed. Before meeting one highly assaultive inmate, for instance, I read that he had been arrested with a load of artillery: rifles, shotguns, automatics, a Baretta, a .32 revolver. When I met him, however, he insisted (in what is by no a familiar litany for me and for readers of this book) that, aside from a coupl black eyes he had given his wife, "My temper's good. I'm just not violent." The inmate's father, by the way, also was not violent: "He just had rules. He wasn't sadistic." His father "only" beat him with a knife sharpening strap and a board. After the stories I had heard, I was almost willing to agree that his father's behavior "wasn't serious," which goes to show how quickly one can become defensively inured to repugnant narratives, a countertransference problem that has been discussed in the sexual abuse literature (Davies & Frawley, 1994). This victim-turned-perpetrator blames himself for what happened in childhood: "I was sadistic; [after my parents divorced] I tried beating my father's wives and his other sons." But then he qualifies this statement too: "Nothing serious," he asserts. "After all, I didn't try to drown them."

This man could not bear the awareness of his own sadism or his paternal object's rage; in his commentary, agency for violent acts is ping-ponged between them. His angry projections justify the gargantuan mistrust to which his huge arsenal testifies. It seemed only a matter of time before his weaponry would be put to catastrophic use. I tell his story to illustrate the way that, in contemporary life, this inmate's projections were visited on and responded to in new interpersonal relationships, including ones with forensic personnel. His angry projections provided the spark for the retaliatory rage of staff members, which, of course, confirmed the accuracy of the initial projections.

A particular kind of interpersonal dynamic colors interventions with aggressive persons, whether they are behind prison walls, are in mandated community-based treatment programs, or are simply private clients. When they are provocative, controlling, and dissimulative, aggressive people call out one's own rage, and can make you forget the distal contributors to their aggressive enactments. I suspect there is no one who has worked with abused children who does not sometimes want to hurt them, and no one who works with rapists and murderers who does not at times want to kill them. Crime stories can be such a riveting distraction from the offender's overall life story, and aggressive posturing can so overwhelm the therapeutic discourse, that clinicians may fail to realize that it is the same psychical dust being kicked up in engagements with criminals as is stirred in dealings with maltreated children, or nonviolent adults abused in childhood.

The more that countertransferential feelings can be used as clues in identifying the offender's internal cast of characters, instead of merely as barometers of his or her aggression, the closer the clinician can get to correcting parataxic distortions and helping to integrate dissociated experiences. Doing so requires examining one's own "unfortunate patterns," as well as the offender's (Sullivan, 1949, pp. 5, 12).

For criminals, dissociating their rage is likely the stock and trade of offending. Meloy (1997a) for example, notes that, although committing a violent sexual assault might physiologically arouse the attacker and reveal the affective power propelling it, the perpetrator will often have no conscious experience of anger (p. 89). It is this rage that a therapist is made to hold, and it can seem as though one were holding a colostomy bag. Some clinicians may deny the potency of these contents or disregard their own revulsion.

Robert Winer (2001) has opined that therapists' difficulty in empathizing with such patients amounts to a refusal to examine their own destructiveness. It is in treatment, during transference, that the offender has an opportunity to experience his or her hatred[6] as an affect instead of as a dislocated sensorium, and perhaps even own the more gratifying aspects of it. This agency will make dissociated rage less fearsome, less fragmenting, and less likely to be enacted. But the process requires the clinician to examine his or her own aggression in particularly challenging ways.

For example, I have sometimes found myself in the strange situation of needing to form questions in a way that would make the recitation of childhood events tolerable for the offender (e.g., after hearing how "bad" a child the offender was, my research protocol dictated my saying, "Sounds as though you were a real handful. Did your parents ever lose their cool and go further than they meant?). But then, forgetting my own pragmatic initiative, I sometimes became entangled in the bramble of who did what to whom first, or who was the worse. I soon could find myself siding with the abuser, which is exactly what the victim-perpetrator's projective identification is destined to accomplish. With an inexperienced researcher or evaluator, this can happen even in an initial session, as one's own survival dynamics take over in the face of persistent baiting. As long as you remain stuck in your own dissociation, the offender will keep pickpocketing your rage and fear and throwing it back at you, in ever-more toxic form. This is a familiar playground for an abused child, now grown up, particularly where unbridled rage has been the dominant enactment.

On the other hand, it may be difficult to discriminate between what is merely a countertransferential affect on the part of the interviewer and what is an actual threat emanating from the client in real time (Strasburger, 1986). Obviously, with aggressive persons, threats must be evaluated and managed both in the context of a specific hostile engagement and in the overall treatment paradigm, if one is to be attempted.

If psychotherapeutic interventions are going to be used with people who have already committed an offense, transferential issues around anger will be the foremost concern, because the cessation of aggressive behavior (leading to lowered recidivism rates) is the only measurement in which institutions are interested. This, and not judgments of the offender's personal happiness or insight, will be the criterion for the continued funding of treatment programs and for attempts to repatriate offenders into the larger community.

---

[6]Kernberg (1992) defines hatred as "the consequence of the incapacity to eliminate frustration through rage, and it goes beyond rage in a lasting need to eliminate the object" (p. 213).

CAN TREATMENT WORK?

The idea that aggressive or criminal persons are not amenable to treatment is a popular one. Clearly, they are not ideal candidates for insight-oriented therapies, since they have such great difficulty offering up for interpretation any semblance of an internal world. Join their empty prose and superficially aimless behaviors with an edgy demeanor and total inability to fathom divergent perspectives and you do not generally find clinicians lining up to offer psychotherapy services. The ones who do are sometimes attracted to the work because of their own voyeuristic yearnings for power or because they find gratification in being the one person in whom the bad guy confides, the object he will not or cannot destroy. Most likely, treatment providers will be drawn from the ranks of newly minted forensic psychologists, a field whose ranks are swelling owing to the current explosion of media attention given forensic profilers and their criminal subjects. Forensic graduate programs tend to be heavy on training psychologists to testify in court, to conduct quantitative research, and to institute, oversee, and evaluate behavior modification programs for inmates. I do not know of any forensic programs in the U.S. that emphasize psychoanalytic theories or techniques.

Given the general pessimism, even fatalism, that greets most program initiatives with violent offenders, I am always buoyed to read the words of experienced forensic clinicians who, while acknowledging the insidious difficulties of engaging destructive people, nonetheless believe that many of them are quite treatable—and not only through cognitive or behavioral methods (Lion & Bach-y-Rita, 1970; Lion & Leaff, 1973; Strausburger, 1986; Meloy, 1997a; Goldberg, 2000). We need a way to think about practical methods of treatment, both inside and outside the criminal justice system, as well as the kind of preventive initiatives that should be undertaken if we wish to lower the general rate of social aggression. To do so, we must incorporate multiple perspectives.

Being a fan of Sullivan's writings about his work with the seriously mental ill, I have been delighted to discover how applicable Sullivan's inpatient milieu and group therapeutic models are to work with criminal offenders. Indeed, many successful European programs incorporate his techniques, with or without crediting the source of their inspiration.

MAXIMUM SECURITY

For most offenders, violence is the just background noise in their interpersonal world; it becomes audible only in moments of crisis. So, the first thing of importance to remember is that the offender is not the equivalent of the rap sheet, in the same way that a hospitalized schizophrenic is not the same as his or her delusional system. This non equivalency may seem obvious but is easy to conflate the two, given the overriding institutional focus on maintaining discipline and control within the prison population and forestalling future aggression on the outside.

The therapist, attempting to alter the esteem in which an offender places a certain antisocial act, needs to address the totality of what Sullivan (1949) called the "evaluative system," which includes how someone values or devalues himself or herself, and how he or she justifies the use of certain behaviors—in this case, violent ones—to meet urgent needs. As difficult as it may be to do, early traumas must be addressed in the context of how they have affected the offender's lack of self-control and driven his or her quest for personal valida- tion, despite the astronomical costs. This said, particularly with in-custody persons, the defensive system must be dismantled at an extraordinarily slow pace. Nowhere does an inmate need primitive defenses more than in prison. The penitentiary recapitulates the offender's childhood prison, where paranoia and violence were as adaptive for the innocent child as they are now for the convicted adult.

What Sullivan (1962) contained in his programmatic design for milieu ther- apy was the idea that the therapeutic environment can promote change only when it maintains a sense of interpersonal security through the management of client's anxiety—difficult under the best of circumstances but seemingly impossible in treating people already confined under the worst imaginable circumstances. How can you lessen someone's anxiety when his life is truly endangered, as it is every day in jail? How can you put a paranoid person at ease when he is heavily surveilled?

With the hypervigilant, little things count. Sullivan (1970) used to arrange the chairs in his interview room so that hospitalized schizophrenics would not be forced into a level of eye contact that would likely unsettle them. I learned early on that, contrary to accepted wisdom regarding seating arrangements with violent offenders (tradition dictated always giving yourself quick access to the exit) the best thing to do was to make sure that the offender had a way to leave the interview room, thus lessening the extent to which he or she would feel cornered and have to lash out. After all, people attack when they perceive no other way out of a situation; that is the offender's life story. The job of the prac- titioner is to demonstrate, at first concretely (as in the seating arrangements) but then with increasing abstraction, the availability of alternate routes out of combustible situations.

Empathic engagement makes accessible the parts of the offender that are enough on the cusp of consciousness for him to engage in a dialogue about aggressive acts. As Sullivan (1953a) was fond of reminding his staff, genuine emotional contact would include abandoning neutrality when dramatic expe- riences are related, rather than attempting to demonstrate to the offender how impervious one is to shocking material. In my opinion, texts about working with offenders, or nonincarcerated "sociopaths," are unnecessarily littered with instructions about how to present oneself as powerful, pokerfaced, and a clev- erer manipulator than the criminal offender in order to gain his "respect." While the ability to exercise thoughtful clinical restraint and demonstrate a kind of receptive composure is imperative, I do not see how mimicking the very failures of impersonality we are hoping to correct in the offender furthers the therapeutic collaboration. We are after all, hoping that dialogue, rather than one-upmanship or bullying, will become the new interpersonal currency. As King wrote about working with violent juveniles, "Frank descriptions of one's own reaction to violent individuals, given spontaneously, have the remarkable therapeutic effect of helping them separate themselves from . . . an illusory omnipotence and to see themselves in a realistic mirror" (as quoted in Strasburger, 1986, p. 19).

The economic and space limitations of the correctional system have instilled a reliance on the briefest possible interventions at the lowest cost. But with offenders, so much negative transference has to be worked through before a good therapeutic relationship can be internalized that brief therapies may not have a real chance to dismantle the dissociative structure that hides the trauma that incited violence. (Parker, 2003). In this regard, art and writing therapies can be a great adjunct, with proven effectiveness in eliciting trauma-relevant information that has been denied, repressed, or dissociated. Beth Mirriam (1998), who runs art programs with female offenders, notes that, for inmates who have little ability to verbalize their experiences, creative venues may provide a nonthreatening way to share difficult material, actualize memories, and offer a container for destructive emotions.

In recent years, cognitive modalities have been joined with behavioral ones in treatment initiatives aimed at offenders. However, like behavior modification through aversion, techniques aimed solely at correcting isolated cognitions about particular criminal acts "risk depicting violent men as faulty thinkers", normal aside from some glitch in their information processing system (Gadd, 2004 p. 187). Such interventions may protect the therapist from the potentially corruptive wellspring of aggressive offenders' perversion and hatred, but they are unlikely to have long-term success rates. If affective and dynamic systems are ignored, cognitive techniques can work only until the boundary of what feels like manageable threat to the potential offender is crossed. For example, the preoffending sexual tension aroused in a pedophile may be forestalled by counting to 10, thinking of England, calling a hotline, or installing a mental "firewall" just as the therapist instructed. But these technique are effective only until some chance encounter provokes such an intense level of anxiety that the pedophile must dissociate from it and, in this dissociated state, offend again. Thus, the integration of dissociated memories and affects must be a primary goal of therapy. Over time, as anxiety is diminished, actions may become internally negotiable, and perhaps amenable to the strictures of cognitive-behavioral retraining, the only kind of longer term intervention that offenders are likely to receive.

PROGRAMS THAT WORK

Grendon Prison: A Therapeutic Community

One of the most interesting therapeutic communities is Grendon, in the UK. Grendon's program is based on the observation that most offenders have trouble sustaining meaningful relationships and tend to resolve conflicted relations through antisocial means (Cullen, 1997). The "therapy" at Grendon explores the correspondences among contemporary relational behaviors, early relationship dynamics, and offending behaviors. For example, how does an interaction with a guard resemble a youthful interaction with the inmate's father or teacher, the boss who fired him, his last assault victim? What do his conversations with a female staffer reveal about his expectations, fantasies, needs, or fears relative to the other women in his life—those he married and those he has raped? More broadly, how does the social role adopted by someone in a prison population (demonstrated by his interactions in the microcosmic prison therapy group) mirror his interpersonal interactions outside jailhouse walls?

The belief is that small-group therapy will supplant the usual hierarchical culture of prison. Group interaction potentially strengthens bonds among inmates and between inmates and staff. It changes the definition of "narrative" from a falsely compliant presentation, or a scripted regurgitation, or a sign of weakness, to one of engagement. As with most prison therapeutic communities, there is a highly statistically significant change in in-house deviance, and the longer the stay, the better the outcomes.[7] Grendon, in fact, has the lowest rate of prison offending of any prison in its category (very violent offenders) in the UK. with regard to security, Grendon also has the best record in the UK, with only one escape in 34 years.

Of course, what happens in the artificial environment of a prison is of less concern to most people than the effect that treatment may or may not have on recidividism. Here the picture is murkier but still positive. Longer stays at Grendon (more than 18 months) are correlated with lower reconviction rates than are matched controls, especially if convicts are released directly into supervision in the community rather than back to regular prison as a prerequisite for final release. The unexpected icing on the cake is that Grendon is actually less expensive to run than are more traditional prisons.

PREP: A Family Systems Therapy

Another good example of interweaving personal introspection in the context of interpersonal dynamics with cognitive models toward behavior change is the PREP program. PREP (The Prevention and Relationship Enhancement Program) is a skills-based curriculum that began in a variety of noncustodial settings—from drug rehabilitation centers to high school auditoriums to army bases and church pews—in the belief that the exploration of power dynamics and the development of communications skills would benefit anyone grappling with intimacy issues (Freedman et al., 2002). The PREP program in Oklahoma offers couples counseling for inmates, with the idea that even those who will never leave prison to set up housekeeping with a spouse or domestic partner can benefit from an exploration of familial dynamics, particular those interactions which trigger abandonment fears or uncontrollable rages.

The Violence Prevention Project: A Residential Treatment Program

The Violence Prevention Project was begun 1987 in New Zealand as an attempt to stem the growing tide of violent offending (Polaschek & Dixon, 2001).

---

[7]One such community in Scotland, now disbanded, boasted a reduction of in-prison disturbances from 176 extremely violent episodes, some involving hostage taking, to a mere 11 behavioral conflicts of which the majority involved prisoners' barricading themselves in their cells. See Cooke (1997) for a more detailed account.

Montgomery House, a residential treatment offshoot of the program, is designed specifically to address violence through social learning principles (Barry, 2003). It is an intensive program, consisting of six learning modules, each centered on specific issues, such as group communication, nonviolent peer confrontation, and family dynamics. Each participant is required to spend 47 hours per week, for 10 weeks, attending group sessions that incorporate role playing, self-disclosure, didactic teaching, and role modeling.

The most interesting aspect of the program is the attempt to match its highly trained staff's ethnicity to that of its offender population, which at the time of this writing was mostly Maaori. Psychologists and lay facilitators (both Maaori and European) are educated in the Maaori language, myths, and traditions, which helps foster greater trust and understanding among staff and program participants.

Initial program evaluations (Barry, 2003) document that offenders attending the program had 35% fewer reconvictions than did controls over the 16 month post-program assessment period, and that their offenses tended to be less serious, although even Montgomery's program designers and evaluators stress that only ongoing care in multiple spheres can eventuate in the huge drops in violence that the program seeks.

FINAL REFLECTIONS

Meltzer (1992) has written about man imprisoned in his mind, with no affective linkages, convinced of, and therefore authoring, his own fraudulence, communicating only in rehearsed lies and transparent evasions. When emotion, known only by its physiological correlates, threatens, "confabulation[s are] constructed to forestall thought" (p. 120). The narratives are representations, symbols presented by culture and appropriated to substitute for created, personally meaningful ones. Sullivan (1953a), commenting on those who have had "insuperable difficulties in living," likened their performances to dreams narrated "by shadowy figures, for a shadowy audience, with one luminously real person, the actor" (p. 54). Plots are woven, generic tales of woe or bliss, populated by mock (sometimes mocking) inhabitants affecting personhood. These are the social suits of the antisocial person, what Cleckley (1941) called their "masks." Of course they are not much different from the operational façades that most people adopt to protect their psychic boundaries: the mask is just more so—more rigid, more opaque, and wrapping something more lurid.

There is a range of ways in which the various shadows of subjectivity are, or are not, assimilated into identity, and there are a variety of cultural supports for what are considered their appropriate expression. People assume aliases on the Internet and find themselves irretrievably "becoming" their sobriquets; church leaders conduct secret lives of debauchery; high school dropouts impersonate doctors, lawyers, and train conductors. In most cases there is not only deception but self-deception, a dissociative impasse at which the person rejects (perhaps transjects is a better word) certain aspects of his or her identity.

Helene Deutsch (1955), famed for her work on imposture, believed that the pathological falsification of a life story is created when a person strongly needs to withdraw from the past and activates a fanciful, desirable history, which, through repeated performance, takes on the mantle of authentic experience. Bollas (1987) observed that liars lie "in order to actualize dissociated self experience" (p. 175), which is another way of saying that habitual lying is a kind of enactment, similar to imposture or dissociated identity, but intermittently more conscious. Some thinkers, Lifton (1983; 1986) and Rank (1971) among them, believe that pluralistic identity is itself a defensive response to the fear of death and a guarantee of immortality under the direst circumstances. This makes sense when one looks at the traumatic origins of plurality and at the contemporary interpersonal conditions that support or reanimate it.

An almost surreal case in point is that of Christian Longo, who, as his life of thin deceptions began to crumble, murdered his wife and three young children and then brazenly appropriated the identity of a *New York Times* reporter while on the run from authorities. Longo, whose ultrareligious parents had quashed his academic aspirations, seems to have desperately wanted recognition and respect, even in the aftermath of committing crimes that would bring him far more notoriety than any journalism career might have. In a truth-is-stranger-than-fiction twist, however, Longo's imposture did end up immortalizing him, as Michael Finkel (2003), the impersonated *Times* reporter, revived his own compromised credibility and flagging career (he had been fired from the newspaper for falsifying an article) by turning Longo's life into a well-regarded book. The juxtapositioning of Finkel's journalistic deceptions with Longo's tale of pathological deceit, homicide, and imposture is as much a psychological meditation on the ubiquity of the false self as one is likely to find in the true-crime genre.

For the full-fledged imposter, as well as the habitual liar (Cleckley's, "so called psychopath," among others), the rankness of the real is monitored and manipulated through the magical, omnipotent contrivances that replace it. This engineered, more palatable virtual reality becomes the currency of all contemporary object relationships; what is enacted in the imposture or in serial lying is a human connection that was never fully achieved with primary caretakers.

> When the liar creates a world for the other, he believes in that world himself, and he feels both more alive and closer to someone who shares the world with him. When the truth dispels the lie, it takes with it the world of self and object representations created by the liar. What is present is the shocking trauma of a shocking departure of a shared reality (Bollas, 1987, p. 182).

Lying sustains the exciting, precarious tension of the tightrope from which one may at any moment fall; when the rope breaks, any tie to others is severed. Such aloneness is in itself a retraumatization that may ignite the most obscene of dissociated enactments. For imposters unveiled, abandonment fears sometimes activate homicidality; the dread of being exposed and deserted dwarfs any imagined consequence of the desperate deed.

TWO DOCTORS

Jean-Claude Romand

Jean-Claude Romand was a brilliant and powerful doctor, an international financier, a well-known humanitarian, and a dutiful family man the day that his wife, children, and elderly parents were gunned down. By daybreak, though, a different man was revealed to authorities: Jean-Claude was, in actuality, a "doctor" without a diploma and a financial sponsor with no funds (in fact, no job). Admittedly, Romand's only humanitarian act was to spare the life of the mistress who had discovered his fraudulence, even as he decided to take the lives of so many other intimates. The heroic identity that Romand had so effortlessly worn was incinerated in the fire he set to cover his crimes. He left his friends to contemplate the dimensions of the dream-drama into which they had been coopted for over 20 years. Interviewed by the writer Emmanuel Carrere (2000) who pursued Romand after his arrest for the murders, Jean Claude

> mentioned no memories, made only distant and abstract allusions to 'the tragedy', none to those who had been his victims, but willingly went on at length about his own suffering, his impossible grief, and the psychoanalytic writings of Lacan, which he had begun reading in the hope of better understanding himself [p. 29].

Mark Hacking: Romand Manqué

Twenty-nine-year-old Mark Hacking also led a double life. He had a devoted wife, a child on the way, a faked university degree, and a bogus letter of acceptance to medical school. One evening his wife, Lori, challenged Mark with questions about their impending relocation to North Carolina, after she had called the medical school that had supposedly accepted Mark. She was told that they had never heard of him. In a tortured confession, Mark disclosed his many lies, leaving Lori overwhelmed, confused, and despairing. As Hacking admitted in court, he went to pack his things, serendipitously came across his gun, returned to the bedroom, and shot his wife. He wondered afterward if he had been dreaming. "I killed her and my unborn child. I put them in the garbage. I can't explain why I did it. I know I wasn't myself that night" (Thompson & Reavy, 2005).

For Hacking, like almost every violent perpetrator I have come upon, it is not that is insisted upon, innocence, but existential absence, and acts for which no self bears witness. Yet in the violent enactment, what can't or won't be known draws the eye repeatedly to its most private parts, showing itself in flagrante, demanding recognition, and a reckoning.

CONCLUDING NOTE: MAKING STORIES MAKE SENSE

I said earlier that what is dissociated is destined to be enacted, if only to make it thinkable. It seems to me that, in the violent act, the awesome matter that previously escaped private symbolization becomes animated and potentially recognizable. Let us say fear, or guilt, or shame, or rage has been dissociated in a particular situation. The person feels only a sense of mounting tension or anxiety as similar past experiences revisit him and eventually coalesce in a cumulative experience "so painful that it threatens to overwhelm [the about-to-be perpetrator] and bring about the death of the self, cause him to lose his mind, his soul, or his sacred honor" (Gilligan, 1996, p. 102). In reply, the person beats someone senseless, rapes her, ends her life. Once performed, the violent act exists in an independent, objective reality. The backdraft of the enactment—whatever is not simultaneously dissociated—makes conscious and intelligible previously formless self-experience. The unformulated, now objectified, can be signified. Aggression now offers a reason to be afraid, or ashamed, or guilty. The effect has produced the illusion of causality. It is an "Aha!" moment of the most profound kind, where what has been elusive is actualized and is made meaningful. Melanie Klein (1952) said, "Violence liberates anxiety" (p. 260). In the process, it bends the unformulated toward a particular narrative explanation, one that lends authority, significance, and momentum to the story of a life.

During Dennis Rader's final statement at his trial, he chose to showboat, speaking of his victims, interrogators, and legal counselors almost as if they were admirers or friends, and of himself as someone who was beginning "a new chapter" in his life. Spectators were suitably aghast at his performance, and the families hurled the expected invectives against Rader: animal, monster, devil, demon. Yet, only months earlier, Rader had been considered righteous enough to be made the president of the local Christ Lutheran Church, and trustworthy enough to lead a troop of Cub Scouts. He had been married for 32 years to the same woman and had raised two children, it appears, without incident. Still, he did not seem sorry to be captured, to be able to share his exploits with the police and, by extension, the public, to "bond" finally with a circle of humanity that had eluded his grasp in all but the few fateful moments of his crimes. He loved to talk and to relive the moments where he stole someone's breath and felt briefly alive himself.

The well-known celebrated killers, like Rader and Bundy and Longo, Hacking, and Romand, scrawl their narratives large on the collective consciousness. Their stories are published, offering an oppurtunity for roundtable discussions, scholarly dissections, barroom chatter, and endless renarrativizing by a second wave of interpreters. Conversely, the majority of violence happens in obscurity, in acts penned by authors known only to their victims, their families, and their friends. They bear a greater than marginal resemblance to more mythic violators, however—these widgets caught in a frozen moment with an internalized object that, like a plastic duck in a carnival shooting gallery, keeps popping up, begging to be silenced. In real time, the violence is precipitated by the comeliness of the prey but enabled by the blind, the psychic shelter in which the hunter hides. I will leave you with one last pathetic story.

CASE FILE

A man follows his adolescent stepdaughter to a play date. As she is returning home from her friend's house, he grabs her from behind, covers her eyes, and pulls her into the bushes. He orally sodomizes her and forces her to fellate him. At the emergency room where her mother takes her after she reports the assault, the girl tells ER personnel that the rape reminded her of a "nightmare" she had been having since childhood: in it a man came into her room and molested her in exactly the same way.

It is perhaps too late for the man perpetuating the nightmare, but maybe we can awaken the girl. No one yet knows how her story will end.

References

Abel, G. G. & Blanchard, E.B. (1974), The role of fantasy in the treatment of sexual deviation. *Arch. Gen. Psychiat.*, 30(4): 467–475.

Albright, D. (1994), Literary and psychological models of the self. In: *The Remembering Self: Construction and Accuracy in the Self-Narrative*, ed. U. Neisser & R. Fivush. London: Cambridge University Press, pp. 19–40.

Allison, R. (1981), Multiple personality and criminal behavior. *Amer. J. Foren. Psychiat.*, 2: 32–38.

Arlow, J.A. (1991), Derivative manifestations of perversions. In: *Perversions and Near Perversions in Clinical Practice: New Psychoanalytic Perspectives*, ed. G.I. Fogel & W.A. Myers. New Haven, CT: Yale University Press, pp. 59–74.

Atwood, G., Orange, D. & Stolorow, R. (2002), Shattered worlds/psychotic States: A post-Cartesian view of the experience of personal annihilation. *Psychoanal. Psychol.*, 19, 281–306.

Bach, S. (1991), On sadomasochistic object relations. In: *Perversions and Near Perversions in Clinical Practice: New Psychoanalytic Perspectives*, ed. G.I. Fogel & W.A. Myers. New Haven, CT: Yale University Press, pp. 75–92.

Baily, W.C. (1976), Use of the death penalty v. outrage at murder. *Crime & Delinq.*, 22: 31–40.

Balint, E. (1963), On being empty of oneself. *Internat. J. PsychoAnal.*, 44: 478–480.

Balint, M. (1968), *The Basic Fault: Therapeutic Aspects of Regression*. Evanston, IL: Northwestern University Press.

Barahal, R., Waterman, J. & Matin, H. (1981), The social cognitive development of abused children. *J. Consult. & Clin. Psychol.*, 49: 508–516.

Barbaree, H.E., Seto, M.C., Serin, R.C., Amos, N.L. & Preston, D.L. (1994), Comparisons between sexual and nonsexual rapist subtypes: Sexual arousal to rape, offense precursors, and offense characteristics. *Crim. Just. & Behav.*, 21: 95–114.

Barrett, D. (1994), Dreaming as a normal model for multiple personality disorder. In: *Dissociation: Clinical and Theoretical Perspectives*, ed. S.J. Lynn & J.W. Rhue. New York: Guilford Press, pp. 123–135.

Barry, S. (2003), Stopping violent offending in New Zealand: Is treatment an option? *New Zealand J. Psychol.*, 32: 92–100.

Becker, E. (1973), *The denial of death.* New York: Free Press.

Benjamin, J. (1995), *Like Subjects, Love Objects: Essays On Recognition And Sexual Difference.* New Haven, CT: Yale University Press.

Bentham, J. (1791), *An Introduction to the Principles Of Morals And Legislation*. New York: Hafner, 1963.

Bettleheim, B. (1989), *The Uses of Enchantment: The Meaning and Importance of Fairytales*. New York: Vintage Books.

Bion, W. (1977), *Second Thoughts: Selected Papers On Psychoanalysis*. New York: Aronson.

Blair, R., Sellars, C., Strickland, I. & Clark, F. (1995), Emotion attributions in the psychopath. *Personality & Individ. Diff.*, 19: 431–437.

Bliss, E. (1986), Sociopathy and criminality. In: *Multiple Personality, Allied Disorders, And Hypnosis*, ed. E. Bliss. New York: Oxford University Press, pp. 175–183.

Blum, H. P. (1991), Sadomasochism in the psychoanalytic process, within and beyond the pleasure principal: Discussion. *J. Amer. Psychoanal. Assn.*, 39: 431–450.

Bollas, C. (1987), *The Shadow of the Object: Psychoanalysis of the Unthought Known.* NY: Columbia University Press.

Bollas, C. (1991). *Cracking Up: The Work of Unconscious Experience.* NY: Farrar, Strauss & Giroux.

Bonne, O., Bachar, E. & Denour, A. K. (1999), Childhood imaginary companionship and mental health in adolescence. *Child Psychiat. & Human Devel.*, 29: 277–287.

Bourke, J. (1999), *An Intimate History of Killing: Face to Face Killing in 20th-Century Warfare.* New York: Basic Books.

Bowlby, J. (1973), *Attachment and Loss, Vol. 2: Separation, Anxiety, and Anger.* New York: Basic Books.

Bradbury, R. (1948), *Fever Dream.* New York: St. Martin's Press, 1987.

Bradford, J. & Smith, S. (1979). Amnesia and Homicide: The Padola case and a study of thirty cases. *Bull. Amer. Acad. Psychiat. & the Law*, 7: 219–231.

Breuer, J. & Freud, S. (1893–1895), Studies on hysteria. *Standard Edition, vol. 2.* London: Hogarth Press, 1955.

Bromberg, P. (2005), Talking with "me" and "not me": A dialogue. *Contemp. Psychoanal.*, 40: 409–464.

———— (2004), One need not be a house to be haunted: On enactment, dissociation, and the dread of "not-me"—A case study. *Psychoanal. Dial.*, 13: 689–709.

———— (2003), Something wicked this way comes: Trauma, dissociation and conflict: The space where psychoanalysis, cognitive science, and neuroscience overlap. *Psychoanal. Psychol.*, 20: 558–574.

———— (1998), *Standing in the Spaces: Essays on Clinical Process, Trauma and Dissociation.* Hillsdale, NJ: The Analytic Press.

Brooks, P. (2001), *Troubling Confessions: Speaking Guilt in Law and Literature.* Chicago, IL: University of Chicago Press.

Brooks, P. (1995). *The melodramatic imagination: Balzac, Henry James, melodrama, and mode of excess.* New Haven, CT: Yale University Press.

Brown, A. P. (2003), From individual to social defences in psychosocial criminology. *Theoret. Criminol.*, 7: 421–437.

Brown, C. (2003), The man who mistook his wife for a deer. *The New York Times Magazine*, February 2, pp. 34–47.

Bruner, J. (1994), The remembered self. In: *The Remembering Self: Construction and Accuracy in the Self Narrative*, ed. Uric Neisser & Robin Fivush. London: Cambridge University Press, pp. 41–54.

Bucci, W. (1997), *Psychoanalysis and Cognitive Science: A Multiple Code Theory.* New York: Guilford Books.

———— (2002), The referential process, consciousness, and the sense of self. *Psychoanal. Inq.*, 22(5), 766–793.

Burgess, A. (1988), *Clockwork Orange.* New York: Norton.

Burgess, A.W., Hartman, C.R. & McCormack, A. (1987), Abused to abuser: Antecedents of socially deviant behaviors. *Amer. J. Psychiat.*, 144: 1431–1436.

————, ————, Ressler, R. K., Douglas, J. E. & McCormack, A. (1986), Sexual homicide: A motivational model. *J. Interpers. Violence*, 1: 251–272.

Carey, B. (2005), "For the worst of us, the diagnosis may be 'evil.'" *The New York Times*, 8 Febuary, sec. f, p 1.

Carlisle, A. C. (2000), The dark side of the serial-killer personality. In: *Serial Killers*, ed. L. Gerdes. San Diego, CA: Greenhaven Press.

Carlson, E. B. & Putnam, F. W. (1986), Development, reliability, and validity of a dissociation scale. *J. Nerv. & Ment. Dis.*, 174: 727–733.

Carrère, E. (2000), *The Adversary: A True Story of Monsterous Deception.* Trans. L. Coverdale. New York: Metropolitan Books.

Carveth, D. L. (2001), The unconscious need for punishment: Expression or evasion of the sense of guilt. *Psychoanal. Studies*, 3: 9–21.

Chasseguet-Smirgel, J. (1991), Sadomasochism in the perversions: Some thoughts on the destruction of reality. *J. Amer. Psychoanal. Assn.*, 39: 399–415.

Cicchetti, D. & Rogosch, F. A. (2001), The impact of child maltreatment and psychopathology on neuroendocrine functioning. *Devel. & Psychopathol.*, 13: 783–804.

———— & White, J. (1990), Emotion and developmental psychopathology. In: *Psychological and Biological Approaches to Emotion*, ed. N. Stein, B. Leventhal & T. Trebasso. Hillsdale, NJ: Lawrence Erlbaum Associates, pp. 359–382.

Cleckley, H. (1941), *The Mask of Sanity: An Attempt to Clarify Some Issues about the So-Called Psychopathic Personality*. Augusta, GA: Mosby, 1988.

Cohen, S. (1989), The reality in fantasy-making. *The Psychoanalytic Study of the Child*, 44: 57–72. New Haven, CT: Yale University Press.

Coleman, R. L. (1988), Solace in a psychotic patient: Delusion, fantasy, imaginary companions, and identification as progressive stages of transitional phenomena. In: *Solace Paradigm: An Eclectic Search for Psychological Immunity*, ed. P.C. Horton, H. Gerwirtz. Madison, CT: International Universities Press, pp. 381–399.

Cooke, D.J. (1997). The Barlinnie Special Unit: The rise and fall of a therapeutic experiment. In: *Therapeutic Communities For Offenders*, ed. E. Cullen, L. Jones & R. Woodward. New York: Wiley, pp. 101–120.

Cooper, A.M. (1991). The unconscious core of perversion. In: *Perversions and Near Perversions in Clinical Practice: New Psychoanalytic Perspectives*, ed. G.I. Fogel & W.A. Myers. New Haven, CT: Yale University Press, pp. 17–35.

Costello, S.J. (2002), *The Pale Criminal: Psychoanalytic Perspectives*. London: Karnac Books.

Crepault, C. & Couture, M. (1980), Men's erotic fantasies. *Arch. Sex. Behav.*, 9: 565–581.

Crimmins, S.M. (1995), Early childhood loss as a predisposing factor in female perpetrated homicides. Ph.D. thesis, 1995. The City University of New York, Criminal Justice.

Cullen, E. (1997), Can a prison be a therapeutic community: The Grendon template. In: *Therapeutic Communities for Offenders*, ed. E. Cullen, L. Jones & R. Woodward. New York: Wiley, pp. 75–100.

Daleiden, E. L., Kaufman, K. L., Hiliker, D. R. & O'Neil, J. N. (1998), The sexual histories and fantasies of youthful males: A comparison of sexual offending, non-sexual offending, and non-offending groups. *Sex. Abuse: A J. Res. & Treatment*, 10: 195–209.

Damasio, A. (1999), *The Feeling of What Happens: Body and Emotion in the Making Of Consciousness*. New York: Harcourt.

———— , Tranel, D. & Damasio, H. (1990), Individuals with sociopathic behaviors caused by frontal damage fail to respond autonomically to social stimuli. *Behav. Brain Res.*, 41: 81–94.

Dateline/NBC (2005, August 12), "31 Years of the BTK Killer," correspondent E. Magnus.

Davies, J.M. & Frawley, M.G. (1994), *Treating The Adult Survivor Of Childhood Sexual Abuse: A Psychoanalytic Perspective*. New York: Basic Books.

DeBellis, M.D. (2001), Developmental traumatology: The psychobiological development of maltreated children and its implications for research, treatment and policy. *Devel. & Psychopathol.*, 13: 539–564.

———— , Keshavan, M. S., Clark, D.B., Casey, B. J., Giedd, J., Boring, A. M., Frustaci, K. & Ryan, N. D. (1999), Developmental traumatology, part II: Brain development. *Biolog. Psychiat.*, 45: 1271–1284.

Dell, P. & Eisenhower, J. W. (1990), Adolescent multiple personality disorder: A preliminary study of eleven cases. *J. Amer. Acad. of Child & Adolesc. Psychiat.*, 29: 359–366.

Della Femina, D., Yeager, C. & Lewis, D. O. (1990), Child abuse: Adolescent records versus adult recall. *Child Abuse & Neglect*, 14: 227–231.

DeMause, L. (2002), The childhood origins of terrorism. *J. Psychohist.*, 29: 340–348.

Dentan, R.K. (1995), Bad day at Bukit Pekan. *Amer. Anthropolog.*, 97: 225–231.

Depue, R.L. & Scindehette, S. (2005), *Between Good and Evil: A Master Profiler's Hunt for Society's Most Violent Predators*. New York: Warner Books.

Dershowitz, A. (1995), *The Abuse Excuse: Cop Outs, Sob Stories, and Other Evasions of Responsibility*. Boston, MA: Little, Brown.

Deutsch, H. (1955), The imposter: Contributions to ego psychology of a type of psychopath. *Psychoanal. Quart.*, 24: 483–505.

Diamond, D. (1989), Father-daughter incest: Unconscious fantasy and social fact. *Psychoanal. Psychol.*, 6: 421–437.

Dietz, P.E., Hazelwood, R. R. & Warren, J. (1990), The sexually sadistic criminal and his offenses. *Bull. Amer. Acad. Psychiat. & Law*, 18: 163–178.

Dodge, K. A. (1990), The structure and function of reactive and proactive aggression. In: *The Development of Childhood Aggression*, ed. D.J. Pepler & K.H. Rubin. Hillsdale, NJ: Lawrence Erlbaum Associates, pp. 201–218.

———— & Newman, J.P. (1981), Biased decision-making processes in aggressive boys. *J. Abn. Psychol.*, 90: 375–379.

———— & Somberg, D.R. (1987), Hostile attributional biases among aggressive boys are exacerbated under conditions of threat to the self. *Child Devel.*, 58: 213–224.

Duncan, M.G. (1994), In slime and darkness: The metaphor of filth in criminal justice. *Tulane Law Review*, 68: 725–802.

Eigen J.P. (2003), *Unconscious Crime: Mental Absence and Criminal Responsibility in Victorian London*. Baltimore, MD: The Johns Hopkins University Press.

Elin, M. (1995), A developmental model for trauma. In: *Dissociative Identity Disorder*, ed. L. Cohen, J. Berzoff & M. Elin. Northvale, NJ: Aronson, pp. 223–259.

Ellenberger, H. (1970), *The Discovery of the Unconscious: The History and Evolution of Dynamic Psychiatry*. New York: Basic Books.

Enders, J. (1999), *The Medieval Theatre of Cruelty: Rhetoric, Memory, Violence*. Ithaca, New York: Cornell University Press.

English, D. J., Widom, C. S. & Brandford, C. (2001), *Childhood Victimization and Delinquency, Adult Criminality, and Violent Criminal Behavior: A Replication and Extension*. Washington, DC: U.S. National Institute of Justice.

Fagan, J. & McMahon, P. (1984), Incipient multiple personality in children: Four cases. *J. Nerv. Ment. Dis.*, 172: 26–36.

Fairbairn, W. R. D. (1940), Schizoid factors in the personality. *Psychoanalytic Studies of the Personality*, London: Tavistock Press, pp. 3–27, 1952.

——— (1952), *An Object Relations Theory of the Personality*. New York: Basic Books.

Fenichel, O. (1945), *The Psychoanalytic Theory of Neurosis*. New York: Norton.

Ferenczi, S. (1927), The problem of the termination of psychoanalysis. In: *Final Contributions to the Problems and Methods of Psycho-Analysis*, ed. M. Balint (trans. E. Mosbacher). London: Hogarth Press, pp. 77–86.

——— (1933), Confusion of tongues between adults and the child. In: *Final Contributions to the Problems and Methods of Psycho-Analysis*, ed. M. Balint (trans. E. Mosbacher). London: Karnac Books, 1980, pp. 156–167.

Finkel, M. (2003), *True Story*. New York: Harper Collins Publishers.

Fisher, C. & Dement, W. (1963), Studies on the psychopathology of sleep and dreams. *Amer. J. Psychiat.*, 119: 1160–1168.

Flynn, K. (2002), "Suspect in rape absorbed pain and inflicted it." *The New York Times*, 7 December sec. A, p.1 Metropolitan Desk.

Fonagy, P., Gergely, G., Jurist, E. L. & Target, M. (2002), *Affect Regulation, Mentalization, and the Development of the Self*. New York: Other Press.

Foucault, M. (1977), *Discipline and Punish: The Birth of the Prison 1st Edition*. New York: Pantheon Books.

Freedman, C. M., Low, S. M., Markman, H. J. & Stanley, S. M. (2002), Equipping couples with the tools to cope with predictable and unpredictable crisis events: The PREP program. *Internat. J. Emergency Ment. Health*, 4: 49–56.

Freud, S. (1893), Charcot. *Standard Edition*, 3. London: Hogarth Press, 1962.

——— (1896), The aetiology of hysteria. *Standard Edition*, 3:191–221. London: Hogarth Press, 1962.

——— (1900), The interpretation of dreams. *Standard Edition*, 4: 1–338. London: Hogarth Press, 1952.

——— (1905), Three essays on the theory of sexuality. *Standard Edition*, 7: 130–243. London: Hogarth Press, 1953.

Friedman, R. A. (2002), "Behavior: Like drugs, talk therapy can change brain chemistry." *The New York Times*, 27 August sec. F, p.5, col.2, Health & Fitness.

——— (1913). Totem and Taboo, *Standard Edition*, 13: 1–161. London: Hogarth Press, 1955.

——— (1916), Some character types met with in psychoanalytic work. *Standard Edition*, 14: 311–333. London: Hogarth Press, 1957.

——— (1919), A child is being beaten. *Standard Edition*, 17: 179–204. London: Hogarth Press, 1955.

——— (1923), The ego and the id. *Standard Edition*, 19: 12–66. London: Hogarth Press, 1961.

——— (1926), Inhibitions, Symptoms and Anxiety. *Standard Edition*, 20: 87–175. London: Hogarth Press, 1959.

——— (1930), Civilization and its discontents. *Standard Edition*, 21: 64–145. London: Hogarth Press, 1961.

——— (1940), An outline of psycho-analysis. *Standard Edition*, 23: 144–207. London: Hogarth Press, 1964.

Gacono, C. B. & Meloy, J. R. (1994), The Rorschach Assessment of Aggressive and Psychopathic Personalities. Hillsdale, NJ: Lawrence Erlbaum Associates, Inc.

Gadd, D. (2004), Evidence-led policy or policy-led evidence: Cognitive-behavioural programmes for men who are violent towards women. *Crim. Just.*, 4: 173–197.

Geberth, V.J. (1996), *Practical Homicide Investigation: Tactics, Procedures, and Forensic Techniques*, 3rd Ed. Boca Raton, FL: CRC Press.

Gerrard, N. (2003, December 21). Holly and Jessica—We'll never know. *Observer*.

Gilligan, J. (1996), *Violence: Our Deadly Epidemic and Its Causes*. New York: Putnam's Sons.

Gillstrom, B. J. & Hare, R. D. (1988), Language related hand gestures in psychopaths. *J. Personality Dis.*, 2: 21–27.

Goldberg, C. (2000), *The Evil We Do: The Psychoanalysis of Destructive People*. Amherst, New York: Prometheus Books.

Goldsmith, R. E., Barlow, M. R. & Freyd, J. J. (2004), Knowing and not knowing about trauma: Implications for therapy. *Psychother. Theory, Res., Prac., Training*, 41: 448–463.

Gottlieb, R. M. (1997), Does the mind fall apart in multiple personality disorder? Some proposals based on a psychoanalytic case. *J. Amer. Psychoanal. Assn.*, 45: 907–932.

Grady, D. (1998), "Studies of Schizophrenia Vindicate Psychotherapy." *The New York Times*, 20 January, sect. F; P. 9, Col. 1, Science Desk; Health Page.

Grand, S. (2000), *The reproduction of evil: A clinical and cultural perspective*. Hillsdale, NJ: The Analytic Press.

Gray, N. S., Watt, A., Hassan, S. & MacCulloch, M. J. (2003), Behavioral indicators of sadistic sexual murder predict the presence of sadistic sexual fantasy in a normative sample. *J. Interpers. Violence*, 18: 1018–1035.

Grinker, R. & Spiegel, J.P. (1963), *Men Under Stress*. New York: McGraw-Hill.

Grotstein, J.S. (1990), Nothingness, meaninglessness, chaos, and the "black hole" II. *Contemp. Psychoanal.*, 26: 377–398.

———— (1995), Orphans of the "real": I. Some modern and postmodern perspectives on the neuro-biological and psychosocial dimensions of psychosis and other primitive mental disorders. *Bull. Menninger Clin.*, 59: 287–312.

———— (1997a), Integrating one-person and two-person psychologies: Autochthony and alterity in counterpoint. *Psychoanal. Psychol.*, 66: 403–430.

———— (1997b), Internal objects or chimerical monsters?: The demonic third forms of the internal world. *J. Anal. Psychol.*, 42: 47–80.

———— (2001), Some reflections on the psychodynamic theory of motivation: Toward a theory of "Entelechy," *Psychoanal. Inq.*, 21: 572–586.

Guay, J., Prouix, J., Cusson, M., & Ouimet, M. (2001),. Victim-choice polymorphia among serious sex offenders. *Arch. Sex. Behav.*, 30: 521–533.

Guntrip, H. (1969), *Schizoid Phenomena, Object Relations And The Self*. New York: Basic Books.

HBO (2003, July 23). *The Iceman and the psychiatrist*. HBO documentary films, Arthur Ginsberg (director).

Haga, C. (2003), "Charges dropped in Dalquist case." *Minneapolis Star Tribune*, 1 February, Metro News, p. A1.

Hagen, M. A.: (1997), *Whores of the Court: The Fraud of Psychiatric Testimony and the Rape of American Justice*. New York: Regan Books.

Halttunen, K. (1998), *Murder Most Foul: The Killer and the American Gothic Imagination*. Cambridge, MA: Harvard University Press.

Hare, R.D. (1993), *Without Conscience: The Disturbing World of the Psychopaths Among Us*. New York: Guilford Press.

———— & Jutai, J. (1988), Psychopathy and cerebral asymmetry in semantic processing. *Personality & Individ. Differences*, 9: 329–337.

Havill, A. (2001), *Born Evil: A True Story Of Cannibalism And Serial Murder*. New York: St. Martin's True Crime Classics.

Harlow, C.W. (1999), *Prior Abuse Reported by Inmates and Probationers*. Washington, DC: Bureau of Justice Statistics.

Heidigger, M. (1927), *Being and Time*, trans. J. Macquarrie & E. Robinson. New York: Harper, 1962.

Henry, V. E. (2004), *Death Work: Police, Trauma, and the Psychology of Survival*. New York: Oxford University Press.

Herman, J.L. (1992), *Trauma and Recovery: The Aftermath of Violence-From Domestic Abuse to Political Terror*. New York: Basic Books.

———— & van der Kolk, B.A. (1987), Traumatic antecedents of borderline personality disorder. In: *Psychological Trauma*, ed. B.A. van der Kolk. Washington, DC: American Psychiatric Press, 111–126.

Hermans, H.J.M. (1996), Voicing the self: From information processing to dialogic interchange. *Psychol. Bull.*, 119: 31–50.

———— (1999), The polyphony of the mind: A multi-voiced and dialogic self. In: *The Plural Self*, ed. J. Rowen & M. Cooper. Newbury Park, CA: Sage. pp. 107–131.

Holcomb, W. & Daniel, A. (1968), Homicide without an apparent motive. *Behav. Sci. & the Law*, 6: 429–437.

Hopkins, J. (1991), Failure of the holding relationship: Some effects of physical rejection on the child's attachment and inner experience. In: *Attachment Across the Life Cycle*, ed. C.M. Parkes, J. Stevenson-Hinde & P. Marris. New York: Routledge, 187–198.

Howell, E.F. (1996), Dissociation in masochism and sadism. *Contemp. Psychoanal.*, 32: 427–453.

—————— (1997), Masochism: A bridge to the other side of abuse. *Dissociation*, 10: 240–245.

Howes, C. & Espinoza, M.P. (1985), The consequences of child abuse for the formation of relationships with peers. *Child Abuse & Neglect*, 9: 397–404.

Hsu, B., Kling, A., Kessler, C. Knapke, K., Diefenbach, P. & Elias, J. E. (1994), Gender differences in sexual fantasy and behavior in a college population: A ten-year replication. *J. Sex & Marital Therapy*, 20: 103–118.

Hyatt-Williams, A. (1998), *Cruelty, Violence and Murder: Understanding the Criminal Mind*. Northvale, NJ: Aronson.

Janet, P. (1889), *L'Automatisme Psychologique*. Paris: Alcan.

Jutai, J., Hare, R. D. & Connolly, J. F. (1987), Psychopathy and event related brain potentials (ERPs) associated with attention to speech stimuli. *Personality & Individual Differences*, 8: 175–184.

Kafka, F. (1912), The judgment. In: *Selected Short Stories*, trans. W. Muir & E. Muir. New York: Modern Library.

Karstedt, S. (2002), Emotions and criminal justice. *Theoret. Criminol.*, 6: 299–317.

Kassin, S. M. (1997), The psychology of confession evidence. *Amer. Psycholog.*, 52: 221–233.

Kermode, F. (1980), Secrets and narrative sequence. *Crit. Inq.*, 7: 83–101.

Kernberg, O.F. (1992), *Aggression in Personality Disorders and Perversions*. New Haven, CT: Yale University Press.

—————— (1998), The psychotherapeutic management of psychopathic, narcissistic and paranoid transferences. In: *Psychopathy: Antisocial, Criminal, and Violent Behavior*, ed. T. Millon, E. Simonsen, M. Birket-Smith & R.D. Davis. New York: Guilford Press, pp. 372–392.

Keyes, D. (1981), *The Minds of Billy Milligan*. New York: Random House.

Khan, M. M. R. (1979), *Alienation in Perversion*. New York: International Universities Press.

Kirkland v. State, 166 Ga. App. 478, 304 2d 561, 1983.

Klein, B. R. (1985), A child's imaginary companion: A transitional self. *Clin. Soc. Work*, 13: 272–282.

Klein, M. (1921), The development of a child. In: *The Writings of Melanie Klein, Vol. I: Love, Guilt and Reparation and Other Works 1921–1945*. New York: Free Press, 1975, pp. 1–53.

—————— (1933), The early development of conscience in the child. In: *The Writings of Melanie Klein, Vol. I: Love, Guilt and Reparation and Other Works 1921–1945*. New York: Free Press, 1975, 248–257.

—————— (1935), A contribution to the psychogenesis of manic depressive states. In: *The Writings of Melanie Klein, Vol. I, Love, Guilt and Reparation and Other Works, 1921–1945*. New York: Free Press, 1975, pp. 262–289.

—————— (1946), Notes on some schizoid mechanisms. *Int.J. Psychoanal.*, 27: 99–110.

—————— (1952), *Developments in Psychoanalysis*. London: Hogarth Press.

—————— (1975), *Envy and Gratitude and Other Works, 1946–1963*. New York: Free Press.

Knight, R. A. & Prentky, R. A. (1990), Classifying sexual offenders: The development and corroboration of taxonomic models. In: *The Handbook of Sexual Assault: Issues, Theories, and Treatment of The Offender*, ed. W. L. Marshall, D. R. Laws, & H. E. Barbaree. New York: Plenum Press, pp. 23–52.

Krafft-Ebing, R. (1886), *Psychpathia Sexualis*. New York: Arcade, 1998.

Kruttschnit, C. & Dornfeld, M. (1992), Will they tell: Assessing reports of family violence. *J. Res. Crime & Delinquency*, 29: 136–147.

Krystal, H. (1988), *Integration and Self Healing: Affect, Trauma, Alexithymia*. Hillsdale, NJ: The Analytic Press.

Lachker, J. (2002), The psychological make-up of a suicide bomber. *J. Psychohistory*, 29: 349–367.

Lachmann, F.M. (2000), *Transforming Aggression: Psychotherapy with the Difficult-to-Treat Patient*. Northvale, NJ: Aronson.

Laing, R.D. (1959), *The Divided Self: An Existential Study In Sanity And Madness*. London: Penguin Books, 1990.

Lalumière, M. L., Quinsey, V. L., Harris, G. T., Rice, M. E. & Trautrimas, C. (2003), Are rapists differentially aroused by coercive sex in phallometric assessments? *Annals of the New York Academy of Sciences*, 989: 211–224.

Lansky, M.R. (2003), The incompatible idea revisited: The oftinvisible ego-ideal and shame dynamics. *Amer. J. Psychoanal.*, 63: 365–376.

Lefer, L. (1984), The fine edge of violence. *J. Amer. Acad. Psychoanal.*, 12: 253–268.

Leitenberg, H. & Henning, K. (1995), Sexual fantasy. *Psycholog. Bull.*, 117: 469–496.

Lejeune, Robert (1977), The management of a mugging. *Urban Life*, 6: 123–148.

Leman-Langlois, S. (2003), The myopic panopticon: The social consequences of policing through the lens. *Policing and Society*, 13: 43–58.

Lempert, R. 1983). The effects of executions on homicides: A new look in an old light. *Crime and deling.*, 29: 88–136.

Lewis, D. O. (1992), From abuse to violence: Psychophysiological consequences of maltreatment. *J. Amer. Acad. Child & Adolesc. Psychiat.*, 31: 383–391.

——— (1998), *Guilty by Reason of Insanity: A Psychiatrist Explores the Minds of Serial Killers.* New York: Fawcett-Columbine.

——— Augur, C., Swica, Y., Pincus, J.H. & Lewis, M. (1997), The objective documentation of child abuse and dissociation in twelve murderers with Dissociative Identity Disorder. *Amer. J. Psychiat.*, 154: 1703–1710.

——— & Bard, J. S. (1991), Multiple personality and forensic issues. *Psychiat. Clin. of North Amer.*, 14: 741–756.

Lifton, R.J. (1976), *The Life of the Self.* New York: Simon and Schuster.

——— (1983), *The Broken Connection: On Death and the Continuity of Life.* New York: Basic Books.

——— (1986), *The Nazi Doctors: Medical Killing and the Psychology of Genocide.* New York: Basic Books.

Lion, J. & Leaff, L. (1973), On the hazards of assessing character pathology in an outpatient setting. *Psychiat. Quart.*, 47: 104–109.

Lion, J. & Bach-y-Rita, G. (1970), Group psychotherapy with violent patients. *Internat. J. Group Psychother.*, 20: 185–191.

Litman, R.E. (1997), Bondage and sadomasochism. In: *Sexual Dynamics of Antisocial Behavior*, ed. L.B. Schlesinger & E. Revitch. Springfield, IL: Thomas, pp. 252–270.

Litowitz, B. E. (1998), An expanded developmental line for negation: Rejection, refusal, denial. *J. Amer. Psychoanal. Assn.*, 46: 121–148.

Ludwig, A. (1983), The psychobiological functions of dissociation. *Amer. J. Clin. Hyp.*, 26: 93–99.

Lykken, D.T. (1955), *A Study of Anxiety in the Sociopathic Personality.* Unpublished doctoral dissertation, University of Minnesota. Ann Arbor, MI: University Microfilms, 1955, no. 55–944.

——— (1957), A study of anxiety in the sociopathic personality. *J. Abnorm. & Soc. Psycholog.*, 55: 6–10.

Lynn, S. J., Pintar, J., Stafford, J., Marmelstein, L. & Lock, T. (1998), Rendering the implausible plausible: Narrative, construction, suggestion and memory. In: *Believed-In Imaginings: The Narrative Construction of Reality*, ed. J. de Rivera & T.R. Sarbin. Washington, DC: American Psychological Association.

Mahler, M.S. (1968), *On Human Symbiosis and the Vicissitudes of Individuation.* New York: International Universities Press.

Main, M. & George, C. (1985), Responses of abused and disadvantaged toddlers to distress in age-mates: A study in the day care center. *Develop. Psychol.*, 21: 407–412.

———, Kaplan, N. & Cassidy, J. (1985), Security in infancy, childhood and adulthood: A move to the level of representation. In: *Growing Points of Attachment: Theory and Research*, ed. I. Bretherton & E. Waters. Monogr. Society for Research in Child Development, Serial no. 209, Volume 50, Nos. 1–2, pp. 66–104.

Malone, K.R. (1996), Rape prevention. *J. Psychoanal. Culture & Society*, 1: 162–165.

Marcus, B. (1989), Incest and the borderline syndrome: The mediating role of identity. *Psychoanal. Psychol.*, 6: 199–215.

Marshall, W. L. & Marshall, L. E. (2000), The origins of sexual offending. *Trauma, Violence & Abuse*, 1: 250–263.

Maruna, S., Matravers, A. & King, A. (2004), Disowning our shadow: A psychoanalytic approach to understanding punitive public attitudes. *Deviant Behav.*, 25: 277–299.

Masson, J.M. (1984), *The Assault on Truth: Freud's Suppression of the Seduction Theory.* New York: Farrar, Strauss & Giroux.

Mattingly, C. (1998), *Healing Dramas and Clinical Plots: The Narrative Structure of Experience.* Cambridge: Cambridge University Press.

McAdams, D. (2003), Identity and the life story. In: *Autobiographical Memory and the Construction of a Narrative Self*, ed. R. Fivish & C. Haden. Mahwah, N.J.: Lawrence Erlbaum Associates, pp. 187–207.

McCracken, G. (1988), *The Long Interview: Series on Qualitative Methods, Vol. 13*, Newbury Park, CA: Sage.

McDougall, Joyce (1972), Primal scene and sexual perversion. *Int. J. Psycho-Anal.*, 53: 371–384.

——— (1978), Primitive communications and the use of the countertransference. *Contemp. Psychoanal.*, 14: 173–209.

McKinney, M. (2005), Brainerd man pleads guilty in Erika Dalquist's death. Minneapolis Star Tribune, 14 October Metro News, p. 7B.

McWilliams, N. (1994), *Psychoanalytic Diagnosis: Understanding Personality Structure in the Clinical Process*. New York: Guilford Press.

Meloy, J.R. (1997a), *The Psychopathic Mind*. Northvale, NJ: Aronson.

——— (1997b), The psychology of wickedness: Psychopathy and sadism. *Psychiatric Ann.*, 27: 630–637.

——— (1998), *Violent Attachments*. Northvale, NJ: Aronson.

——— (2000), The nature and dynamics of sexual homicide: An integrative review. *Aggress. & Violent Behav.* 5: 1–22.

Meltzer, D. (1975), Adhesive identification. *Contemp. Psychoanal.*, 11: 289–310.

——— (1992), *The Claustrum: An Investigation of Claustrophobic Phenomena*. Roland Harris Trust library #15, Great Britain: The Clunie Press.

Melzack, R. (1973), *The puzzle of pain*. New York: Basic Books.

Merriam, B. (1998), To find a voice: Art therapy in a women's prison. *Women & Therapy*, 21: 157–171.

Meyers, H.C. (1991), Perversion in fantasy and furtive enactments. In: *Perversions and Near Perversions in Clinical Practice: New Psychoanalytic Perspectives*, ed. G.I. Fogel & W.A. Myers. New Haven, CT: Yale University Press, pp. 93–108.

Miller, S. B. (1989), Shame as an impetus to the creation of conscience. *Int. J. PsychoAnal.*, 70: 231–243.

Miller, S. J. (2003), Analytic gains and anxiety tolerance: Punishment fantasies and the analysis of superego resistance revisted. *Psychoanal. Psychol.*, 20: 4–17.

Millon, T., Simonsen, E., Birket-Smith, M. & Davis, R.D. (1998), *Psychopathy: Antisocial, Criminal, and Violent Behavior*. New York: The Guilford Press.

Mills, J. (2003), Lacan on paranoiac knowledge. *Psychoanal. Psychol.*, 20: 30–51.

Minneapolis Star, February 4, 2003. Brainerd man leads police to body.

Mitrani, J. L. (1994), On adhesive object relations. *Contemp. Psychoanal.*, 30: 348–366.

Modell, A. H. (2003), *Imagination and the Meaningful Brain*. Cambridge, MA: MIT Press.

Morrison, H. & Goldberg, H. (2004), *My Life Among the Serial Killers: Inside the Minds of the World's Most Notorious Murderers*. New York: Avon Books.

Moskowitz, A.K. (2004a), Dissociative pathways to homicide: Clinical and forensic implications. *J. Trauma & Dissociation*, 5: 5–32.

——— (2004b), Dissociation and violence: A review of the literature. *Trauma, Violence & Abuse*, 5: 21–46.

Muller, R. (2000), When a patient has no story to tell: Alexithymia. *Psychiat. Times*, 17: 7.

O'Connell, B.A. (1960), Amnesia and Homicide. *Brit. J. Delinq.*, 10: 262–276.

Ogden, T. (1989), *The Primitive Edge of Experience*. Northvale, NJ: Aronson.

Ohio v. Grimsley, 3 Ohio App. 3rd 265, 444 N.E. 2d 1071, 1982.

Orwell, G. (1949), *Nineteen Eighty Four*. San Diego, CA: Harcourt Brace Jovanovich.

Pardes, H. (1986), Neuroscience and psychiatry: Marriage or co-existence? *Am. J. Psychiat.*, 143: 1205–1212.

Parker, M. (2003), Doing time: A group analytic perspective on the emotional experience of time in a men's prison. *Group Anal.*, 36: 169–181.

Partwatiker, S. D., Holcomb, W. R. & Menninger, K. A. (1985), The detection of malingered amnesia in accused murderers. *Bull. Amer. Acad. Psychiat. & the Law*, 13: 97–103.

Patrick, C., Bradley, M. & Lang, P. (1993), Emotion in the criminal psychopath: Startle reflex modulation. *J. Abn. Psychol.*, 102: 82–92.

——— Cuthbert, B. N. & Lang, P. J. (1994), Emotion in the criminal psychopath: Fear image processing. *J. Abn. Psychol.*, 103: 523–534.

Person, E. S., Terestman, N., Wayne, A. M., Goldberg, E. L. & Salvadori, C. (1989), Gender differences in sexual behaviors and fantasies in a college population. *J. Sex & Marital Ther.*, 15: 187–198.

Polaschek, D. L. L. & Dixon, B. G. (2001), The violence prevention project: The development and evaluation of a treatment programme for violent offenders. *Psychol., Crime and Law*, 7: 1–23.

Porter, S., Birt, A. R., Yuille, J. C. & Herve, H. F. (2001), Memory for murder: A psychological perspective on dissociative amnesia in legal contexts. *Internat. J. Law & Psychiat.*, 24: 23–42.

Prentky, R., Burgess, A., Rokous, F., Lee, A., Hartman, C. Ressler, R. & Douglas, J. (1989), The presumed role of fantasy in serial sexual homicide. *Amer. J. Psychiat.*, 146: 887–891.

Pye, E. (1995), Memory and imagination: Placing imagination in the therapy of individuals with incest memories. In: *Sexual Abuse Recalled: Treating Trauma in the Era Of The Recovered Memory Debate*, ed. J.L. Albert. Northvale, NJ: Aronson, pp. 155–184.

Quay, H. C. (1987), Intelligence. In: *Handbook of Juvenile Delinquency*, ed. H. C. Quay. New York: Wiley, pp. 106–117.

Radden, J. (1996), *Divided Minds and Successive Selves: Ethical Issues in Disorders of Identity and Personality*. Cambridge, MA: MIT Press.

Radwin, J. O. (1991), The multiple personality disorder: Has this trendy alibi lost its way? Law & Psychol. Rev., 15: 351–373.

Raines, A. O'Brien, M. Smiley, N., Scerbo, A. & Chan, C. (1990), Reduced lateralization in verbal dichotic listening in adolescent psychopaths. *J. Abn. Psychol.*, 99: 272–277.

────── (1993), *The Psychopathology of Crime: Criminal Behavior as a Clinical Disorder*. San Diego, CA: Academic Press.

Rank, O. (1941), *Beyond Psychology*. New York: Dover Publications.

────── (1971), *The Double: A Psychoanalytic Study*. NC: University of North Carolina Press.

Reik, T. (1945), *The Unknown Murderer*. New York: Prentice-Hall. Inc.

Reiser, M.F. (1984), *Mind, Brain, Body: Toward a Convergence of Psychoanalysis and Neurobiology*. New York: Basic Books.

Ressler, R. K. & Schactman, T. (1992), *Whoever Fights Monsters*. New York: St. Martin's Paperbacks.

────── Burgess, A. W. & Douglas, J. E. (1992), *Sexual Homicide: Patterns and Motives*. New York: Free Press.

──────, ──────, ──────, Hartman, C. R. & D'Agostino, R. B. (1986), Sexual killers and their victims. *J. Interpers. Violence*, 1: 288–308.

──────, ──────, Hartman, C. R., Douglas, J. E. & McCormack, A. (1986). Murderers who rape and mutilate. *J. Interpers. Violence*, 1: 273–287.

Revitch, E. & Schlesinger, L. B. (1989), *Sex Murder and Sex Aggression.: Phenomenology, Psychopathology, Psychodynamics and Prognosis*. Springfield, IL: Thomas.

Rhodes, R. (1999), *Why They Kill: The Discoveries of a Maverick Criminologist*. New York: Knopf.

Rhue, J. W. & Lynn, S. J. (1987, Fantasy proneness: Developmental antecedents. *J. Personality*, 55: 121–137.

Richards, H. (1998), Evil Intent: Violence and disorders of the will. In: *Psychopathy: Antisocial, Criminal and Violent Behavior*, ed. T. Millon, E. Simonsen, M. Birket-Smith & R. Davis. New York: Guilford Press, pp. 69–94.

Ricoeur, P. (1967), *The Symbolism of Evil*. New York: Harper & Row.

────── (1980), Narrative Time, Crit. Inq., 7: 169–190.

Rieber, R. W. & Vetter, H. (1994), The language of the psychopath. *J. Psycholing. Res.*, 23: 1–28.

Rivard, J. M., Dietz, P., Martell, D. & Widowski, M. (2002), Acute dissociative responses in law enforcement officers involved in critical shooting incidents: The clinical and forensic implications. *J. Forens. Scis.*, 47: 1093–1100.

Saks, E. R. (1997), *Jekyll on Trial*. New York: New York University Press.

Sarbin, T. R. (1989), Emotions as narrative emplotments. In: *Entering the Circle: Hermaneutic Investigations in Psychology*, ed. M. J. Packer and R. B. Addison. New York: State University of New York Press, pp. 185–201.

────── (1995), A narrative approach to "repressed memories." *J. Narr. & Pers. Hist.*, 5: 51–66.

Rokach, A., Nutbrown, V. & Nexhipi, G. (1989), Content analysis of erotic imagery: Sex offenders and non-sex offenders. *Internat. J. Offender Ther. & Compara. Criminol.*, 32: 107–122.

Satten, J., Menninger, K., Rosen, I. & Mayman, M. (1960), Murder without apparent motive: A study in personality organization. *Amer. J. Psychiat.*, 117: 48–53.

Schafer, R. (1980), Narration in the psychoanalytic dialogue. *Crit. Inq.*, 7: 29–53.

Schlesinger, L. B. & Revitch, E. (1997), *Sexual Dynamics of Antisocial Behaviors*, 2nd ed. Spingfield: IL: Thomas.

────── (2000), Serial homicide: Sadism, fantasy and a compulsion to kill. In: *Serial offenders: Current thought, recent findings*, ed. L. B. Schlesinger. New York: CRC Press, pp. 3–22.

────── (2001), The potential sex murderer: Ominous signs, risk assessment. *J. Threat Assess.*, 1: 47–72.

Searles, H. F. (1960), *The Non-Human Environment*. New York: Internat. Univ. Press.

Sebold, A. (1999), *Lucky*. New York: Scribner.

Shengold, L. (1989), *Soul Murder: The Effects of Childhood Abuse and Deprivation*. New York: Ballentine Books.

────── (1999), *Soul Murder Revisited: Thoughts About Therapy, Hate, Love, and Memory*. New Haven, CT: Yale University Press.

Siegel, D.J. (1996), Cognition, memory, and dissociation. *Child & Adolesc. Clin. North Amer.*, 5: 509–536.

Silverstein, J. L. (1994), Power and sexuality: Influence of early object relations. *Psychoanal. Psychol.*, 11: 33–46.

Sizemore, C. & Pittilo, E. (1977), *I'm Eve*. New York: Doubleday.

Socarides, C.W. (1973), Sexual perversion and the fear of engulfment. *Internat. J. Psychoanal. Psychother.*, 2: 432–448.

Solnit, A. J. & Kris, M. (1967), Trauma and infantile experiences. In: *Psychic Trauma* , ed. S. S. Furst. NY: Basic Books, pp. 175–220.

Snow, M. S., Beckman, D. & Brack, G. (1996), Results of the dissociative experiences scale in a jail population. *Dissociation*, 9: 98–103.

State v. Badger, 551 A. 2d 207, NJ, 1988.

State v. Darnell, 47 Or. App. 161, 614 P. 2d 120, 1980.

State v. Rodrigues, 679 p. 2nd 615 Hawaii, 1984.

Stein, A. (2000), *Dissociation and Crime: Abuse, Mental Illness and Crime in the Lives of Incarcerated Men*. Dissertation Abstracts International, A Humanities and Social Sciences, 61(4–A), 1626, US: University Microfilms International.

—— (2001), Murder and memory. *Contemp. Psychoanal.*, 37: 443–451.

—— (2002), Sensation seeking. In: *Encyclopedia of Crime and Punishment, Vol. 4*, ed. D. Levinson. Newbury, CA: Sage, pp. 1467–1470.

—— (2003), Dreaming while awake: The use of trance to bypass threat. *Contemp. Psychoanal.*, 39: 179–197.

—— (2004), Fantasy, fusion, and sexual homicide. *Contemp. Psychoanal.*, 40: 495–517.

—— & Lewis, D.O. (1992), Discovering abuse: Insights from a follow-up study of delinquents. *Child Abuse & Neglect*, 16: 523–531.

Steinberg, M. & Schnall, M. (2000), *The Stranger in the Mirror: Dissociation-The Hidden Epidemic*. New York: Cliff Street Books.

Stern, D. B. (1997a), Dissociation and constructivism. In: *Memories of Sexual Betrayal: Truth, Fantasy, Repression and Dissociation*. ed. R.B. Gartner. Northvale, NJ: Aronson.

—— (1997b), *Unformulated Experience: From Dissociation to Imagination in Psychoanalysis*. Hillsdale, NJ: The Analytic Press.

—— (2003), The fusion of horizons: Dissociation, enactment, and understanding. *Psychoanal. Dial.*, 13: 843–873.

—— (2004), The eye sees itself: Dissociation, enactment, and achievement of conflict. *Contemp. Psychoanal.*, 40: 197–237.

Stevenson, R.L. (1896), *The Strange Case of Dr. Jekyll and Mr. Hyde*. Chicago: M.A. Donahue & Co.

Stoller, R.J. (1973), *Splitting: A Case of Female Masculinity*. New York: Quadrangle.

—— (1976), *Perversion: The Erotic Form of Hatred*. Cambridge, MA: Harvester Press.

—— (1985), *Observing the Erotic Imagination*. New Haven, CT: Yale University Press.

—— (1986), *Sexual Excitement: Dynamics of Erotic Life*. Washington, DC: American Psychiatric Press.

Stolorow, R.D. (2003), Trauma and temporality. *Psychoanal. Psychol.*, 20: 158–161.

Stone, A. A. (1993), Murder with no apparent motive. *J. Psychiat. & Law*, 21: 175–189.

Stone, M. H. (1998), Sadistic personalities in murderers. In: *Psychopathy: Antisocial, Criminal and Violent Behavior*, ed. T. Millon, E. Simonsen, M. Birket-Smith & R.D. Davis. New York: Guilford Press, 346–355.

Straker, G. & Jacobson, R. (1981), Aggression, emotional maladjustment, and empathy in the abused child. *Development. Psychol.*, 17: 762–765.

Strasburger, L. (1986), Treatment of antisocial syndromes: The therapist's feelings. In: *Unmasking the Psychopath*, ed. W. Reid, D. Dorr, J. Walker, & J. Bonner. New York: Norton, pp. 191–207.

Sullivan, H.S. (1949), The theory of anxiety and the nature of psychotherapy. *Psychiatry*, 12: 3–12.

—— (1953a), *Conceptions of Modern Psychiatry*. New York: Norton.

—— (1953b), *The Interpersonal Theory of Psychiatry*. New York: W.W. Norton.

—— (1956), *Clinical Studies in Psychiatry*. New York: Norton.

—— (1962), *Schizophrenia as a Human Process*. New York: Norton.

—— (1970), *The Psychiatric Interview*. New York: Norton.

—— (1972), *Personal Psychopathology: Early Formulations*. New York: Norton.

Suskind, P. (1991), *Perfume*. New York: Simon & Schuster.

Swihart, G., Yuille, J. & Porter, S. (1999), The role of state dependent memory in "red-outs." *Internat. J. Law & Psychiat.*, 22: 199–212.

Tanay, E. with Freeman, L. (1976), *The Murderers*. Indianapolis, IN: Bobbs-Merrill.

Taylor, P. J. & Koppelman, M. D. (1984), Amnesia for criminal offenses. *Psycholog. Med.*, 14: 581–588.

Thigpen, C. & Cleckley, H. (1957), *Three Faces of Eve*. New York: McGraw-Hill.

Thompson, L. & Reavy, P. (2005), Tearful ending-Mark hacking gets 6-to-life prison term. *Desert Morning News*, Salt Lake City, UT: June 7.

Tillman, J. G., Nash, M. R. & Lerner, P. M. (1994), Does trauma cause dissociative pathology? In: *Dissociation: Clinical And Theoretical Perspectives*, ed. S. J. Lynn & J.W. Rhue. New York: Guilford Press, pp. 395–414.

Trujillo, K., Lewis, D. O., Yeager, C. A. & Gidlow, B. (1996), Imaginary companions of schoolboys and boys with dissociative identity disorder/ multiple personality disorder: A normal to pathologic continuum. *Psychiat. Clin. North Amer.*, 5:, 375–392.

van der Kolk, B. A. (1996), The body keeps score: Approaches to the psychobiology of posttraumatic stress disorder. In: *Traumatic Stress: The Effects Of Overwhelming Experience On Mind, Body And Society*, ed. B. A. van der Kolk, A. C. McFarlane & L. Weisaeth. New York: Guilford Press, pp. 214–241.

—— McFarlane, A. C. & Weisaeth, L., ed. (1996), *Traumatic Stress: The Effects Of Overwhelming Experience On Mind, Body And Society*, New York: Guilford Press.

—— van der Hart, O. & Marmer, C. (1996), Dissociation and information processing in post traumatic stress disorder. In: *Traumatic Stress: The Effects Of Overwhelming Experience On Mind, Body And Society*, ed. B. A. van der Kolk, A. C. McFarlane & L. Weisaeth. New York: Guilford Press, 303–327.

Volkan, V. (2002), September 11 and societal regression. *Group Anal.*, 35: 456–483.

von Broembsen, F. (1986), The two-way journey: pathological and adaptive aspects of symbolizing activity. *J. Mental Imagery*, 10: 87–94.

von Franz, M.L. (1964), The process of individuation. In: *Man and His Symbols*, ed. C. G. Jung, M. L. von Franz, J. L. Henderson, J. Jacobi & A. Jaffe New York: Dell, pp. 157–254.

Vronsky, P. (2004), *Serial Killers: The Methods and Madness of Monsters*. New York: Penguin.

Wade, N. (2005), "Exploring a hormone for caring." *The New York Times*, 22 November, sec. F, p. 5, Health and Fitness.

Wegner, D.M. (2002), *The Illusion of Conscious Will*. Cambridge, MA: MIT Press.

Weiss D. S. & Marmar C. R. (1997), The Impact of Event Scale—Revised. In: *Assessing Psychological Trauma and PTSD: A Practitioner's Handbook*, ed. J. P. Wilson and T. M. Keane. New York: Guilford Press, pp. 399–411.

White, G. D. (2004), Political apathy disorder: Proposal for a new DSM diagnostic category. *J. Humanist. Psychol.* 44: 47–57.

Whitman, T.A. & Akutagawa, D. (2004), Riddles in serial murder: A synthesis. *Aggress. & Violent Behav.*, 9: 693–703.

Widom, C. S. (1989), The cycle of violence. *Science*, 244: 160–166.

Wilber, C. (1985), The effect of child abuse on the psyche. In: *Childhood Antecedents of Multiple Personality*, ed. R. Kluft. Washington, DC: American Psychiatric Press, pp. 21–36.

Wilgoren, J. (2005), "In gory detail, prosecution lays out case for tough sentencing of B.T.K. killer." *The New York Times*, sec. A; col. 1, p. National Desk; P. 16, 18 August.

Wilson, S.C. & Barber, T.X. (1981), Vivid fantasy and hallucinatory abilities in the life histories of excellent hypnotic subjects ("somnambules"): Preliminary report with female subjects. In: *Imagery, Volume 2: Concepts, Results, And Applications*, ed. E. Klinger. New York: Plenum Press, pp. 341–387.

Winer, R. (2001), Evil in the mind of the therapist. *Contemp. Psychoanal.*, 37: 613–622.

Winnicott, D.W. (1958), The capacity to be alone. In: *The Maturational Process and the Facilitating Environment: Studies in the Theory of Emotional Development*. London: Karnac Books, pp. 29–36.

—— (1960), Ego distortion in terms of true and false self. In: *The Maturational Process and the Facilitating Environment: Studies in the Theory of Emotional Development*. London: Karnac Books, pp. 140–152.

—— (1969), The Use of An Object and Relating Through Identifications, *Int. J. Psychoanal.*, 50: 711–716.

—— (1984), Deprivation and Delinquency. London: Routledge.

Wolfgang, M.E. (1958), Patterns In Criminal Homicide. Philadelphia, PA: University of Pennsylvania Press.

Wulffen, E. (1926), *Kriminalpsychologie*. Berlin, Germany: P. Langenscheidt.

Wurmser, L. (2003a), "Abyss calls out to abyss": Oedipal shame, invisibility and broken identity. *Amer. J. Psychoanal.*, 63: 299–316.

——— (2003b), The annihilating power of absolutness: superego analysis in the severe neurosis, especially in character perversion. *Psycholanal. Psychol.*, 20: 214–235.

Yochelson, S. & Samenow, S. (1976), *The Criminal Personality*. Northvale, NJ: Aronson.

Zeddies, T.J. (2002), More than just words: A hermeneutic view of language in psychoanalysis. *Psychoanal. Psychol.*, 19: 3–23.

Zelikovsky, N. & Lynn, S.J. (1994), The aftereffects and assessment of physical and psychological abuse. In: *Dissociation: Clinical and Theoretical Perspectives*, ed. S. J. Lynn & J. W. Rhue. New York: Guilford Press, pp. 190–214.

Acknowledgments

Half the trick is in being well-mentored. I have been especially fortunate in this regard.

My earliest mentor, forensic psychiatrist Dorothy Otnow Lewis, sparked my enduring interest in the connections among child maltreatment, dissociation, and crime. She is a pioneer in her field, a role model for clinicians and researchers, and a constant source of personal inspiration to me. Some of the original research for this book was conducted with monies from the Harry Frank Guggenheim Foundation under a grant administered by Dorothy and her remarkably talented associate, Catherine A. Yeager. I thank them both for schooling me in the art of interviewing behind bars.

The distinguished scholar Robert Jay Lifton supervised my doctoral work at the City University of New York. Robert's theories regarding the protean self, the construction of meaning, and the psychology of survival have greatly influenced my own approach to the study of violence. While many told me that doctoral work was about "just doing a little piece of science," Robert Lifton's dedication to influencing criminal justice policies has kept me mindful of the broader uses toward which "a little science" could, and should, be put.

More than anyone perhaps, I am indebted to Donnel B. Stern. Despite the fact that I am not an analyst and my research is outside the journal's usual purview, both Jay Greenberg and Donnel Stern took a chance on publishing my early work in *Contemporary Psychoanalysis.* Donnel's own book, *Unformulated Experience,* is a template for thinking about dissociation in everyday life, and started me on a journey through the interpersonal and relational literature that has enriched my writing as well as my relationships with the people about whom I write. He encouraged me to chronicle my experiences and it is clear to me that I could not have brought the project to fruition without Donnel's deft hand at the editorial helm. He has honored me by writing the foreword to this book.

At John Jay College of Criminal Justice, Dean James Levine has offered me unwavering support, pragmatic advice, and a number of key introductions to people who later proved pivotal in my academic career. Jim always included me in, when I surely would have been left out: this is the best mentorship for which anyway can ask. One of the critical introductions that Jim made was to Elizabeth Hegeman, psychoanalyst and anthropologist, who initiated me into new ways of thinking about how culture shapes consciousness, and suggested that I submit my early papers to the psychoanalytic journals. And speaking of psychoanalysts, I am ever so grateful for the friendship of my colleague, Dr. Katie Gentile, whose experience with first time authorship serendipitously paralleled my own, and who, throughout the writing process, graciously served as sounding board for issues both scholarly and personal.

Michael Blitz has been by turns my teacher, my mentor, my colleague, my chairperson, and my friend now for over ten years. He seems to show up in almost all of my professional dreams, and has helped make many of them come true. My colleagues in the Interdisciplinary Studies Program at John Jay College of Criminal Justice: Andrea Balis, Meghan Duffy, Carol Groneman, Elizabeth Gitter, Jerry Markowitz, Shirley Sarna, and Dennis Sherman have each added immeasurably to my professional and personal life. They taught me that to become a great teacher one must stay a perennial student. Christina Czechowicz was a beacon of light through some dark days.

My own students have inspired me, instructed me, and gently interrupted me when I was professing instead of teaching. In particular, I want to thank the research assistants who helped me compile and code the law enforcement files used for this project: Paul Kogan, Miguelina Guzman, Lisa Shehata, Lindsey Harriman, and Amanda Gil.

Of course, I am indebted to the sixty-four incarcerated men whose narratives provided the impetus for this work. In addition, my deepest thanks to members of the FBI's Behavioral Science Unit for their participation in the collaborative research on patterns of criminal behavior that informs the analysis of the narratives in this book.

At The Analytic Press, I thank Paul Stepansky for seeing the potential of a psychoanalytic book on criminal violence, Lenni Kobrin for adding polish and grace to the product, Shari Buchwald for her professional and personal generosity, and Nadine Simms for seeing it through to completion.

In one way or another, you have all been my mentors. Thank you for your guidance and support.

Index